THREE KING

Three Kings in Baghdad
The Tragedy of Iraq's Monarchy

Gerald de Gaury

Preface by Philip Mansel
Introduction by Alan de Lacy Rush

I.B. TAURIS
LONDON · NEW YORK

Published in 2008 by I.B.Tauris & Co Ltd
6 Salem Road, London W2 4BU
175 Fifth Avenue, New York NY 10010
www.ibtauris.com

First published by Hutchinson & Co. Ltd in 1961
Copyright © 1961, 2008 Gerald de Gaury

Cover image: 'The Emir Faisal' by Augustus John © The Ashmolean Museum of Art
and Archaeology
In Paris the Emir Faisal wore the special head-dress of the Hashemites and traditional
Hejazi dress to impress the delegates to the Peace Conference of 1919. As King of
Iraq after 1921, however, he generally wore modern clothes or military uniform.

In the interests of consistency, all names and place names have been spelt using
Gerald de Gaury's transliteration, rather than modern spellings.

ISBN: 978 1 84511 535 7

A full CIP record for this book is available from the British Library
A full CIP record for this book is available from the Library of Congress

Library of Congress catalog card: available

Printed and bound in India by Thomson Press India Limited

The banks of the Euphrates echo with ghostly alarums; the Mesopotamian deserts are full of the rumour of phantom armies; you will not blame me if I passed among them 'trattando l'ombre come cose salda'.

From a letter to Lord Cromer in the foreword of *Amurath to Amurath* by Gertrude Bell.

Contents

Illustrations

Author's Foreword

This book, at the publishers' request, is not a day-to-day history or even a year-to-year one; and without access to Foreign Office and Air Ministry records, which are not yet made available, it would be difficult to write a full story of the monarchy in Iraq. My intention has been merely to evoke the characters of the three Kings, and of the Regent of Iraq, ruling from Baghdad between 1921 and 1958, and to revive something of the atmosphere in their days.

Persons concerned to denigrate their worth and that of Nuri al Said, so often the Chief Minister, may lift some words of mine from their context in an attempt to prove what cannot be proved from the whole. The Regent and Nuri were humanly imperfect and being Arab were dissimilar in character to Europeans. If Arabs decry them, they decry themselves. History will amply prove, if it has not done so already, that the country was happier and better ruled in their day than it has been since the revolution. It was not their fault that hard as they strove on behalf of their people they and theirs were caught and destroyed 'in the gale of the world'.

G. de G.

Acknowledgments

I am most grateful for help and encouragement from Major-General J. M. L. Renton, Air Marshal Sir Robert Foster, Dr. R. Dixon Firth, Sir Harry Sinderson Pasha, Group Captain P. Domville, Colonel W. H. Hargreaves and Albert Haurani.

Among others who kindly aided me were Mr. Eric Caparn, Mr. Malan, Mr. T. F. Coade, Miss Borland and Miss Lucie Smith, all of whom helped by giving me their recollections of events or providing contributions or suggestions.

The admirable volumes of S. Longrigg, Ernest Main, Philip Ireland, C. J. Edmonds and Henry A. Foster on Iraq are indispensable to anyone interested in the days of the Monarchy and I gratefully acknowledge the use of their works and others in the text.

I am indebted to Messrs. George Harrap & Co. Ltd. for the use of material about the 1941 Revolt in Iraq, from my book *Arabian Journey*, published by them.

G. DE G.

Preface
The Lost Kingdom

THE Hashemite Kings of Iraq, like their cousins in Jordan, were a dynasty of realists. According to their interests and the needs of the moment, they have served and used Islamic traditions, the Ottoman, British and American empires and Arab nationalism. Installed by the British government after the defeat of the Ottoman Empire, three Hashemites reigned as kings of Iraq: Faisal I 1921–33), his son Ghazi (1933–39) and grandson Faisal II (1939–58). When the Hashemites arrived in Iraq it was a backward corner of the Ottoman Empire under British occupation. By 1958, the year of their murder, Iraq had been transformed into one of the most modern states in the Middle East.

The Hashemites' realism was partly due to confidence. Descendants of the Prophet Mohammed, they felt their dynasty was, as one of their admirers wrote in 1916, 'the oldest reigning house in the entire world'. As Emirs of Mecca, they had ruled in the two holy cities of Islam, Mecca and Medina, since the thirteenth century. In 1516 they had welcomed Ottoman suzerainty in the Hijaz, as the best protection from Portuguese attacks in the Red Sea. During the following four hundred years of Ottoman rule, the Emirs of Mecca remained semi-sovereigns, helping to organise Muslims' annual pilgrimage to the two Holy Cities, sending ambassadors even as far as Delhi. They bought property in Constantinople, where they were encouraged by the Ottoman government to reside.

Tension between Turks and Arabs, however, was always in the background. In 1703 one Hashemite was said to have denounced the Ottoman Sultan as 'son of a Christian whore' (dynastic pride meant that, until the late nineteenth century, Hashemites married only each other) and to have threatened to transfer allegiance to the Sultan of Morocco. In 1880, thirty-six years before the outbreak of the long-foretold Arab revolt, the British ambassador in Constantinople was informed by 'an Arab gentleman' that discontent prevailed in the Ottoman Empire's Arab provinces and that Arabs would rise under 'their real religious head' the Emir of Mecca – if they could depend on British support.

Finally in June 1916, after much hesitation, such an uprising was launched with the longed-for British support, by Faisal I's father Sherif Hussain. The oppressive wartime rule of the Young Turk government, and the famine threatened in the Hijaz by the British wartime blockade, were motives as strong as desire for a complete break with the Ottoman Empire. From his entry into Damascus on 1 October 1918, until his expulsion by French forces on 1 August 1920, the Emir Faisal ruled in Syria. He had no connection with Iraq, a country that he had never visited – unlike the Hijaz, Syria or Constantinople, where he had spent his youth and had sat as deputy for Mecca in the Ottoman parliament.

When he arrived in Basra on a British battleship on 24 June 1921, Faisal was intended to serve as a monarchical safety-valve, to defuse Iraqi nationalist anger at British rule, expressed in the rising of 1920, which had been suppressed only by repeated RAF bombing raids on Iraqi villages. The Hashemite alternative seemed the best solution to the Colonial Secretary Winston Churchill and his advisers T.E. Lawrence (long an admirer of the Emir Faisal) and Gertrude Bell: earlier that year they had accepted the establishment of Faisal's brother Abdullah in Transjordan, where his great-grandson Abdullah II rules today. Few Iraqis at first accepted Faisal I. If they voted for him in the British-organised plebiscite, it was on British instructions. As de Gaury relates, on his first railway journey from Basra to Baghdad, Faisal found not welcoming crowds, but empty platforms.

Gerald de Gaury first came to Iraq in 1924 as a young British officer. He returned frequently, when no longer on active service, as a friend of the Royal Family. He knew all three kings – Faisal I from the 1920s, Ghazi in the 1930s and Faisal II since he was a baby as well as Faisal II's uncle and Regent Abdulillah, since he was twelve years old. De Gaury writes as an eyewitness as well as a historian, intending to evoke their characters, the decoration of their palaces and the 'atmosphere in their days', as much as the political record. He describes Baghdad in the 1920s as 'an ancient oriental hive... nearly oblivious of the Western world' and King Faisal I's 'large liquid eyes', his fondness for bridge, champagne and unexpected descents in Baghdad.

De Gaury was a particular friend of King Faisal I's brother ex-King Ali of the Hijaz, in whose house on the Tigris he lived when writing his history of the Hashemite Rulers of Mecca, and of King Ali's son the Regent Abdulillah. The Hashemites appreciated East and West at the same time. The Regent Abdulillah's pride in English friends such as Churchill and Lady Cunard, and love of Bond Street shops, did not stop him, in Iraq, from receiving streams of callers and devoting himself to government business. During the reign of his young nephew he was the dominant figure in his country. When warned of his unpopularity, and advised to let the young King Faisal II reign on his own, he would reply: 'How can I leave Faisal among these barbarians?'

Three Kings in Baghdad is a memorial, not only to the Iraqi Royal Family but also to 'the British moment in the Middle East'. De Gaury shows the kinder side of British imperialism. He was well informed (his Arabic was excellent), modest and honest. He did not profit from the exploitation of Iraqi oil by British companies. He is too polite to tell all he knew. You will not learn in these pages, what one Iraqi officer exiled in London told me, that the hounds of the Royal Hunt were fed on the same rations as the soldiers of the Royal Guard. You will learn that Faisal II, who had a British nanny, governess and tutor and enjoyed his education at Harrow, was 'as nearly a British product as it is possible for a foreigner to be' – higher praise, perhaps, when printed in 1961 than it would be today. Such excess of anglophilia helps explain why the Royal family became isolated from Iraqis, and why Iraqi soldiers were ready to shoot them down on 14 July 1958, as de Gaury describes in his harrowing chapter 'Murder on a Summer Morning.' It was de Gaury who organised their memorial service, and delivered the eulogy, at the Chapel Royal of the Savoy two weeks later.

Three Kings in Baghdad is a defence of monarchy in general, as well as the Iraqi monarchy in particular. De Gaury points out that the 1958 revolution also removed or killed hundred of ministers, civil servants, deputies and senior officers. Continuing the Iraqi-British connection, many left for exile in London. Some readers may be reminded, in de Gaury' s account of the virtues of the murdered Royal Family and the crimes of their assassins, of similar memoirs written after the French and Russian revolutions, by courtiers of their decimated dynasties. He depicts the Iraqi monarchy as no more absurd, certainly less sanguinary, than the revolutionary and socialist regimes which succeeded it. Until Nasser's radio began its nightly denunciations of the Hashemites as 'hounds of the imperialists', and the Franco–British–Israeli invasion of Egypt in 1956 revealed Great Britain to be pro-Israeli rather than pro-Arab, the Iraqi monarchy had become popular – especially in the reign of the nationalist idol King Ghazi. During the 1948 Arab–Israeli war, the ladies of the Iraqi Royal Family had been the first in Arab history to help in army canteens and hospitals. The monarchy was a modernising regime, with a modern constitution and education system. After they had been obliged to leave for Israel as a result of the Arab–Israeli conflict, many Iraqi Jews missed life in their former homeland. At Faisal II's coming of age celebrations in the streets of Baghdad on 2 May 1953, floats advertising female emancipation had been especially widely cheered. Oil revenues were spent carefully. When Hugh Trevor-Roper visited it in 1957 he found it 'a land of secularism and reason ... efficient, energetic, prosperous, complacent: a Levantine Switzerland.'

The success of the Hashemites' cousins in Jordan, the

persistence of monarchies in the Arabian peninsula and the emergence of neo-dynastic regimes in Iraq, Syria and, more recently, Egypt, based on the families of Saddam Hussein (who built more palaces than the Hashemites ever owned), Hafez al-Assad and Hosni Mubarak, suggest that the Regent Abdulillah's belief that monarchy, with its spirit of continuity, is 'best for the East' is not unfounded. Even before the catastrophe of the US-led invasion of 2003, many Iraqis considered the years of the monarchy as a golden age – as de Gaury had prophesied they would. At the moment *Three Kings in Baghdad* is republished, they have little prospect of another.

Philip Mansel

Introduction

There scarcely exists on the earth a community
of provinces of which the interests and prejudices
are more discordant than that for which we
have accepted the burden of a mandate.
Perceval Landon, *Daily Telegraph*,
3 May 1921

GERALD de Gaury's *Three Kings in Baghdad*, first published in 1961, challenges the generally negative view
of Iraq's kings and their links with Britain. Instead it
suggests that, given all the obstacles of which we are now
so fully aware, no other regime could have established the
Iraqi state more successfully. This view is endorsed by most
Iraqis old enough to remember those distant days. For them
the overthrow of the monarchy in a *coup d'état* on 14 July
1958 was a tragedy that spawned the dictatorship of Saddam
Hussein and Iraq's later crises.

Gerald de Gaury wrote *Three Kings in Baghdad* soon
after the *coup*. He received the news through a telephone
call to his flat in London. Army rebels had gunned down the
Royal Family in the palace garden; Iraq's most powerful
political leader, Nuri al Said, had also been killed; Iraq had
been declared a republic. While jubilant crowds – including criminals released from prison – dragged the corpse of
Crown Prince Abdulillah through Baghdad's streets, de
Gaury was appalled by the impending collapse of the state
edifice that had taken thirty-seven years to build. He could
see that, without the monarchy's centralising influence, Iraq
must inevitably revert to the oscillation between dictatorship
and ethnic and sectarian violence that had plagued the region
since the Mongol destruction of the Abbasid civilisation in

7

the thirteenth century. It was an historic moment when he felt bound to record what had just become a chapter of Iraq's history.

De Gaury spent most of his working life in Iraq as a soldier, intelligence officer and friend of the Royal Family. Born in London on 13 May 1897, he was the son of a stockbroker, Hubert Stanley de Gaury, and of Hilda Simpson, whose father was a surveyor and land agent. Nothing else is known of his antecedents. Contemporaries suspected that he thought them too dull to mention; others whispered that he was the illegitimate son of the hero of Omdurman, Field Marshal Lord Kitchener. Commissioned as a 2nd Lieutenant in the Hampshire Regiment in 1914, he fought at Gallipoli, then in France in the trenches around Arras and the Somme. Wounded four times, he was awarded the Military Cross in 1917.

His passion for the Arab world began while receiving medical treatment at a convent in Malta. Fascinated by an Arabic dictionary by his bedside, he studied the language and persevered until he gained a first-class interpretership in the Civil Service Commission's examination. In Iraq he first served in 1924 as a regular officer under secondment to the Arab Levies. Later, he became an intelligence officer attached to the British Royal Air Force, an assignment involving surveillance of political and tribal developments and liaison duties with the British High Commission and the palace. He also undertook intelligence work in Iran and Saudi Arabia, sometimes travelling in regions previously unvisited by western explorers. In 1935 he and the British Minister visited King Abdul Aziz in Riyadh, and four years later he returned as a special emissary charged with encouraging the King to remain strictly neutral during the Second World War. From 1936 to 1939 he resided in Kuwait as British representative, or Political Agent, charged with monitoring internal affairs and preserving the sheikhdom as an exclusively British preserve. In 1941, he raised a Druze cavalry regiment that helped drive the Vichy French from Syria.

It was soon after arriving in Iraq in 1924 that de Gaury

met its first king, Faisal I (r. 1921–33) son of the head of the Hashimite family, Sherif Hussain of Mecca, who had fought alongside T.E. Lawrence during the Arab Revolt. Needing a bridge partner, the Royal Chamberlain invited him to join in a game with the king and his attractive English companion, the wife of a locally employed British engineer. Palace connections were extended at evening receptions in the Secretariat garden where King Faisal mingled with Iraqi dignitaries, high-ranking visitors and British officials headed by the High Commissioner and Gertrude Bell. In later years, de Gaury, always a romantic, forgot the heat and the mosquitoes, recalling only the lawn with its 'dusty look against which uniforms, polished buttons, light dresses and a sprinkling of women's jewellery shone and glimmered doubly luminous'. It was on such an occasion in 1926 that he spoke to King Faisal's brother, King Ali of the Hijaz, whose ancestral land had recently been conquered and annexed to the territories of Abdul Aziz. In planning a comeback, King Ali needed British support and welcomed de Gaury's overtures. By the time he died in 1935, his only son, Abdulillah, then aged twenty-three, had become de Gaury's friend.

Though not a memoir, *Three Kings in Baghdad* is permeated with de Gaury's memories and observations. The result is a superbly sharp picture tempered by lapses of objectivity. His disparaging presentation of Iraq's second king, Ghazi (r. 1933–39) clearly reflects Abdulillah's antagonism towards him. True, King Ghazi was no match for his illustrious father. Promiscuous and a heavy drinker, he threw wild parties and adored aeroplanes and fast cars. But one senses that de Gaury would have forgiven him if he had been an anglophile and had not neglected his wife, Queen Aliya, who was Abdulillah's sister. Certainly most Iraqis forgave his faults and admired his support for Palestinian rights and Arab unity, and for plans to counter British dominance with German help. De Gaury acknowledges that young Iraqis carried his photograph in their wallets and 'cheered him wherever he went'. He also concedes that his speeches, broadcast from his private radio station, attracted enthusiastic

audiences not just in Iraq, but in Kuwait, Jordan and Saudi
Arabia. Yet he dismisses them as mere attempts 'to bemuse
the conservative public and upset foreigners'.

Also noteworthy is de Gaury's failure to mention that he
was residing in Kuwait as the British Political Agent in 1938
when dissidents there requested King Ghazi's help in removing their despotic ruler, Sheikh Ahmad al-Jaber al-Sabah, or
forcing him to grant reform. Some even wanted Iraq and
Kuwait to unite. King Ghazi seemed about to invade when
he was killed in a car crash in April 1939. Was the crash a
genuine accident, as claimed? Some suspected it had been
arranged by the British Secret Service or by the pro-British
Prime Minister, Nuri al Said, or both, to prevent an Iraqi
takeover of oil-rich Kuwait and remove a pro-German king
in the run-up to the Second World War. Others accused
King Ghazi's enemies within the palace. De Gaury refutes
these well-known suggestions, yet provides none of the extra
evidence one might expect from a friend of the Royal Family
who occupied a key position at the time. Even when I
questioned him years later, he added nothing to his published account. One fact was, however, confirmed by my
later research – that de Gaury's removal from Kuwait within
weeks of King Ghazi's death resulted directly from his
vilification by the previous British Political Agent, H.R.P.
Dickson, and other supporters of Sheikh Ahmad, who
emerged from the crisis almost unscathed.

De Gaury again skates over thin ice regarding
Abdulillah's appointment as regent for King Ghazi's four-
year-old son and successor, Faisal II (r. 1939–58). He
nowhere mentions what he surely knew – that there was an
alternative candidate, the late king's competent uncle, Emir
Zaid, who had fought in the Arab Revolt, studied at Oxford
and been Iraq's ambassador in Berlin. Nuri al Said hated
King Ghazi and more than once asked Zaid to control him
or take his place. Although Zaid refused to usurp the throne,
his daughter assured me that he would have accepted the
regency if Nuri had felt able to oppose Queen Aliya. The
choice of her brother, Abdulillah, was in most people's
opinion disastrous. As for Nuri's desire to depose Ghazi, it

surely justifies the fears that haunted the king in the months preceding his violent death – fears that de Gaury attributes to hypochondria.

By emphasising the Anglo–Iraqi alliance, de Gaury encourages the notion that the Hashimites were puppets of the British government. In fact, Faisal I, despite his friendly behaviour, infuriated British diplomats by his persistent demands for Iraqi independence – a goal that he achieved, at least on paper, in 1932. As for King Ghazi, he was, as de Gaury admits, an Arab nationalist *par excellence*. Only in the reign of Iraq's third king, Faisal II (1939–58), did the Hashimite monarchy lose its Arab nationalist credentials and become wholly subservient to Britain following a crisis during the Second World War.

In April 1941, a pro-German revolt forced Abdulillah to flee from Iraq to Jerusalem. Soon afterwards, de Gaury, on a secret-service assignment in Tehran, received orders to join him as his *charge d'affaires*. So began the adventure in which British troops and the Arab Legion restored Abdulillah to power in Baghdad.

De Gaury shared all the dangers up to the moment when Abdulillah was reunited with the boy-king, Faisal II, who had been detained in northern Iraq.

Nothing could have delighted de Gaury more than the way this episode clinched his friendship with Abdulillah. For below the veneer of a professional soldier and intelligence officer lurked an ardent royalist and aesthete. In *East is West*, Freya Stark admires de Gaury's sophistication and describes a dream in which he suggested that she should smile less as smiling was 'no longer fashionable'. How could such a man not relish intimacy with an Arab prince of the Hashimite family that had controlled Mecca and Medina for centuries?

Not surprisingly, *Three Kings in Baghdad* provides a more attractive picture of Abdulillah than most people would accept. Effeminate and shy, he appeared arrogant and was never popular. Although he reminded Freya Stark of Shelley, Desmond Stewart, who taught English in Baghdad in the 1950s, found him 'sometimes fawnlike, more often suspicious

and chinless' (Stewart, *New Babylon: A Portrait of Iraq*, 191).
Cecil Beaton, found him 'like a dancing instructor', while the
ambassador to the Soviet Union and future Warden of New
College, Oxford, Sir William Hayter, thought him 'faintly
sinister' (Hayter, *A Double Life*, 158). Yet Lord Astor,
'Chips' Channon and many others welcomed him and de
Gaury into their country houses and London drawing-rooms.
In London, de Gaury helped Abdulillah look for a suitable
wife for the young King Faisal and another to replace
Abdulillah's beautiful Egyptian wife, Malik, who had
returned to Cairo after a boring *mariage blanc*. More to his
taste – and de Gaury's – were the handsome young men to
whom de Gaury also introduced him.

De Gaury's *Three Kings in Baghdad* is essentially a family
story. It includes revealing references to women such as
Abdulillah's sisters and his formidable and ambitious mother,
ex-Queen Nafisa of the Hijaz. He also draws a moving
portrait of the innocent king, Faisal II, destined to be murdered at the age of twenty-three. Despite a cosseted childhood, he had emerged as a capable young man. 'All those
about him,' writes de Gaury, 'foresaw a brilliant future'.
Longing for him to take his rightful place when he attained
his majority in 1953, Iraqis were furious when Abdulillah
failed to step aside.

Yet Iraq was progressing well. Despite all the problems
and political repression, contemporary accounts support
de Gaury's view that Iraq was enjoying an economic and
cultural boom and enormous development of its infrastruc-
ture thanks to the well-run Development Board and soar-
ing oil revenues. Thus the dangers to the regime lay less in
the internal situation than in foreign policy.

De Gaury's friendship with Abdulillah mirrored that
between Britain and Iraq. The cordiality seemed splendid at
the time. In fact, it isolated the monarchy from the Iraqi
people and became an increasing liability. After the overthrow of King Farouq of Egypt in 1952, Gamal Abdel
Nasser, as second president of the new republic, denounced
Iraq's membership of the pro-western, defensive organisa-
tion, the Baghdad Pact, and became the hero of the Arab

masses by nationalising the Suez Canal in July 1956. When Britain, France and Israel retaliated by invading Egypt, international uproar and humiliating troop withdrawals highlighted Britain's decline as an imperial power. Clearly it was urgent for the Iraqi regime to seek local support. Instead Abdulillah and Nuri al Said relied on martial law and remained defiantly pro-British.

De Gaury omits to mention Abdulillah's meddling in Syrian politics. His father's kingdom of the Hijaz was now part of Saudi Arabia. The Hashimite throne of Jordan was held by his cousin, King Hussain, and being more than twenty years older than Faisal II, he was unlikely ever to become king of Iraq despite being Crown Prince. He therefore aimed to revive the Hashimite monarchy in Syria where his uncle, Faisal I, had briefly ruled before being evicted by French forces and moving to Baghdad in 1921. Nuri al Said mocked this aspiration, but wanted to stifle Egyptian influence in Damascus. Both men therefore conspired with Syrian royalists and opportunists, American, British and Turkish diplomats and anti communist operatives, often behind the façade of Baghdad Pact meetings. Opposition to their machinations provoked the union of Egypt and Syria in February 1958 which in turn triggered the formation of the rival Hashimite Federation of Iraq and Jordan. These conspiracies figure in Patrick Seale's classic work, *The Struggle for Syria*, and in files held in British and French government archives and in the Bureau de Documentions Arabes in Damascus. Why then are they not mentioned in *Three Kings in Baghdad*? Was de Gaury unaware of them? Perhaps he knew but kept silent, knowing how greatly they antagonised Iraq's Free Officers and contributed to their decision to destroy the monarchy.

In his last years de Gaury lived in an elegant regency square in Brighton and mixed with a social set that included the playwright, Terence Rattigan, writers such as Robin Maugham and Derek Patmore, the artist Count William de Belleroche and his friend Gordon Anderson, plus others with whom he had more in common than he dared to admit. There were also visitors from London and the continent, including his devoted friend, Princess Eugenie of Greece, daughter of Freud's disciple, Marie Bonaparte. Active to the end, he painted excellent watercolours and added an autobiographical volume, *Traces of Travel* (1983), to earlier classic works including *Arabia Phoenix* (1946), *Arabian Journey* (1950) and *Rulers of Mecca* (1951).

After de Gaury's death in January 1984, his papers proved to have been well 'weeded'. Despite his writings, he was a secretive man who took many unanswered questions to his grave. Nevertheless, in *Three Kings in Baghdad*, he casts a brilliant light on a forgotten corner of Britain's vast realm of imperial influence in the twentieth century.

Alan de Lacy Rush

I

Giants in Retreat

. . . But as to the Iraqi there is no manner of doubt that his whole phenomenal life is one kaleidoscope of changing emotions—uncontrolled and, while they last, absolutely sincere.

The Ins and Outs of Mesopotamia

T. LYALL

THE steamship was small and old-fashioned, with punkahs swinging slowly in the dining saloon and small electric fans whirring only in the best cabins.

A whale was travelling with the ship and every now and then scratched its back against the hull. The rigging had given up its vibrant singing in the Indian Ocean. The native passengers began to remain in the sun above board, and the smell of the mutton fat with which they cooked on deck was pungent.

We leant over the rails and talked of the land ahead of us, Mesopotamia, recently renamed Iraq and given a monarchy by the British Government, which had found direct rule there over-costly in lives and specie. The military occupation was past history and the garrison, including some sixty thousand Indians and twice that number of camp-followers, was rapidly moving away.

'The late Lord Kitchener,' said a British military fellow traveller, 'hoped to be the first Viceroy of the Arab East'; and it did not sound absurd to have had that aim in 1914. In much of the area, including Mesopotamia, the people in general were illiterate, unused to administration and with characters unsuited to it.

15

By the end of the war Kitchener was dead and Britain tired, and though Ottoman Turkey had collapsed there were obligations which ruled out a foreign Viceroyalty in its place. Britain had encouraged the Grand Sherif of Mecca to revolt against his Turkish master. A little later during the war Britain made promises to the Zionist Jews and to the French. The three commitments were irreconcilable, but in Iraq she was doing her best to keep her word to the Arabs, her recollection of it jogged by a rebellion on the Euphrates in 1920. She was setting up a regime under Faisal, son of the Grand Sherif of Mecca, supported by the Mesopotamians among his followers who had fought with Lawrence.

The still-young Royal Air Force was to undertake the security of his State, something then astonishing—and irritating to its predecessor the Army; and the Arab levies raised for guard duties during the war, with some Kurdish and Assyrian levies, were to be its ground force.

The Iraq levies were in consequence added to the list of units overseas to which regular officers of the British Army could be temporarily seconded. It was an arrangement blessed by officers who looked for adventure and for better pay than they would receive at home, and I for one became bound for Iraq.

The Arab world possessed a romantic air; Baghdad with its long history, the city of Haroun al Rashid, had a lure in its name. Moreover, Iraq was a young country, though in an old land; its newly formed military units might lend military duties unusual interest, and it was a place worth knowing about politically and strategically.

The way from the West to Iraq in 1924 was still by ship to Bombay and then by another slower one up the Persian Gulf. 'Al Iraq Arabi' and 'al Iraq Ajem' it was called on old maps, a basin of fertile silt constantly enlarged and scoured by three rivers, the Tigris, Euphrates and Karun. When first seen from the Persian Gulf, the land is only a thread on the horizon where mud meets brackish brown water; but, richly fertile, under hot sun and humid sky, it was a granary of the ancients. Mongol invaders in the thirteenth century broke down the irrigation canals, and afterwards its only export of value was dates from the date-gardens of Basra, the biggest in the world—the Ottoman Turks, successors of the Mongols, having done next to nothing to repair the irrigation system.

However romantic Baghdad might sound, southern Mesopotamia, 'between the rivers', was mostly a barren, sorry land, subject to violent sandstorms and to almost annual epidemics of cholera, loathed by soldiers of the wartime army.

It was such a long and roundabout way to Basra, the port of Iraq, via Bombay, that I had enquired from the War Office before leaving England if I might travel by a new route, across the Syrian desert by car. The reply was curt. It was clearly considered foolhardy. The only alternatives were primitive—by raft down the Euphrates or by camel caravan or carriage along its bank. The accepted route for Service travellers was by ship and then by a railway—planned by the Germans and built by the British—to the new capital.

As the train neared Baghdad, it passed great mounds of bare earth, all that has remained of Babylon, site of the Tower of Babel. Babil, as it is called today, was still in a polyglot land.

In the South there were many Indians; traders, moneylenders and menials. A hundred thousand persons in the North used Turkish as their only language. The merchants engaged in the important carpet-transit trade spoke Persian; and the first Minister of Education had written only Persian and no one considered it very extraordinary that he should do so. In the North-East were Kurds who spoke their own language, as did a whole refugee people, the Assyrians. Nearly a third of the population of Baghdad were Jews and the first Minister of Finance was a Jew. There were smaller minorities such as the Sabeans, silversmiths and canoe-builders in the South, and Yazidis, 'devil-worshippers', in the North.

Even the Muslims were divided into sects and various orders.[1] Antipathy was often marked between them when it came to receiving orders from a representative of another group. A new Arab King, hitherto unknown in the country, would have a hard

---

[1] The Sunna are the adherents of the main Muslim orders; the Shiahs throughout the world are less numerous, though in Iraq they are nearly equal in numbers. The Shiahs regard Ali, son-in-law of the Prophet, as the first Caliph (Khalifa) or successor to the Prophet, and Hassan and Hussain, his sons, as second and third rightful successors, rejecting the first three Caliphs of the Sunni Muslims and usurpers, and there are other differences in both tenets and observances between them.

B

task in welding together so many elements in a new nation unless supported by a strong outside power. In the Orient, where little of importance happens without foreign pressure, the new countries of the Arab East, that were hitherto parts of the Turkish Empire, were given shape by the Allies and the League of Nations and even so their frontiers and homogeneity were at first uncertain.

To Europe, Faisal was known only as a leader in an episode of the War in the East, the Arab Revolt, but it was a romantic one compared to the slogging match in France, that left those who took part in it with few of the chivalrous notions of war they had had at the start. So Faisal had an unusually exotic air about him, which mystery heightened. *The Times* of 7th August 1920 had headed a long article about him, 'The Emir Faisal— Creator of the Arab Army—a modern Saladin', and had gone on to say that 'his character and personality remained a closed book, even after the peace conference . . . the Press had seen his picturesque figure and heard only the more romantic side of his war service'. In 1918 Faisal had been acclaimed as King in Syria, but was obliged to leave Damascus in 1920 when the French entered it. *The Times* article added that 'he was suspected by the French of having been set up in Syria and secretly supported by Great Britain as part of an insidious scheme to spread British influence. . . .'

T. E. Lawrence had published an article on him in *Landmark* in October 1921, in which he gave a few more particulars. Faisal was 'thirty-seventh in direct line from the Prophet . . . and had been brought up among the bedouin for hardening purposes, since he was delicate as a boy'. As a young man he had been a Deputy in the Ottoman Parliament and had fought with an Arab contingent in the Yemen for the Turks. In the revolt against the Turks in 1916, Faisal had led the bedouin in person. 'At the time they had few rifles and no stores and he had to keep up the spirit of the men with the thought of material rewards to follow, by filling his treasure-chest with stones and ostentatiously loading it upon a powerful camel. . . .' With the rapid success of the coast operations, the British Fleet was able to bring him arms and stores, and his army put itself on a more businesslike footing.

'His work of course culminated,' Lawrence continued, 'in the wonderful burst of national enthusiasm that ran through Syria when the Turkish forces were destroyed by the Allied armies. Faisal's force entered Damascus on 30th September 1918 as the vanguard of Allenby's armies. . . .

'Faisal has again and again in public acknowledged the debt he owes to Great Britain.'

T. E. Lawrence himself was almost unknown when he wrote this article. It was the American writer Lowell Thomas' book which began to give him fame as the hero of the bedouin campaign. His own book had not yet been published.

Better known than Lawrence, from her writings before the war, was Miss Gertrude Bell, a traveller in Arab lands and Persia, who, it was said, was an ardent supporter of Faisal, now in Baghdad. I must see her there, friends in England had said, as soon as possible, but my very haste to present a letter of introduction on arrival in Baghdad led to a delay in meeting her.

No sooner was I done with reporting at military headquarters in Baghdad, in a house used by the German General Staff during the war, than I returned to question my hotelkeeper, a Christian with unctuously attentive manners, as to her whereabouts. To keep his building as cool as might be, the courtyard had been covered with a ceiling of tentage that could be sprayed by coolies from the roof-top. In summer this device may have had a comforting effect. In winter it led to a chilling gloom, accentuated by dark-green paint on the walls. A verandah ran round the court, as it did in all the older houses in Baghdad, supported by palm trees cut into slender columns and topped by rudimentary stalactite capitals. The general effect was that of being in the depths of a palm grove as painted by an inartistic child. Dark corridors ran out of the courtyard and gave on to brick stairways leading up to bedrooms or down to underground rooms devised as retreats in midsummer. These cavernous entrances were uninviting. The hotelkeeper waved his white hand towards them. 'Miss Bell—he live 'ere.'

Miss Bell, who belonged to a well-known Yorkshire family, was the most distinguished British subject in Mesopotamia or perhaps in the whole Arab East. Her literary work revealed her learning and sensitivity. She had played an able part in the war and been in the counsel of proconsuls and Ministers. If she had been a man, she would have been one of them, and she was in fact the Oriental Secretary and Adviser to the High Commissioner in Baghdad. It was strange that she lived in this Baghdad inn, mostly frequented by hard-bitten English traders or by passing young officers like myself.

She had after all, I reflected, been an explorer and an archaeologist, and must have ridden alone with Arabs and Persians on long desert journeys. A year or more, without relief, in bedouin camps and weeks spent on a raft coming down the Euphrates might, I supposed, alter one's feelings about comforts and surroundings. 'Miss Bell now in room on river,' the Armenian hotel-owner said decisively, holding out his hand for the letter in mine. So that was it. There was perhaps a suite with a good view down the Tigris.

The letter went and I waited; but not for long. With pleasing informality, I was bidden to join Miss Bell at once, in her rooms on the riverside. The winter sun was glaring off the water and into the room. On a small table, set in the middle, were several bottles of alcohol, the nearest a well-known brand of gin, glasses, some of them used, a swizzle stick and the apparatus for the serious drinking of spirits; and to the right, stretching towards the table, on a low stool, was a large leg, plastered to the thigh. My letter, torn open, was on the floor.

'Come in, my dear, and help yourself to a drink. You'll need it. You are wanting to see Miss Bell? I am Mrs. Bell. Have you just arrived? No, much more than that, dearie. Give yourself a man's drink and sit down here and tell me about yourself.'

Mrs. Bell was impatient of her convalescence and delighted that chance had brought her a young officer, whom she had, as it were, captured from Miss Bell, a lady she clearly did not much like.

My mistake was made worse by a second one. I wrote a note to Miss Bell and, instead of saying simply that I had lost the letter of introduction, explained briefly what had happened. That there could be a mistake made between her and anyone else was not calculated, I later realized, to please Miss Gertrude Bell, and the particular characteristics of the other lady would not have improved the matter. The wife of a racecourse manager was in any case not to be confused with her. Possibly it was not the first

time that there had been a mistake made between them. Had the
racy Mrs. Bell even maliciously told the hotelkeeper to show up
to her all the visitors who asked for 'Bell'? It would have been
like her to do so. Hers was a bold and simple humour, near to the
horseplay of the characters designed to give the light relief in
Shakespeare's plays—very necessary between heroic scenes,
murders and other intensity.

Mrs. Bell was by no means unpopular with the younger
officers. She diverted them in a country in which most of them
found little diverting save their work. She did rather more for
them than the arch-politician, able writer, *grande dame* and justly
admired authoress, Miss Bell.

If, therefore, I did not meet Gertrude Bell at once, I sometimes glimpsed her in the distance, at receptions, and once, riding
home on the evening of a hot day, I saw her on the road to Kadhimain, north of Baghdad. Preceded by two sowars of Indian
cavalry, a large car was approaching along a narrow dirt-track
through the palm groves. As the heavy vehicle slowly lurched
over the successive small bridges across irrigation conduits, little
clouds of dust rose. From them emerged at intervals a single
mounted figure in a dark habit, riding side-saddle in a masterly
fashion on a prancing Arab mare. Drawing level, I saw the Union
Jack, and the High Commissioner seated in the car, and saluted.
Miss Bell put up her riding-whip vertically to the brim of her
tricorne in reply and, setting spur to her mount, went forward at
a hand-gallop, followed by a pair of bounding salukis, to direct
the sowars.

After a quite long pause, to mark, no doubt, her displeasure
at the contretemps over the letter, I was bidden one spring
evening to her house, a low, mud-brick building in a rose garden
near the South Gate. There was a high mud wall round it, and
at a wooden door you rang and waited for her Muslim servant
to open and conduct you to the long French windows that gave
on to a small room made to resemble as much as possible an
English drawing-room. There were many knick-knacks and
photographs and a plant with wide leaves filled the fireplace.

She was noticeably thin, and when she rose held herself very
erect. Her seeming angularity was accentuated by an unusually

long, thin, straight nose, of the kind traditionally held to show
unusual intelligence. Her hair, of a sandish-gold colour fading
to grey—she was fifty-six—was arranged in the Edwardian style,
coiffed up straight from the forehead. Her evening dress was
made of cream lace, heavily flounced, and she wore with it a
muslin shawl. She was credited with getting her hats, dresses
and parasols from Paris, then considered ultra-mondaine for an
Englishwoman in the East.

The manner of her reception was only just not proconsular.
I was a little early and the other guests had not arrived. She sat
upright in a small, plush-covered, Victorian armchair and gently
drew me out about myself in an Edwardian rather than the
modern way—by leading and not direct questions—until the
others arrived.

She had, I knew, only three years earlier, at the Cairo Conference held by the Colonial Secretary, Winston Churchill, with
T. E. Lawrence as an Adviser, been the enthusiastic supporter
and promoter, as it were, of Faisal's kingship, and her opening
words to the first political officer she met on her way back from
the Conference were 'We've pulled it off.'[1] Faisal had much
needed such support then and had thanked her and been grateful
to her. She was full of enthusiasm and had enjoyed king-making.
'Isn't it wonderful?' she had written to her father from Baghdad
at that time. 'I sometimes think I must be in a dream.' There had
been difficulties to overcome. The people had been mostly cool
about Faisal before he came, if only through ignorance of him.
In the southern urban centres a new prosperity had followed the
military occupation and they were not much in favour of a
change from British rule. The desert bedouin were lukewarm at
first, and in June 1921, just before Faisal's arrival, she had
written: '. . . but it is rather a comic position, to be telling people
over and over again that, whether they like it or not, they must
have Arab, not British, government'.

After he came she had still to impress them that Faisal was
the right man. At a great meeting of the bedouin of the western
Iraq desert, when Faisal had spoken to them in their own language—'he spoke in the great tongue of the desert, sonorous,
magnificent, no language like it. He spoke as a tribal chief to his

[1] *Not in the Limelight* by Sir Ronald Wingate. Hutchinson; p. 95.

feudatories'—even then Fahad, ancient Patriarch and Paramount of the Anaza of Iraq, and Ali Sulaiman, Paramount of the Dulaim tribes, had said to his face: 'O Faisal, we swear allegiance to you because you are acceptable to the British Government.' The Kurds, too, had needed even more persuading, and there were others, minorities, and some British officials, who were doubtful or opposed to him. Sir Ronald Wingate thought that 'this enchanting piece of political enthusiasm of T. E. Lawrence, and, I am afraid, the romantic penchant of Gertrude Bell for the bearded and robed Sheikh of the desert, combined with the understandable wish of our rulers not to let a friend down . . . would produce a continually unstable political situation in Iraq'. H. St. John Philby[1] was in favour of a republic, and there were others with the same view.

The referendum went in favour of Faisal—the British official figure was ninety-six per cent in favour—but it had been, in fact, an uncertain business, and without the British political officers' explanations and management would have gone otherwise. One of them would afterwards relate that many of the illiterate people in the North had thought that they were voting, not for a King, but for more sugar, then in very short supply, and some Shiahs in the South had thought that he was a Shiah and not a Sunni Muslim.

Gertrude Bell's guests at dinner, my first night with her, were two of her warmest friends in Iraq: Captain Iltid Clayton, an artilleryman with the new Iraq Army, and Kinahan Cornwallis, who had come to Iraq with Faisal, at his request, and had stayed on with him as Adviser in the Ministry of the Interior. Like Gertrude Bell, both were keen supporters of the new regime. Cornwallis spoke of the initial lack of enthusiasm, how Faisal had been ready for great receptions at the stations between Basra and Baghdad, and the train had in fact often passed nearly empty platforms.

'When at long last it reached Hilla,' said Cornwallis in his slow, deep voice, 'I told Bertram Thomas,[2] Political Officer there, that it was the policy of H.M.G. to support Faisal, and that

---

[1] Indian Civil Service, Political Officer, well-known explorer and author.
[2] The explorer who later, while Finance Minister to the Sultan of Muscat and Oman, was the first European to cross the Empty Quarter of Arabia.

he had better, if he valued his job, get his notables together and bring them to Baghdad as soon as possible, as a delegation of welcome.'

Cornwallis was a giant of a man, well over six feet tall, with a distinguishedly large nose, who had been a runner of renown at his university. During the war he had been in the Arab Bureau at Cairo, under the famous Arabist, Dr. Hogarth, and afterwards liaison officer between Faisal and the British Commander in Syria. His quiet manner and gigantic size were impressive.

He had returned, when Faisal left Syria on being sent adrift by the French, to the Ministry of Finance in Cairo, but when, in 1921, Faisal had agreed to offer himself as a candidate for the throne of Iraq, he had asked if Cornwallis might rejoin him, at Suez. At Jedda a number of Iraqis who had fled their country after the failure of the 1920 rebellion against the British came aboard and attached themselves to Faisal. As Cornwallis said sardonically: 'They doubtless had much to tell him about their country.' Faisal spent most of his time on board talking to them, in the course of which they would not have spared the British. It was fortunate that he had Cornwallis with him. Although he had only been lent for attachment to Faisal by the Egyptian Government for three months, he was to stay in Iraq, with hardly any interval, until he left it as retiring British Ambassador twenty years later. He, more than others, kept the difficult balance between the Iraqi Government and the British authorities during most of those years and had, more than any other Englishman, the confidence of Faisal.

The King's first arrival in Baghdad, in June 1921, did not go according to plan in timing, owing to a diversion which he had wished to make to the Holy Shiah cities. Assembling in the early morning of the 29th June at the railway station in Baghdad, Sir Percy Cox, the High Commissioner, and the British and Arab notables had learnt that he would not reach the city until midday. It was already midsummer and Sir Percy firmly sent everyone away until the evening and a message to the King to delay his arrival until then. He and Cornwallis had to spend most of the day waiting for Baghdad instead of Baghdad waiting for them.

So, in a slightly makeshift way, but in consonance with our

wartime promise, began the reign of the Hashimites[1] from Mecca in Iraq.

Faisal was 'bitterly disappointed', as he told Cornwallis, at the cool reception on his arrival in Iraq. He had been led to suppose, he said, that there was 'a real feeling for independence and unity among the people of Iraq' and that 'they really wanted' him, but he had 'seen little sign of it'. He felt that 'the first thing to do, if Iraq was to become an independent State, was to create this feeling'. He leaned very much, therefore, on Jaafar al Askari and Nuri al Said, young ex-Ottoman and Iraqi-born officers who were with him during the Arab Revolt. It was Nuri who preceded him to Iraq and had organized what little enthusiasm was shown to him on arrival.

It was not the first time Faisal had met with rebuffs and subsequently succeeded in making some headway, with the help of the British. When he went in a British warship to France, his first visit to western Europe, just after the war, as a representative of the Arabs to the Conference at Versailles, he was met at Marseilles by French officials who informed him that their government did not recognize him as head of a delegation and suggested that he should, instead, visit the battlefields. From them he went on to England, and the British induced the French to accept his presence at the Conference. He was, meanwhile, received by the King, given the Chain of the Victorian Order and hospitably entertained.

He had been accompanied to the Conference by Rustam Bey Haidar and Tahsin al Qadri, both Syrians, and Nuri al Said, then thirty, three years younger than himself. In those days Faisal still wore his Arab clothes and head-dress. The *Figaro* described him on arrival at Boulogne-sur-Mer as being met by the Sous-Prefet 'in the name of the Government and by Captain Pisani from the Ministry of Foreign Affairs, who remained attached to him during the Conference.[2] French troops and a band paid honour to him and the Emir dined with the Sous-Prefet and afterwards went to the theatre in the box of the Sous-Prefet to see *La Favorite*.'

[1] Amir-Hashim was a great-grandfather of the Prophet Muhammad, from whom the Sherifs or nobles of the ruling clan of Mecca descend and take their name.
[2] Captain Pisani had been in Arabia during the Arab Revolt.

Later, in mid-January 1919, in Paris, he was invited to an official reception in the Hôtel de Ville, 'wearing the Legion of Honour, and a head-dress reminding one in the distance of that of an Egyptian Sphynx'. He signed the Golden Book of the city and was given 'a splendid sporting gun damascened with gold inlay', a reception which can hardly have atoned for the initial rebuff at Marseilles on his very first arrival in western Europe or for the very little headway he was able to make at the Conference. Still less would he be able to forgive having been forced out of Syria—which he had hurried to enter triumphantly at the beginning of October 1918 and where he had been proclaimed King—by General Gourand with the French Army in 1920.

At the Conference dreams of complete and immediate independence and unity for the Arabs died away. Thus, when Faisal came to Iraq in 1921 for the first time, at the age of thirty-six, he was wary of Allied promises, believing more in the help that was obtainable from a few individuals and relying upon the activities of his Mesopotamian Arab followers, former junior Turkish officers he had known in the war, most of whom had taken a part in the Arab rebellion in Iraq in 1920.

To them the British presence in Iraq rankled.

If the people of Baghdad were on the whole glad to receive Faisal as their King in 1921, the city was hardly one prepared for a monarch. There were no palaces or even palatial buildings which could be easily adapted for his use. Baghdad had not been a true capital city for nearly seven centuries, since the day when the last Caliph of the Abbasid dynasty trustingly walked out with his family in surrender to the Mongol Army and was slaughtered then and there; at a point very near where Faisal's own descendants were to be slaughtered thirty-seven years after his accession.

There were only three bridges of boats. It was a superstition of the simpler people that when it had five bridges, as in the days of the Caliphs, the city would fall. They said, seeking to prove their tale, that the British Army put up for a time two extra pontoon bridges.

The Ottoman Governors of the Wilayat or Province of Baghdad had usually lived in the Citadel, by the North Gate of the city; that, together with other gates and a partly ruined wall and rampart, marked the city limits when Faisal arrived. It was thus to the Citadel that he went to live. He drove in a car provided by the British through the only street, one cut through a maze of lanes and teeming, covered bazaars that made up Baghdad. The German High Command had insisted on cutting the road through the city for military-supply purposes and it had been done with military directness. Along it some houses were halved, with bits of furnishing and furniture still showing several years later.

The street, renamed after the British General Maude, who had died in Baghdad of cholera in 1917, was unpaved, and when bursts of rain came in winter the city was almost impassable. Inconvenient as rain might be, it was a rare pleasure, and people would run out to be drenched. Lurish porters from the Customs quay, temporarily put out of work, then lined up to carry Iraqi notables and Europeans across the street for a few annas. They were used to shifting the heaviest loads, packing-cases and even girders, and so made light work of carrying human beings pick-a-back. As they made their way across, their short tunics tucked in their belts, knee-deep in the slush, they laughed and joked and engaged in ribaldry.

The houses were unstable, being made of mud brick, though often with very thick walls, for coolness' sake. Hardly anything had survived from the days of the Caliphs and most old houses had been rebuilt, refaced and re-roofed.

A limited middle class was made up of rich merchants and religious leaders and there were a few powerful families whom Faisal would have to persuade to be his supporters; their names accordingly recurred in lists of Ministers until 1958, although less frequently as time went on. Their chief was the Naqib, head of the Qailani family, whose influence extended from China to the Atlantic through his followers of the Qadiri order of dervishes, and there were some twenty other leading families.[1] Often they

[1] That of Fuad al Daftari, of Shaikh Ibrahim al Rawi, Rifaat al Chadirchi, of Musa al Pachachi, of Yusif al Suwaidi, of Abdul Majid al Shawi, of Muhammed Jawad and Muhammad Jaafar Abu Timman, of Abdul Ghani al Kubba, of Fakhri Jamil-Zadé, of Shaikh Daud, the families of Naib and Chorbachi, of the Utaifa of Kadhimain, the Kudhairi, the Urfali and Shahbandar family, the latter headed by Mahmoud al Shahbandar, and that of the distinguished Abdul-Rahman al Haidari, from Erbil. From the countryside the outstanding names were those of the Emir Rabia, titular head of the Anaza Confederation, of the Paramount of the Shammar, of the Sa'adun family of the Muntafiq Confederation, and of the Baban family from Kurdistan. All except the Shaikh of the Shammar were settled on estates.

were in opposition to each other, as in the Italian cities of the Middle Ages. A number of them had members living in Constantinople, a connection from the days before the war, when it was their imperial capital. In the whole new capital of Baghdad there were hardly any other families of note except that of a former acting Governor and Ottoman Commander-in-Chief, Field Marshal Muhammad Fadhil Pasha al Daghestani, a Caucasian, descendant of the autonomous Ruler of Daghestan, who on retirement had acquired estates in Mesopotamia.

In the city they had huge, rambling houses, whose great extent was concealed behind heavy, brass-studded doors and windowless ground floors in the narrow lanes. Some of the families were of Turkish origin with forbears who had come down in the army of Sultan Murad the Conqueror and had been rewarded for their services with grants of land, and some were of Persian origin. Others were rich through trading and had the customary honorific for such persons of *Chelebi* after their names. Only about half, or less, of the leading families and one-third of the people of Baghdad had predominantly Arab blood, and even they must have had ancestry from men of the ancient empires and invading armies of the long past.

The heads of the great families were bearded, turbanned and dressed in long gowns, walking slowly, weighing their words, conserving their wealth and concealing its extent. Even their sons still inclined to wear ankle-length shirts in midsummer, though they wore suits and red tarbooshes for most of the year. As a sign of independence and emancipation, Western-style suits were increasingly considered 'the thing', and out of a laudable intention to foster 'progress and Westernization', Faisal and his young followers from the days of the Arab Revolt encouraged it and invented a new national headgear, a fore-and-aft cap.

Of city 'utilities' there were almost none. Lighting and sanitation were primitive, though water from the Tigris was laid on to most quarters of the city and to the bigger houses. The tap in big houses was in the middle of the courtyard, with perhaps another in the private Turkish bath. Otherwise it was fetched by hand or on donkeys, in leather skins, from the river and left to cool in porous earthen jars, each big enough to contain a boy or one of 'the forty thieves'.

A fleet of Victoria carriages was the only general form of public transport in the city; their drivers wore as head-dress a twisted kerchief, one end projecting over an ear, making a small turban known as a *charawi*. The cabmen, the boatmen and their kind—the *charawiya*—were considered by other Baghdadis as rough and immoral, but good-humoured and amusing. There were hardly any artisans except jewellers, silversmiths, boat- and house-builders and the lusty coppersmiths, whose art lay largely in their strength of arm. When Faisal arrived there had been no government or administration except the provisional Council of State under the Naqib and the British quasi-military political service. There were hardly any persons qualified to act as administrative clerks, except those who had fled with the Turks and might not return, and some Jewish secretaries or Christian and Indian clerks in the merchant firms, the majority of whom were already fully engaged. Nearly all the great Muslim families had Jewish secretaries and *hommes d'affaires*, and nearly all their sons were circumcised, when their time came, a little before puberty, by Jewish rabbis. Christians, Indians and Jews between them filled roles that the Muslims scorned or were incapable of performing.

In short, Faisal's new capital was an ancient oriental hive, well integrated in its own still largely mediaeval way, nearly oblivious of the Western world or, indeed, of distant parts of its own new kingdom.

The proclamation of Faisal as King of Iraq was announced for the 23rd August at 6 a.m. in the open space in the middle of the Citadel. He was fetched from his quarters in the Citadel by the High Commissioner, Sir Percy Z. Cox, and the General Officer Commanding-in-Chief, Sir Aylmer Haldane, Sayid Mahmoud al Gailani, the son of the Naqib of Baghdad, himself too old to attend, and Hussain Afnan, the Secretary of the Council of State. His A.D.C. was the Syrian Captain Tahsin al Qadri. The party—the King in khaki uniform—advanced along a path of carpets to a dais, also carpeted, on which were some chairs and a throne, on the model of that at Westminster, but hastily knocked up from packing-case wood that still showed the signs of its origin. 'Asahi Beer', a Japanese product, they are said to have been.

The proclamation by the High Commissioner was read in Arabic by Sayid Mahmoud and Faisal read a reply. The band played 'God Save the King' (of England). The Guard of Honour of the 1st Battalion the Dorsetshire Regiment presented arms and a twenty-one-gun salute was fired. The spectators had been admitted to the Citadel by invitation card only and *The Times* photograph published on 6th October shows that nearly all the first three rows of spectators were British, half of them men and half women, the men in solar topees and military caps. A *Times* correspondent wrote that some local notables, who 'strolled along late', were 'rightly not admitted to the ceremony'. As the party retired in the same order the new national flag of Iraq was hoisted on the Citadel and government buildings.

A constitution worked upon by a British lawyer, Sir Edgar Bonham Carter, then by a British and an Iraqi Committee, was to go before the Constituent Assembly whose task it was to pass it before being dissolved and replaced by Parliament.

The Parliament was to have a Senate and a Chamber of Deputies, the members of the latter to be elected by persons themselves to be elected by primary electors. There was to be no women's suffrage. The King was declared to be a Constitutional Monarch, with less full powers than the British had desired for him, though in fact he was in a sufficiently strong position to call and dismiss Cabinets at his own pleasure.[1]

Kinahan Cornwallis, as Chief Adviser in the Ministry of the Interior as well as a Personal Adviser to the King, undertook to shape as quickly as might be an Iraqi Civil Service and to organize the core of British political officers, who later became Advisers to the various departments when Iraqis were able to take over executive posts. Mesopotamians who had been in the service of the Turks were offered amnesty and the opportunity of returning, and a number did so.

Some of the British did not, for one reason or another, stay long, but others decided to throw in their lot with that of the new Arab State and served it painstakingly for many years. In

[1] See chapter on 'The Machinery of Government', p. 10 et seq. of *Independent Iraq* by M. Khadduri, for a full description of the steps taken in framing the written Constitution of Iraq.

the early days some of them enjoyed a life of discovery and unusual responsibility, though with discomfort and danger, in the outlying corners of the land; in the mountains of Kurdistan or in the far deserts. Others, based upon the towns, were soon engaged in the routine of government and the many laborious tasks which were required before there could be tranquillity; such matters as plans for irrigation, the settlement of long-outstanding tribal disputes, a national land-settlement scheme, the working of new departments, the tactful training of inexperienced Ministers, the completion of records of the inhabitants.

It was not long before Iraqi politicians began to say in public that the services of British officials were of no great value or that they took too many decisions, usurping a Minister's privilege. The Press later became scurrilous about them on occasions. But the truth was that in the early years their work was essential to the young State's continued existence, an additional reason, perhaps, for their unpopularity. In private most of the politicians gave other and truer views. They depended upon the British for unbiassed opinions and hard and quick work.

From the very first days of his reign the King had extremists, Arab Nationalists, whom as a matter of policy he was bound to countenance if not encourage, on the one side and the British on the other. Without the Nationalists there could be no hope of independence and without the British the State could not exist. He was obliged to run with the hare and hunt with the hounds and seemed to find nothing very difficult about it at first. He had learnt that habit in his youth in Ottoman Turkey.

When he was twenty-three, in 1908, his father Hussain had been called upon by the Sultan to return to Mecca as its ruler, after seventeen years spent in Constantinople by the Sultan's order. He was to replace a cousin, who had died in Istanbul before he could take up appointment in replacement of the youthful Sherif Ali, swept away for political reasons by the Young Turk movement. It had long been Turkish practice to bring to the capital, to a gilded cage as it were, close relatives and possible rivals of the Sherif ruling in Mecca. They had adopted a similar precaution with other families of standing in their provinces, so that the sons and relatives concerned became used to Turkish ways, to speaking Turkish and to the Court.

If Hussain's sons[1] had thus acquired a wider view of the world in their youth than relatives left behind in Mecca, they also learnt from their father that in Constantinople they must be careful to dissemble, adopt a pleasing and graceful manner, and watch nuances of speech and behaviour in Pashas and foreign Ambassadors.

The rivalries of the Great Powers before 1914 made of Constantinople a chequer-board of politics and intrigue, on which a son of the Sherif of Mecca was no more than a pawn: but a pawn could observe and learn the game, and if he were patient and seemingly amenable he might even contrive to get himself moved in the right direction. The intricacies of Ottoman protocol and the refinements of the Court, the bland approaches and shadowy retreats of diplomacy, the snares of generosity, were subjects in which Faisal was schooled by his father in the old capital founded by the Emperor Constantine and still known to the Arabs as Roum. Brought up in this atmosphere, with the advantage of good looks and the incentive of being only a third son, political ambition became second nature to Faisal.

His first opportunity of pre-eminence as an Arab leader was owed to the increasing despotism of the Sultan Abdul-Hamid of Turkey, followed by the Pan-Turanianism of the Westernized Young Turks after 1908. His father, as the Grand Sherif, or Emir, of Mecca, had had 'at first no separatist policy in regard to the Ottoman Empire', Faisal used to say. He merely hoped, as did the intellectuals of Syria, for 'the right to develop within the Empire and if a few extremists existed, they were not considered serious persons'.

Although Faisal would give this mild account long after the First World War,[2] there had in fact been the Ligue de la Patrie Arabe founded in Paris as early as 1904. It had been sufficiently strong and noticeable for a former French official, Eugene Yung, to write a book called *Les Puissances devant la Revolte Arabe— la Crise Mondiale de Demain* (Hachette) in 1906. On page six of

---

[1] See pedigree.
The Sherif Hussain, born in 1855, had four sons: Ali, Abdulla, Faisal and Zaid. The first three were by his wife Abdiya, a daughter of the Sherif Abdulla, who had also been an Emir of Mecca, and the fourth by a Turkish woman, the daughter of Salah Bey, a son of Fuad Pasha al Kabir. Ali became King of the Hijaz, Abdulla King of Jordan and Faisal King of Iraq.

[2] *King Faisal of Iraq* by Mrs. Stewart Erskine. Hutchinson, 1933.

his book Yung envisages 'the future Arab Nation with a Supreme Head at Mecca or Taif, to which the Muslims of all their world would resort for their instructions'. Sultan Abdul-Hamid of Turkey was reputed to have been fearful of the ambitions of Hussain and his sons, and events proved him to be right.

In June 1913 there had been an Arab Congress in Paris which pressed for attention to Arab rights, and there were several Arab societies. Some were secret, like that for army officers called al Ahad, with its headquarters in Damascus and strong branches in Iraq. Faisal, as a Deputy in the Ottoman Parliament, frequently travelled between Mecca and Constantinople, and was able to keep in close touch with the movement through its active members in Damascus.

In brief, before the war and during its first two years, he had played a dual role, promising the Turks his assistance and that of his father, while secretly working towards a revolt against them.

On the other hand, Ottoman rule had protected the Arab world and Islam from foreign encroachment for four hundred years and had in the past allowed a degree of autonomy to the Arab provinces. Above all, the Ottoman Sultan was *Caliph-al-Islam*, Defender of the Faithful, and the Arabs were proud that the Arabic language remained the spiritual language of the Turks.

To the British Government in India, with its millions of Muslim subjects and an army in which so many of the best fighting men were Muslims, each with the ambition to make the pilgrimage to Mecca, the religion of Islam and therefore Turkey were of high concern. And within the Turkish Empire Faisal's family, the Sherifs of Mecca, who had been ruling there and controlling the pilgrimage for some thirteen hundred years, were of unique standing.

Hussain's second son, Abdulla, had been in touch with the British in Egypt with regard to the future of the Arabs before the 1914–18 War, and he and Faisal, while always deferring to their father, were at the heart of a political movement which was hoping to achieve new status for the Arabs.

At the end of the war and following the Arab Revolt, although many Arabs were not yet 'nationalist' in sentiment,

c

save for pride in their race and a sense of autarchy rather more than was warranted, the movement had been given a fillip from the West.

In 1918, on 11th October, President Wilson's *Fourteen Points* were published and in November 1918 there followed the joint declaration of the French and British governments about 'the freeing of the peoples who had suffered under Turkish oppression', acknowledging their desire for 'complete and final enfranchisement' and giving encouragement to the establishment of native governments. The joint declaration of the 7th November 1918, the terms of the Armistice, and Article 22 of the Charter of League of Nations, all promoted the idea and held out hope to the Arabs of 'self-determination'.

When describing in her Administration Report the conditions in Mesopotamia at the end of the war, Gertrude Bell herself had stressed the contentment of the people with the prospect of British administration. She had thought that the Shiahs would object strongly to an Emir from Mecca. She had, however, added: 'Baghdad, which is a far more active centre of political thought than any other part of Iraq, has not yet spoken.' It was there, in Baghdad, about which she was right to make a reservation, that, with the encouragement given by the President and the Allies, Nationalism had come most alive, though it was less widespread than Faisal had hoped when he arrived.

Largely in consequence, not only was the mandate there unpopular with the extremists but, equally, the sop to them, a proposed Anglo-Iraqi Treaty, to be open to 'periodic, agreed revision'.

In the Treaty, Great Britain undertook to press the candidature of Iraq for the League of Nations 'as soon as possible', and there were subsidiary agreements to the Treaty covering military co-operation and favourable financial terms for Iraq. Great Britain was to fortify the embryo State. Nothing could have seemed more reasonable or helpful for a country that had an inexperienced government and administration, an army that hardly existed, except on paper, few police, recalcitrant feudatories, intransigent prelates, and tribes unused to paying taxes, no proper revenue system, with over half of its frontiers undefined, some of them threatened and the whole country largely unmapped, with hardly any roads and some corners quite unexplored.

The Treaty had a rough passage and an early sign of the way things were to go came at the Levee held on the first anniversary of the King's accession. The High Commissioner, as he entered the Palace, was insulted on the steps by demonstrators led by a Palace official. He demanded and received an apology, but no one was punished. A few days earlier Nationalists in Syria had attempted to assassinate Catroux, the French High Commissioner there, and a visitor, General Gourand, Faisal's old enemy, killing the French interpreter who was riding with them.[1]

The situation in Faisal's capital was rapidly getting out of hand when he was taken ill with appendicitis. Thus the British High Commissioner, obliged to take over the rulership anew while the King was ill, was fortunately in a position to quash the trouble with a firm hand. It was thought, or at least said, by some opponents of the British, that the operation on the King had been arranged to this end. In fact, as the doctors reported, the operation was only just in time.

In the North, after Faisal's arrival in Iraq, the Turks were openly hostile, in spite of the armistice pending the conclusion of peace. As the British withdrew the Turks advanced. Two British officers were callously murdered by Kurds, who then bolted to join the Turks. Since 1921 a Turkish official had been at Rowanduz in the north-eastern mountains with a force of irregulars, stirring up trouble and keeping the whole of Iraqi Kurdistan in a ferment. By November 1923 Iraqi Government prestige there was at the lowest possible ebb. Of this the young Nationalists in Baghdad knew and cared little or nothing.

Faisal appreciated the seriousness of his position. He might lose half his kingdom and if he lost half he might lose all. *The Times* of 19th February 1923 carried a long account of an interview given by the King to its correspondent:

He emphasized his conviction that there was not a vestige of justice in the Turks' claim to Mosul. . . . If they took the first step and

---

[1] *Deux Missions en Moyen Orient* by General Catroux, Librairie Plon, Paris, 1958, has a full account of the circumstances; pp. 1–5 et seq.

were successful, they would subsequently endeavour to recover the whole of Iraq.

The next subject touched upon was the difficult problem raised by the attitude of the Ulema (i.e. religious chiefs) in the holy cities of Kerbela and Nejef, who have been suspected of intriguing against the Government of Iraq, advising tribal leaders not to pay their taxes, and spreading the extraordinary superstition that participation in the forthcoming elections would be an act of war against the Prophet. . . .

'The Peace which appears to prevail in the Middle East . . .' said the King earnestly, 'is an illusion.'

'He gave a message to the British people . . . the Arab nation . . . hopes that the great British people will think of its little Ally in the East. It hopes that Britain will endeavour to safeguard the existence of the nation against the dangers which now threaten its very existence. . . .'

So, in 1923, Air Marshal Sir John Salmond, the British Commander of the Forces, was obliged to undertake operations against the Turkish Forces infiltrating in increasing strength and against Shaikh Mahmoud, a Kurdish leader calling himself King, who was agitating for an independent Kurdistan, as envisaged by the Treaty of Sèvres. Faisal, alarmed for the unity of his kingdom, placed the small Iraq Army under Salmond and undertook to raise an irregular force of tribesmen, horse- and camel-mounted, to harass the flank of the Turkish Forces. His young half-brother, the Emir Zaid, was nominally in supreme command, with his headquarters at Mosul. Meanwhile, at Lausanne, the Turks were claiming the Mosul Province from Britain's representative Lord Curzon. Curzon ably refuted the Turkish arguments and the Conference broke up without their making progress. In northern Iraq the demonstration of strength and the R.A.F. operations brought the Turkish effort to an end. In his despatches on the operation Sir John Salmond wrote enthusiastically of the co-operation by the local forces under his command.

It was the first R.A.F. Command operation in Iraq, one of many, without which the country could not have been held together.

Though Rowanduz—beyond deep gorges reached by dangerous mule-tracks—had been reoccupied and comparatively good order re-established, Kurdistan was not to be peaceful for long. Operations were almost continuous there during Faisal's reign; and the South was only second in number of disturbances. An agreement fostered by the British between the Emir of Nejd and the Iraqis, signed at Ujair in Arabia in 1922, improved the position on the southern frontier by outlining the border and allotting neutral grazing areas to the tribes; but the riverain tribes, inside Iraq, were also trouble-makers and resentful of control from Baghdad, to which they had been largely unused in Turkish days. There, too, R.A.F. strength had to be shown frequently in support of the central Iraq Government. And the Persian frontier was not clearly agreed upon and would require negotiation. Oblivious of the problems of the frontiers and in the provinces, the Nationalists in Baghdad were continuing their outspokenness about British 'interference'.

After much difficulty the first Treaty was in the end accepted, in June 1922, by the Iraq Ministers, and signed by the King in October, but they added that it must be ratified by the coming Constituent Assembly, a proviso the High Commissioner had wished to resist.

The new High Commissioner, Sir Henry Dobbs, like his predecessor, was infinitely patient, explaining again and again the provisions of the Treaty to members of the Assembly.

In the political wrack a Senator and former Minister of Justice, Tawfiq al Khalidi, was assassinated, being shot four times while on his way home from a visit to the High Commissioner on 22nd February 1924, an attack to which Nuri al Said was believed to have been privy. There were stormy meetings in the Iraqi Chamber, pro-Treaty deputies were threatened, some wounded, and, mob terrorism beginning, the troops were called upon to restore order.

At long last, the High Commissioner being immovable in his stand, the Prime Minister, Jaafar al Askari, another of Faisal's young Nationalist ex-officers, managed to assemble a majority, though there were many abstentions owing to threats. The ratifications were not exchanged until December 1924.

In Gertrude Bell's house, on the night in 1925 when I was first entertained by her, I learnt something of the past history of

Faisal, of the roles Cornwallis and she had taken on, and of general conditions in the country, and I looked forward to seeing the King.

It was in a rather unexpected fashion that I first met him. From time to time there were evening parties at his Secretariat—outside the North Gate—to which officers stationed in Baghdad as well as all the notables, senior civil officials and any visiting Shaikhs would be invited. Since the building was small and simple, only a series of low, hutlike, small rooms linked together by covered ways, these parties usually took place in the summer on the lawn in front of it. Miss Bell and Kinahan Cornwallis were always there, as were the officers, Colonel Pearce Joyce, head of the British Military Mission, Jaafar al Askari, Nuri al Said and others who like them were helping to form the new State and had been in the Arab Revolt with Faisal.

The grounds and the palm trees were lit by small coloured lights. The weather was usually hot, with perhaps a lingering haze from a sandstorm, and the leaves of plants and the lawn all had a dusty look, against which white uniforms, polished buttons, light dresses and a sprinkling of women's jewelry shone and glimmered doubly luminous.

The civilian Iraqis arrived wearing the new national fore-and-aft cap, which suited none of them. There was a buffet table, and a military band not yet well trained playing fitfully in the distance.

At one of these parties, Tahsin al Qadri, Faisal's A.D.C., invited me to play bridge as his partner against the King, the fourth being an Englishwoman. The King, wearing a white undress uniform tunic, with blue overalls, was already by the table and received us with a captivating smile. The 'Duchess of Alwiya', as the Englishwoman was known by the British colony in the cantonment of that name, had not had a say in the founding of the State, but she liked to play a prominent role in it socially. The wife of an official, an engineer in the Government's employ, she dressed with care and was a fine-looking woman with social energy and efficiency.

Every now and then, without any good reason, Tahsin would give a giggle habitual to him and say: 'I double you.' And every now and then another A.D.C. would bring a guest across the lawn for a few words with the King. When they left the King or Tahsin would ask again what were trumps. The King spoke in Arabic, using French bridge terms.

The game was going forward erratically, but my partner and I were clearly winning, as I was thankful to find, for the stakes had not been mentioned and Palace stakes might be high. When the rubber at last drew to a close, Tahsin very quickly made some marks on his score-sheet and, before anyone else could finish an addition, said with great firmness: 'We all owe His Majesty five pounds.'

The King rose, smiled wanly and drifted away, bowing his farewells right and left to the general company, warmly shaking hands with the more important guests with whom he had hardly spoken, receiving a curtsy to the ground from Miss Bell. The card game had been only a Court game, a means of avoiding protracted conversations.

Other mock games were played in the Oriental world. It could be amusing to intrigue, or bargain for its own sake as long as possible, and was only upsetting when the adversary did not understand the rules and suddenly wished to add up the score with exactitude and be paid.

Like everyone who met him, I was at once greatly impressed by Faisal. He was very slim with small bones, narrow shoulders, thin fingers and hands, and a rather long face of great beauty in which large, liquid eyes could appeal almost irresistibly. The delicacy of his frame and the gentleness of his movements and manner added to the feeling that he needed help and support, an attribute of a kind that would not be felt throughout the country quickly.

Faisal had settled down to an alternation between encouraging Nationalists and reassuring the British. Sometimes all went smoothly, but now and then there was cacophony in the fugue.

When his Ministers were markedly against the British, the High Commissioner would ask Faisal to remove them, but when they were against Faisal and not against the British, so that he had thoughts of calling upon them to resign, the British would warn him against unconstitutional enterprise.

Though he had been a leader of the Arab Revolt, it was as a

man of manœuvre rather than of action that he was thought of in Iraq. His appeal was to the emotions, and his success, apart from his ability to rouse the emotions of persons close to him, lay in his persistence, though it was the former characteristic that was the more evident. Lord Allenby said of him that he was 'one of the most picturesque of those who took a leading part in the World War. Picturesque, literally as well as figuratively. Tall, graceful; handsome to the point of beauty—with expressive eyes lighting up a face of calm dignity; he looked the very type of royalty.'[1]

Sir Henry Dobbs, the successor to Sir Percy Z. Cox, the first High Commissioner in Iraq, who knew Faisal long and intimately, said that 'he stood in the eyes of the British public as an almost legendary figure, a modern Saladin, endowed with every charm of manner and person. He was and is a truly kingly figure. . . . There can be no doubt that it is mainly to His Majesty that Iraq owes her present political status.'[2]

Gertrude Bell, like Allenby and T. E. Lawrence, who wrote of his first meeting with him in rapturous prose, said that he was tall; and Lawrence added 'pillar like'. *The Times* of 11th December 1918 called him 'tall, dignified and fairer than the usual Arab type'. Perhaps the Arab dress made him look taller than he was, and a comparison with most of his short brother Arabs would have seemingly confirmed it. In fact they were wrong. He was five feet nine and a half inches, the height recorded in the measure book of his London tailors, which agrees with my own recollection of him.

A view of his character is given by Hector Bolitho in his book *The Angry Neighbours*. He wrote of him: 'He talked to me of London, a little boastfully. He was able to juggle with great names of which his brothers did not know. He had read Galsworthy and could say, a little grandly, "When I was talking to the King" and "When I met the Prince of Wales at lunch".' Bolitho describes his hands as slim, his features as fine, but his eyes as cold. It seems doubtful that he could have read Galsworthy in English.

Faisal certainly preferred the indirect approach rather than the frontal attack in politics. He had an equable temper, though at times he could be very angry.

He was angry when a representative of a British newspaper, having attacked him and denounced Britain's policy towards his country, enticed him into giving an interview 'in order that he might correct their views' and then used it merely as an opportunity for a further attack on him. He was angry for days when he was in Paris in 1926 and learnt of the French bombardment of the centre of Damascus. And once he was extremely annoyed with Tahsin al Qadri, his A.D.C., for making a mistake over the dress to be worn at a banquet in Tehran with the result that he had to change quickly into uniform at the last minute.

His relaxations included chess as well as bridge. Chess was popular in the Hijaz and his family had all played it exceptionally well, learning when very young. In Baghdad he tried tennis and liked it, though his way of playing was old-fashioned and quite unacrobatic. He would wait for the ball to come to him, which it did often, for his opponents were more interested in amusing him and being invited to play with him again than in winning and possibly angering him. When the ball did come near him he would give it a sharp stroke or lob it over the net, without any long drives or backhanders. 'Love–fifteen, Your Majesty,' someone would cry out, and he would turn with his charming smile, missing the next shot in consequence.

'Oh dear,' said a woman partner at bridge during a post mortem, 'I went to bed with the King,' and the King, unoffended, laughed heartily. He liked such simple jokes and knew enough English to understand them, though he never spoke or read English well.

Once, in Vichy, he tried golf and liked it sufficiently to arm himself for his return to Iraq with a large bag and numerous clubs of which he did not make use.

He was interested in improving agricultural methods in the country and having tried them out, near his Secretariat in Baghdad, started a model farm of his own at Khanikin on the Persian border, where water was plentiful. He visited it frequently and did more than inspect results, taking a practical role in its management. He was not above physical work, and was once found by a British official at the Palace, where a reception was about to take place and the workmen concerned had left early owing to a religious fasting period, with his coat off, moving furniture about himself.

Faisal's adaptability to European ways was marked. Both personally, in everyday matters, and politically, in important ones, he showed it more than most of his people. He was one of the first Arabians to wear European dress, twitting his conservative elder brothers on not doing so, and if he were offered alcohol when visiting some Christian institution he would himself refuse, though saying: 'You may offer it to the others,' and Nuri al Said and his entourage would then accept it, having his permission. He frequently drank champagne at meals, holding that it must be medicinally valuable, since it was given to invalids.

Leaving Syria after the French occupation in 1920, he stayed gratefully for some days in the Church Missionary Society house at Haifa, a kind of residence to which his more bigoted fellow Muslims would have objected.

Outstanding examples of his political adaptability were his qualified agreement with the Zionists and his meeting with Ibn Saud, conqueror of his homeland, which pride and the Arab leaning to long-standing feuds would seemingly have made an improbable event.

Both Arabs and Ottoman Turks were particularly fond of proverbs and allusions and Sir Henry Dobbs, the High Commissioner in Iraq, told me a story to illustrate that addiction and Faisal's constant preoccupation with politics. They were dining one early summer night at the Residency in the middle of Baghdad. It had a large garden, and, after a dinner during which the conversation kept on coming back to politics, they went to sit on a terrace overlooking it. At such moments, when other guests are at a slightly greater distance away than when at table, confidences can be exchanged and in the East are expected.

As they sat beneath the stars, with darkened palms before them, Sir Henry, a tall and bulky man, looked down at the King and said that it was now almost the time of year for sleeping out of doors.

'Unfortunately,' he added, lowering his voice, 'I am kept awake by cats, whose amours are disturbing in the first half of the night, and by the cooing of turtle doves before the dawn. I am not sure which are the more annoying to me, but in any case Your Majesty can understand that I am reluctant to have them destroyed.'

The King looked puzzled and, according to Sir Henry, said: 'I do not follow you, Sir Henry. Which are we, the Arabs?'

Dobbs did not always see eye to eye with Gertrude Bell, having himself a different approach to Faisal and the political issues in Baghdad. Her position at the High Commission began to be embarrassing. There was always a throng of visitors to see her. Potentates and countrymen, on arrival in Baghdad, would go straight to her before calling elsewhere. The Nationalists viewed her standing in the country without pleasure. As Nuri al Said said long afterwards: 'We objected to her not as herself, but in her role as a man.' Her very enthusiasm, too, could be an embarrassment. She loved being in the forefront and Faisal was beginning to look askance at her ubiquity, as he reluctantly explained to Sir Henry Dobbs. Once at an inspection of troops she made an unforgettable sensation. The King, in khaki uniform on a white horse, had ridden slowly out of palm gardens surrounding the parade ground to take up his position at the saluting base. As he did so there appeared, at full gallop, reining to a halt at his side, a slim figure in white habit on a black mare, Miss Bell.

Moreover, a woman in government service was still said to be an anachronism in the East. Though travellers visiting her, like Vita Sackville West (Lady Nicolson), noticed first 'her radiant ardour and her irresistible vitality', Lady Bell wrote of her: '. . . in truth the real basis of Gertrude's nature was her capacity for deep emotion. Great joys came to her in life, and also great sorrows. How could it be otherwise with a temperament so avid of experience?'

When young she had been very fond of William Lascelles, and she loved and wanted to marry Henry Cadogan, who had died suddenly in Tehran, while she was away from him in England. Was the stealing away to travel with the Arabs in unknown lands largely a palliative for sorrows, with her wartime work and Faisal's advent its romantic culmination?

When the Colonial Office told her that her wartime appointment was soon to come to an end, she must have been profoundly hurt. She still held the honorary directorship of the little archaeological museum which she had begun in Baghdad, although as it grew she must have supposed that that too would be taken over in time by a British or Iraqi official, and Faisal and the Iraqi Ministers were needing her advice less and less, as they felt their knowledge of the country widen.

She habitually had by her some strong pills, so she told a friend, adding that if ever she 'felt the time had come', she would take them. She was not sleeping well in the summer of 1926 and was given an opiate. She seemed to me unhappy and the last letters to her father show that she was, in fact, sad. On 12th July she went for her usual evening bathe in the river and appeared well, but she died that night.

In spite of his standing as a Prince of Mecca and his constant efforts to propitiate them, Faisal still had difficulties with the ultra-religious Shiah prelates at the Holy places in Iraq: Najaf, Karbala and Kadhimain and, of lesser importance, Kufa and Samarra.

They feared, and rightly, that his government would lessen their power over the people. They were influential not only in Iraq, but equally so in Persia, where the Shah was a Shiah and where the population was almost entirely of the Shiah persuasion.

Most of the prelates in Iraq were Persians or Persian in origin and they were paid deep respect by Persians, who visited the shrines in large numbers and sent the bodies of their dead to be buried in the Holy ground of Najaf and Karbala. Their influence could sometimes be unbounded. In the last century the Shiah prelates in Persia had broken the foreign tobacco monopoly by ordering the people not to smoke for six months and they had been obeyed.

The shrines of Iraq were also revered and visited by large numbers of Indian Shiah Moslems and thus in India too the prelates had influence.

It was wise of Faisal to take care to visit Najaf and Karbala immediately on his arrival and again several times later.

The Holy men were feared by the people for their knowledge of the occult and for the judgments they might give in religious courts. They further maintained respect for themselves by appearing rarely, and then in forbidding black clothes and vast turbans.

The shrine of Abbas, who had allegedly been a hot-tempered man, was so feared that accused men were often asked if they would swear their innocence on it. If they agreed and were taken there they sometimes broke down and confessed on nearing it. The sight of heads and limbs hanging from the interior of the dome—where, it was alleged, they had flown up on being torn away from the bodies of false-swearers—and of the shrine itself emitting smoke from the furious Abbas, was too much for them.

Many of the inhabitants of Najaf, built on the edge of a cliff facing the desert, lived underground for the sake of coolness in summer. The chambers beneath the surface were hewn out two or three, or even more, storeys deep, so that some houses were larger below the surface than above it. Here and there the chambers had been connected up with those of neighbouring houses, making it possible to move about the city without being seen. Some of the people used the underground passages for thieving and immoral purposes. Large numbers of visitors may have made such behaviour easy, though the *mita'*, or temporary marriages permissible to Shiahs for as little as a few days, reduce female prostitution among them.

Christians in the Holy cities were anathema. A British political officer had been killed not long before in one of them. Even laymen destroyed glasses and plates used by a Christian before he left their house so that bystanders would report the host's deference to Muslim transcendence. Only a few, more sure of themselves, would receive a Christian without signs of xenophobia. One of the latter kind was Sayid Jaafar al Utaifa, a descendant of the Prophet Muhammad, venerable and rich, an owner of large properties in Kadhimain near Baghdad, an example of the man of dignity in a world that is gone. Distinguished European visitors and senior officers of the British Services visited him and he would even invite them, provided that they agreed to take the precaution of arriving discreetly during the night before, to view the annual Muharram Passion Play of the Shiahs from a window overlooking the Mosque.

When it was only a matter of a courtesy visit, he would receive callers at a garden outside the city. Messages were exchanged with him beforehand, so that he was ready at the large wooden gates of his orchard, itself hidden by a fifteen-foot wall of sunbaked mud and straw. However frequently foreign visitors came, he never refused to see them, and his picturesque appearance and old-world behaviour provided the exotic note which they expected in Baghdad, one which it hardly yielded them otherwise. So Sayid Jaafar had become a kind of 'showpiece' and probably knew and rather enjoyed the position.

Like most men of his standing he wore turban and robe, then an almost obligatory sign of respectability, similar to the bowler hat and umbrella of the City of London and no less reassuring in fact. Strange passions or disturbing rectitude may, of course, belong to wearers of either kind of headgear. The Sayid's turban was billiard-cloth green; his long dress was usually of light-grey face-cloth embroidered in black braid at collar, cuffs and fastenings; his footgear was generally canary-yellow or sealing-wax-red leather slippers with long, curling points; and he always carried a string of amber beads with a silver tassel.

His brows were prominent and large and his nose was equally distinguished. His beard and moustache were hennaed bright red or dyed bootblack black. It might, disconcertingly, be either, according to his whim.

He would hold each of our hands a long time in turn. 'How very gratifying.' 'How welcome and fortunate.' 'Welcome again.' 'How do you do?' 'How goes your health?' 'Again how is your health?' As many times we had to reply. The succession of enquiries and ejaculations would continue as we advanced with him into his garden and until we were seated on long wooden benches covered with Persian rugs, set out on a shady path between the gently gurgling water-channels.

'And how,' he would say, this time with a show of greater earnestness, 'does Sir Henry —— and Sir William —— how are they?' They were names we only knew by hearsay, of military commanders long since gone to England or India. No one, including the Sayid, I fear, really cared a straw. His questions were no more than the safe exchanges of the polite society of a bygone, oriental world.

Formal relations having at last been satisfactorily established, the Sayid ordered his waiting servants to bring the tea. For it we were taken, with the slowness which his dignity demanded, still farther into the depths of the garden, where the shade was so profound from close-set palms, orange trees and pomegranates and the humidity so heavy from the slow-moving water in the channels that it was as dank as a cave. As we moved along at cere-monious pace, in time with the water, it seemed to be the dusty, corrugated palm-trunks that were moving, not us. Ahead, giant frogs, hopping ponderously on the dark mud paths, lowered them-selves into the channels and edged their way obscenely out again when we had passed. The leaves of the fruit trees were grey with the dirt of duststorms; it was the murkiest garden imaginable. Only here and there and far overhead gleamed shafts of sun-light, where fronds of palm trees criss-crossed like prison bars and the doves cooed and fluttered lazily in and out of a zephyr we could not feel below.

There were no more than eight of us and the table was never laid for less than twenty-five. Pride demanded that it should be so. His reputation for generosity and hospitality would suffer were he ready for less than twenty-five guests at one time. 'Is that all we are?' He would peer about him as if some of the party might be lost. We sat in a huddle at one end of the long, empty table while servants poured tea from immense, heavily decorated silver tea-pots into tiny-waisted tea-glasses standing in little china saucers. We nibbled the cakes and crumbled the hard sweets. He would press us to eat more; but even twenty-five guests could have made little inroad into that great quantity of food, laid out so that plate touched plate, over the length and breadth of the table, concealing its fawn, muslin and gold-embroidered cloth.

One visitor, I remember, Sir Hubert Young, who was acting High Commissioner, leant forward when the Sayid was not looking and gently stroked an iced cake. 'Just as I thought— my initials are still there from our last visit,' he said to his guest from Europe, Lady Mountbatten. She turned to ask the Sayid about his harem and about his daughters. But the parting presents, wooden boxes of Persian sweetmeats, were already being brought to us, a signal for departure from his world and century to ours.

Every now and then there would be reviews or galas, of the Police or troops, of Boy Scouts and schoolchildren, which Faisal had to attend. He went to them accompanied always by his three leading favourites and political supporters, Rustam Haidar, Jaafar al Askari and Nuri al Said. They would stand or sit in a row, from time to time exchanging smiles and whispered confidences in Turkish.

Rustam was a cultured, French-educated Syrian, tall and of singularly ascetic appearance. When a youthful student in Paris he had been a founder-member of the Fatat Arab Secret Society, devoted to the liberation of the Arab countries from Turkey or from other alien rule. It was the initiative of the Fatat that led to the Arab Congress in Paris in 1913. After accompanying Faisal to the Peace Conference he had joined him in Syria and then Iraq. He had become an Iraqi, was the King's trusted lieutenant in the Palace and his constant companion at the bridge table. He was one of a small and sophisticated coterie in which were Hussain Afnan, who had been Secretary to the Provisional Council of State when Faisal arrived, and his intelligent and emancipated wife, and Saifullah al Khandan, a well-educated Kurd, and his Austrian wife. They were looked at askance by the rest of Baghdad for their Western habits, then thought uncouth.

Rustam was murdered, when Minister of Finance, in his office by an ex-police-inspector of German sympathies on the 18th January 1940.

Jaafar al Askari, who hailed from Chemchamel near Kirkuk in Iraq, had served in the Ottoman Army until captured by the British in the Western Desert. He was persuaded by Nuri al Said to give his parole and join Faisal as one of his followers in the Arab Revolt, and he and Nuri al Said married each other's sisters. He was Nuri's closest friend.

A brave, heavily built man, of marked personality, with a good sense of humour, Jaafar al Askari had been Governor of Aleppo while Faisal was in Syria. He then returned to Iraq, becoming first Minister of Defence, later taking leave to pass his

Bar examination in England, and was twice Premier of Iraq, becoming Iraq's first representative in London in 1925. While Minister of Defence he was shot dead without parley by Iraq Army officers during a coup d'état on the 29th October 1936 and hastily buried by the roadside between Baghdad and Baquba.

Nuri al Said, many times Premier of Iraq, who on occasions was nevertheless obliged to seek refuge outside Iraq, was the longest survivor of the little band which used to accompany Faisal everywhere in the early days of the State. Born in Baghdad in 1888, he had become an officer in the Ottoman Army, was an enthusiastic member of the secret al Ahad Society, and having been detained by the British in 1914 and taken to India he had elected to join the Arab Revolt. With Jaafar he had done more as the first Chief of Staff than any other Iraqi to bring into being the Army by which they were both murdered. He was an example of extreme intelligence wedded to unusual adaptability and good political sense. He and Jaafar never wavered in loyalty to the dynasty or in their faith in Britain as the supporter of the Arab movement. 'As long as British policy is favourable to Iraqi ideals, my loyalty can be relied upon,' he would say.

In the early days of the kingdom, as an extreme Arab Nationalist, he went through a picaresque period, when he was guarded day and night by a selected gang of toughs, some in the uniform of the Iraqi Military Police; and there were not wanting stories of executions, other rough 'acts of justice', and the promoting of anti-British and anti-Jewish demonstrations by students which they had undertaken on his behalf. At work he was full of nervous energy and high inquisitiveness, usually concealed by a statesmanlike reticence while in official European circles. At the same time he liked to relax in an Oriental way.

Twice he borrowed the use of a house from me, for a night, in order to entertain unofficial visiting Europeans. A succession of dancing girls and performers of various kinds and an Arab band, whose strange instruments he knew as well as the players, were brought along by his bodyguard. On such occasions he would soon become carried away by the music and greatly animated. At the first party given in my house, one rented from Jaafar Pasha, the band repeatedly played to his order the then most popular song—'Cocaine'.

D

It was said of Nuri that he 'never read a file', and, broadly
speaking, it was true. He came to know what he wanted about
any subject by asking those who understood the question best.
I never heard him make an original remark, but I never heard
him make an unwise one. His memory was good and he liked
small jokes. Once at an evening party long after the Second
World War he thrust into my hands twenty pounds in bank-
notes. Astonished, I asked him why. He reminded me in a voice
loud enough to be heard by the bystanders that he had borrowed
it from me when he was penniless in Jerusalem in 1941. On
returning from the United States of America to London after the
war, he was asked by a member of the Foreign Office staff if
there was anything they could do for him. He said that he did
rather urgently want to see Colonel Eadie, who had long been
in the Iraq Military Mission. He did not know his whereabouts.
The War Office staff officer, impressed by a call on the subject
from the Foreign Office, made haste to trace the officer who, as
he later told me, was sent a fast staff car to bring him at once
from the camp where he worked outside London. He was then
ushered into Nuri's presence at his hotel by the Foreign Office
representative. Nuri handed him a bottle of chilis and a bottle of
Cayenne pepper which he had brought with him from the
United States, knowing how fond he was of curry and how short
supplies were in England.

He could also be sentimental, more so than most of his
compatriots. I recall how, arriving in H.M.S. *Ajax* at Istanbul
after the war, he and Daud Pasha al Haidari ran from side to
side of the ship to see the places on the coast and in the city which
they remembered from their youth. I saw that Nuri's eyes were
watering as he pointed out their haunts of long ago, when he
was a youth in the Military College.

He was slim and slightly built, with large marks of Baghdad
boils on his cheek. He was always neat and well dressed and often
carried a chain of amber beads in his hand. As a sign of friendli-
ness he would hook his little finger in that of the person to whom
he wished to show that feeling. Even his enemies admitted that
he had not amassed a large fortune in questionable ways. He was
to be killed in horrible circumstances in July 1958 in Baghdad.
So all three of Faisal's inseparable chief advisers, who were con-

stantly in his company and who, more than any others, helped him to found the State and give birth to Iraqi 'nationalism'—if that is the right word—were in the end murdered by Iraqis.

The King, like his great Caliphial predecessor, Haroun al Rashid, would occasionally sally forth, though usually by day, with these three or others of his staff, to make a surprise descent on, say, the Prefect of Baghdad, who to his mortification would be found out of his office, or to a parade of the Army where he was not expected. Such visits had an excellent effect and his unheralded appearance was gratifying to the ordinary citizens, who liked the interest he showed in them.

Faisal's family had soon been installed by him in Baghdad. Since there was no palace ready for them they lived in first one and then another old and simple house near the North Gate of the city and the Secretariat, or 'Bilat', which he used daily for his work.

His wife, Hazaima, who was his cousin and a sister of the wife of his brother Abdulla, like all the Hashimite family and most Arabians, was small. Humans, and animals, from the Hijaz may perhaps owe their diminutive size to its fierce climate. Only certain insects and reptiles seem to thrive there and grow particularly large. In any case, Faisal's offspring, like other Hijazis, were small.

He had three girls, who were put in charge of an English governess, Miss M. Lucie-Smith, and one boy. His eldest daughter, Azza, reached marrying age without finding a suitor of her own standing and, while spending a holiday in Rhodes, she met and ran off with an hotel servant, who soon deserted her. She lived for several years on a pittance in Italy and it was only on returning from England via Rome after the Second World War that her cousin, the Regent of Iraq, was able to arrange for her to go to Amman, where her uncle's, King Abdulla's, family could keep an eye on her.

Faisal's half-sister married an Iraqi, Ata Amin, who later became a diplomatist.

Another of his daughters, Princess Rajha, also failing to find a suitor of high rank, married an Iraqi Royal Air Force officer, Abdul Jabbar Mahmoud, who, it transpired, had a flair for business deals and became a wealthy man, until the revolution in 1958. They were in Europe then and so escaped harm except for the loss of their property, but she did not survive it for long, dying of Hodgkin's Disease in Lausanne in March 1959.

The youngest child, the Princess Rafia, who was never quite stable—indeed, she was far less than sane—died before the Second World War.

Ghazi, the third child in age and the only son, born in Mecca in 1912, was adored by his mother and had been mewed up by her with the women of the family, until it was almost too late for him to recover from it and go to a school. Just in time, or so it was thought, his father was persuaded to send him to England and Harrow. So, in 1925, when he was thirteen, he set off for England. Mr. Amery, the Secretary of State for the Colonies, who was visiting Baghdad with Sir Samuel Hoare, was dismayed to find that he knew scarcely any English and was quite unprepared for life at an English public school. He therefore found for him a tutor, the Rev. Mr. R. E. Johnson, of Marden Vicarage in Kent, where he was given special preparatory tuition.

On his first night there Ghazi barred the shutters and shut close the windows of his room. The absence of sentries with their comforting stamp outside, and of faithful Negro servants asleep in the corridors, ready to be called, alarmed him.

Very soon he was hankering for a car of his own. Jaafar al Askari, the Minister in London, came down to Marden and dissuaded him. The boy wrote to his father, who cabled to Jaafar: 'Why do you annoy my son? Give him motor-car.' But he had, under English rules, to have a chauffeur. 'On his bicycle, it seemed absurd to him that he should be expected to avoid hitting children in the road, though when the police regulations were explained to him he quite loyally observed them.'[1]

Even with the period of special tuition, the sudden transition from being the darling of his mother in the Royal circle to being a fag and junior boy at an English boarding school could hardly be expected to meet with much success, and it did not do so. In some ways the young Oriental was much in advance of his companions and in others behind them. In schooling he was unable to compete on a level for his age and, galled by failures, he hated

[1] Obituary letter to *The Times* by Rev. R. E. Johnson, 6th April 1939.

the life. When he left he is said to have threatened his house-master that he would return with his army to burn down Harrow-on-the-Hill. It is certain that he was not happy there.

It was appreciated by the school authorities that he might not find life easy in an English public school and he was put to live with a junior master, his wife and their very small daughter, instead of in a school house with other boys. From the first, and the whole time he was at Harrow, he was quite unable to concentrate on his work. At night he still closed up his windows as he had when at Marden Vicarage and slept in an air-pilot's fur-lined cap. When asked why he wore it he explained, lifting the ear-flaps in order to hear the question, that it was so that jinn could not enter his ears while asleep. He had, he said, already experienced trouble with jinn in Baghdad. There were some in the Palace and his father the King exorcized them from the bedroom corridor by reading the Koran in a loud voice.

When without a proper prayer-rug, he used a vest instead. Once he was heard sobbing and gabbling prayers late at night in an almost hysterical manner because he was to receive a whipping from the monitor in charge of outside boys the following day. He was in such an excited condition about it that the master with whom he lived intervened and the beating was postponed indefinitely. So his prayers were answered.

He could be vindictive, saying once: 'You will see what God will do to you,' meaning that the Muslim God would avenge himself on the lady concerned, a housemaster's wife, who was talking to him gently about God's mercy. And he never forgot that Jaafar al Askari had refused him a car when he wanted one; he said at Harrow, more than once, that he hated him.

When he was taken to Spain during the holidays he persisted in thinking that he would meet ruling Moors there and was bitterly upset when he found that in fact there was a Christian church in the mosque at Cordoba.

Years later I was asked by an Arabic-speaking professor of Granada University, who had then recently accompanied King Abdulla, Ghazi's uncle, on a tour in Spain, why it was that Abdulla refused to take an interest in the mosque's architecture and walked through it from beginning to end without once raising his eyes or making a single enquiry. It was, of course, owing to the Arab form of pride. I cannot think that Englishmen will ever walk through New Delhi with averted eyes; though admittedly the Arabs ruled longer in Spain and peopled it more than the British did in India.

Ghazi recovered his spirits in Spain only when he found that he could buy arms and uniforms.

Even Dujaili, his Arab tutor, did not seem able to make him learn much and the English climate affected them both and Ghazi in particular. He was quite unsuited to life in England, did not stay his full time at Harrow, resented the outcome and the whole affair.

From his early youth he took an ardent interest in cars and aircraft and he loved speeding. He had the natural charm of his father with greater exuberance and even as a youth he began to have a following among officers and students. If his lack of respect for their institutions bemused the British there would, it was wrongly thought, be plenty of time in which he might become settled before reaching the throne.

2

Triumph and Defeat

*New political systems and philosophies were
imported into the Near East under the general
term of democracy and grafted artificially into a
society which was feudal in nature and theocratic
in spirit. The results were not happy, and were
often disappointing. The strain and stress produced by maladjustments and by the lack of understanding, and sometimes of appreciation, of the new
political institutions, discredited democracy in the
eyes of many Easterners.*

Anglo-Turkish Relations and the
Emergence of Arab Nationalism

ZEINE N. ZEINE

F AISAL'S plan at first was a simple one: to achieve independence by encouraging the urban Nationalists and
obtaining the support of the tribal Shaikhs and great
riverain landlords by use of the charm and persuasiveness of
which he knew himself to be master. Once he had the backing
of the Nationalists and countrymen of importance he could
cajole the British into agreement and prove the case for early
independence by an occasional, well-timed demonstration of
national solidarity.

The plan proved less easy than it seemed at first. In the
towns the leaders of the new Nationalism were by no means
personae gratae with members of the old families. The latter were
not particularly snobbish, but they found it irksome that men
whose humble beginnings they had in many cases known, or

55

whom they had in some cases actually helped in person, perhaps by a letter of recommendation to a Turkish official, before the war, were now as Ministers able to lord it over them or over their followers.

As men of property they had been on good terms with the Turks, but also—as soon as they arrived—with the British. The young Nationalists had intrigued and fought against the Turks and in 1920 had intrigued and fought against the British, being in some cases involved directly in the slaughter of British officers. The men of property found it difficult to believe that the British would really be prepared to hand over the country to such men, inexperienced in ruling as they were and irresponsibly as they behaved. And it was dangerous, they held, to rouse the people as they did. The countrymen began to feel uneasy. British officials had listened painstakingly to their plaints and sought to redress wrongs and they paid deference to tradition and were fearful of innovation unless it was unavoidable. The Nationalists, on the other hand, were far less careful to avoid offending custom. The King himself, leaning as he did to progressive measures and the modernization of the country, was on the side of the Nationalists. The Shaikhs, however, had a means of appeal, since, as men of standing, they could visit the King and senior British officials. So there were always strings of tribal visitors at the Palace and at the offices of Cornwallis and leading British officials; and they all had to be given attention.

Sometimes the conflict between old and new came to a head in an incident. Exasperated Shaikhs would go back to their lands to brood upon their wrongs, supposed or real, and perhaps attack a tax-gatherer or a Police post and have to be subdued by the R.A.F. and Levies or Iraq Army.

One example of the way that the old and the new pronouncement could clash with evil consequence arose in spite of advice given by the King in person. A preliminary incident was described to me by an English business man staying in a small hotel in the main street of Baghdad, then recently named Rashid Street instead of Maude Street. He had, he told me, complained to the occupant of the room above him, who had prevented him from sleeping for the second night running by walking up and down until dawn. The occupant was a distinguished-looking country Shaikh, a member of the great Saadun family from the South, who had apologized, but continued his pacing. The manager of the hotel said that he could do nothing to stop him for he was a man too important to offend. When the Englishman related this story, I was able to tell him that an hour earlier it had been reported that the same Shaikh had shot dead, in his office, Abdulla al Sana, a senior Iraqi official, just becoming a Minister. The killer had evidently spent two sleepless nights considering his deed; the motive was avowed by him and he did not try to avoid arrest. Abdulla al Sana, son of a slave formerly owned by the Saadun family, having been educated, wished to marry a girl of the Saadun family. He told the King, received his blessing and had done so. This to the Saadun family was an unparalleled dishonour, to be wiped out only by death. The court sentenced the killer to imprisonment, from which he was soon released.

There were continual intrigues among the Ministers and their parties, to a point beyond that which could have been foreseen by Faisal, inured though he was to intrigue. The imposed parliamentary system lent itself to it. Prime Ministers could seldom keep their governments together for long, and during Faisal's reign, lasting twelve years, there were fifteen governments. Of these, nine were headed by members of old families and six by the 'young Nationalists' of the ex-Ottoman officer type. So the Palace was frequented also by the politicians, striving to placate or please the King.

From early morning to late midday the Chamberlain, at first Safwat Pasha and then Tahsin al Qadri, the former A.D.C., who had married a date-garden heiress from Basra and became an Iraqi subject, led in the callers one by one. Sometimes they had to wait more than a day to reach the Royal presence, and there would be careful manœuvring and shifting of the silent notables so that the more important persons or those with pressing reasons could precede visitors who had come before them, and all the time coffee and lime tea would be served with scented or gilt-topped cigarettes and the A.D.C.s would come and go with whispered messages to the Chamberlain.

Across the way, nomad Shaikhs and visitors from Arabia and Trans-Jordan or the deserts of Syria would be similarly marshalled, at a coffee hearth of the kind to which they were used, by a follower of the King from Mecca who knew their bedouin ways. They each had to be given presents—money, clothes, supplies of food, arms, or all four. So day after day, year after year, Faisal was engaged in his almost insupportably hard task as King of a new country of which, so far, he was not, because of the Mandatory Government, the true Sovereign.

Faisal's position as a descendant of the Prophet and a Prince of Mecca might have enabled him to rule in a more aloof, theocratic manner if it had not been for the division in the country between Shiah and Sunni Muslims and the large Christian and Jew minorities. He could only continue his appeal to individuals and make use of the divisions between the young Nationalists, the men of property and the British; and he leant more to the first of the three for the sake of the future.

As Faisal and his Nationalist Governments began to feel their growing strength, supported as they were by the British Royal Air Force, they began to take a stronger line over internal policy. They considered introducing conscription and wished to disarm the tribes of the South, mostly Shiahs, who were ultra-conservative in habit, superstitious and fiercely bigoted in religion. The strength of their feelings was shown in the Muharram Passion Play to which Sayid Jaafar of Kadhimain would invite us annually, it being performed wherever the people were of the Shiah persuasion as opposed to the Sunna order to which Faisal and most of his close supporters belonged.

Gertrude Bell had written soon after Faisal's arrival in Iraq in one of her letters home:

It may have escaped your notice that we are in the middle of Muharram. From the first to the fifteenth the Shiahs mourn for Hussain, the Prophet's grandson, who was invited over from Mecca by the Iraqis to be Khalif, and when he arrived got no support from them, was opposed by the army of his rival Muawiya at the place where Karbala now stands, saw his followers die of thirst and wounds and was killed himself on the fifteenth. One small son escaped and from him Faisal is descended. Incidentally, when Faisal came, the story of his ancestor was always in my mind. The parallel was so complete, the invitation from Iraq, the journey from Mecca, the arrival with nothing but his formal following. If the end has proved different, it's because I said 'Absit omen' so often.

But the end did prove the same for Faisal's grandson, killed with his family by the Iraq Army.

The Muharram mourning for Hussain was greatly reduced by order of successive governments in Iraq, and once they even sent some of the Army to the bridge of Kadhimain, a Shiah shrine and city—the Minister of Defence, Jaafar Pasha al Askari, was present—nominally to support the Police and keep order, though in fact they opened fire and killed many of the participants.

There were processions every night at the beginning of the month of Muharram, with lighted torches and beating of drums. Each night the numbers taking part grew. Each night they showed more fervour, more torches and men with trays of light on their heads, with others leading horses in embroidered caparisons. The men were all in black, most of them bare to the waist, some swinging chain flails with which they beat their backs in unison. During the first days they swung them carefully, with a little jerk at the top of the swing so that the chains only lightly touched their shoulder-blades. The drums marked time and there would be repeated cries of 'Hassan—Hussain—Ali'. Then came breast-beaters, all naked to the waist, beating in unison and with a hollow thud as the blow fell, using a different rhythm to that of the flagellants. Other groups, moving with a curious sideways step, swung swords with which they cut their foreheads, until the practice was forbidden. All this time there would be shrieks and groans from the spectators.

After the first nights there was in addition a procession of actors of the various parts in the Passion Play, some in chain-mail and Persian helmets, with crests of feathers, some carrying great silken war-banners, with more flagellants and beaters. Each night until the tenth of Muharram there were larger numbers, greater emotion and more abandon, finer array for the actors and horses and those taking the part of soldiers in Muawiya's army.

Boys read the story of the battle of Karbala and young men dressed as women took the part of the women of Hussain's family and children those of his children. There was, too, the body of Hussain on a bier, arranged by placing two men, one beneath the other, with plenty of real blood between the 'severed' head and the 'body', a dove tethered on the corpse. The man who took the part of the Christian Ambassador from Roum, the Byzantine capital, who interceded at the Court of the Caliph on behalf of the women prisoners taken in the battle, was dressed in the full uniform of a British naval officer, with the addition of a solar topee and dark glasses, a cigarette hanging on his lower lip in order to emphasize his 'Western' and 'Christian' origin.

The fervour and extent of popular participation in the Muharram mourning ceremonies in southern Iraq and Persia was so remarkable that it seemed to show a popular need for masochism with a complementary delight in sadism. The ceremonies, if such they can be called, were under the general direction of the Shiah prelates and certain old families in each city, town and settlement. Had the Government—instead of aiming at doing away with them—sought to improve and gradually take them over as an annual festival of which all might be proud, just as the Christian Church took over and adapted many festivals from the pagan world, the result might have been less sinister. But such subtleties in the art of governing were beyond the fiery young Nationalists of Baghdad. They feared originality and empiricism, spoke much of 'liberty' while giving it away in favour of uniformity. So year by year the mourning ceremonies of the Shiahs were reduced. Bereft of that more or less controlled outlet by Iraqi governments, which saw it as anachronistic in a modern State, people took perhaps more readily, as a form of substitute, to political mob demonstrations; whatever the truth, it was usually from the Shiah quarter of Baghdad and from among the *charawiya* that the mob first came in later disturbances.

In the early years of Faisal the First's reign the standard of everyday security in Baghdad was not high in spite of an aftermath of Ottoman severity and cruelty. By far the greatest number of murders in Baghdad—about a hundred weekly, according to a British C.I.D. officer during the Mandate—were murders of sisters by their brothers for an alleged affair with a man, dishonouring her whole family. The offending part of the woman's body was cut out with a knife.

These killings were regarded in the same light as are *crimes passionelles* in Latin Europe, and if brought to the notice of the Police and a magistrate were dealt with by a light sentence. As a result of this rigidity of view, boys, rather than women, danced in the Arab theatres and took women's parts in plays until after the advent of the British.

If the Turkish regime was marked by severities, so at the beginning was the British. An officer of the levies, a Kurd, had, just after Faisal arrived, been given so severe a thrashing as punishment for a military offence that he died. Miss Bell, hearing about it, took the matter up and, thanks to her, it was followed by a court martial. On the other hand, beating was still an approved punishment in forces under the Colonial Office, and in the Iraq levies men seemed to prefer a punishment that was soon over to a loss of pay, with its effect on their families, or to imprisonment, which they held to be shameful and almost unbearably irksome.

The arrangements made for a caning, awarded by a commanding officer, were doubtless much the same in all units under the Colonial Office, wherever it might still then be in force. The Arab sergeant-major in the Iraq levies, having paraded the troops and camp-followers, would ask the British officer's permission to begin, and when the punishment was over the man would lean forward to kiss his officer's hand, as a sign of obedience and of absence of revengefulness. He would attempt the same thing with the sergeant-major, who, with the modesty becoming to his lesser rank, would withdraw his hand, waving it towards the officer, like a prima donna indicating the conductor. For a year or two this form of punishment was regularly awarded and carried out.

If Sayid Jaafar al Utaifa, who entertained us in Kadhimain, and others of his ilk were men of a bygone age, there were also Englishmen who were notably and proudly products of their period. The Colonel of the Arab levies, stationed in Baghdad as a unit, though it sent detachments up-country, had long been in the Colonial Office service. He was an immense man, six foot four inches tall, with a drooping, dark Edwardian moustache. He ate voraciously, perhaps necessarily for the support of so large a body, wore a gold-edged cap, even with his khaki, and had boots and accoutrements polished and boned until they reflected like mirror-glass.

All the officers' quarters of the camp—huts built of mud and straw—had windows filled in with a palm-cane lattice entwined with camel-thorn, giving a dim green light. Every hour or so during the midday heat the thorns would be drenched with water, cooling the air indoors and giving off a refreshing smell. The Colonel did not speak much at meal-times, except to give orders to the Arab waiters who, barefooted, were kept nipping about him. Sometimes he would be obliged to send reprimands to the boys who pulled the punkah cords from outside the mud walls of the room and who, every now and then, drowsing in the midday heat, needed slapping into renewed attention and threatening with the Colonel's anger. With the self-confidence of Arab youths, they would squeak some reply to his reminder through the hole in which the cord ran: 'May God cool you, Colonel Sahib,' or some cheekier phrase.

In the orderly room the Colonel was a particularly imposing figure. He held himself bolt upright and seldom spoke except to announce the punishment or dismissal of the offender.

The Colonel's dicta included one about having the cookpots and women close behind native troops in action. 'They only fight to protect their cookpots and women,' he would reiterate. Another of his sayings was that the Arabs always tried to divide the British, and that one should be on one's guard against it. They began gently, with careful insinuation, not going too far at first. If one allowed it, they would then become bolder and make astonishing allegations, hoping to please. It was an age-old characteristic, he said, and it was, indeed, one noticeable later as applicable on a wider basis. Arab politicians would whisper to us about the French in Syria and to the French about us. Still later the Americans had to listen to stories about the British which, I fear, some believed.

When the Arab levies were transferred to the Iraq Army and given a new British Colonel,[1] they were also given an Arab second-in-command from the Iraq Army, Shakir al Wadi, who had been an A.D.C. to King Faisal. He once gave me a reply which his way of life and his career made memorably unexpected.

---

[1] Afterwards Lieut.-General Sir John Evetts. Already exceptionally well disciplined, drilling like British Marines or Guards, he gave them up-to-date field training, and the unit was thenceforth known as the exemplar battalion of the Iraq Army.

Shakir was proud of having been to the Staff College at Camberley and counted friends in the British service. He became Iraqi Minister in London and Minister of Defence in Baghdad, and at the time of his death in a London hospital in 1957 was Iraqi Ambassador to Turkey. He was a good host and prided himself on knowing where to dine well in London and how to choose good wines. In short, he led an occidental life, and I never heard of him praying or visiting a mosque regularly.[1] Yet he reacted strongly about the British Consul in Ahwaz whom the Persian Premier, according to newspapers, had accused of inciting the inhabitants to rebel. Asked: 'Do you know the Consul, a quiet man, whose hobbies are botany and entomology? Is nothing more unlikely than the accusation made against him?' he answered: 'I hate that man!' His words tumbled over themselves in his vehemence. 'He said it to King Faisal the First, to his face! He told him that there was a new and interesting book giving a list of two hundred foreign words in the Koran.'

King Faisal and his A.D.C. had been equally horrified at the inference made.

The belief that the Koran was in God's own words and in the language of Paradise, Arabic, was rooted in their minds, as probably it is in the minds of other seemingly cosmopolitan, non-practising Muslims. That a Christian should suggest that the words in the Koran were not direct from God was blasphemy of the most odious kind.

Shakir's reaction in this case was an eye-opener. It showed how circumspect one should be, how easily one could be misled by seeming sophistication and outward Westernization.

The way the Iraqi democracy worked in the reign of King Faisal was equally an eye-opener to those who, judging it by its written form, expected a parliamentary system working like that of England. In fact it could not do so. There were insufficient experienced men to work such a system had they wished to do so or understood it. When elections were under way, other government business was held up because the administrative

[1] Faisal, unlike the Sultans of Turkey and Morocco, in spite of his descent from the Prophet and his standing in the Muslim world, did not go in State on Fridays to a mosque. His son and his grandson similarly did not parade their religion, though there is no reason to question their beliefs.

officers were busy rigging the elections; and court judgments were often corrupt, the judges being insufficiently highly paid. There were barely half a dozen men of true 'Cabinet rank' in the whole country[1] and it was in fact not a democracy but an oligarchy, with the King at its head.

It was understandable that Faisal felt fatigued and, by way of relaxation, he began to make visits to England through Switzerland and south-eastern France. He visited England in September 1925 and again in the midsummer of 1926; and then in the autumn of 1927, when he was not only tired, but had been feeling ill for some months, he decided to make another journey to England accompanied by Dr. Sinderson. He was extremely thin and wasting so rapidly that the High Commissioner thought that he was dying from an incurable disease. Every kind of ordinary test had failed to reveal the nature of his illness, and after preliminary examinations on arrival in London nothing identifiable was found wrong with him.

On being again examined, by Dr. Clifford Dobell, it was found that he had a chronic amoebic infection. It was at this point, when Dr. Sinderson had only just received Dobell's explanation, that the King said to him: 'Tell me, am I going to die? There is so much I must do for my country.' Sinderson was able to say: 'You are getting better from this moment onwards. I am giving you an injection that will begin your cure.' That Faisal made this remark under fear of death should prove his patriotism, if proof were needed.

The King nearly always wore European dress, but he still used a *Sidara*, the fore-and-aft Iraqi national cap, until, finding it conspicuous in London, he took to a bowler hat, except on official occasions.

Passing the Chelsea football ground at a time when a vast and boisterous crowd was there, he turned to Sinderson and said Bolsheviks? Sinderson explained and said that he would arrange for him to visit the next match. He duly went, was well treated and much amused, but on a visit to a Service exhibition at Wembley, wearing his bowler hat, he was upset when photographed in it by the Press; a brimless hat, in which the forehead

---

[1] Ernest Main: *Iraq from Mandate to Independence*, Allen & Unwin, 1935, confirms this estimate; pp. 166 et seq.

could touch the ground during prayers, still being *de rigueur* for Muslims. Sinderson followed the photographer and offered a posed photograph in the *Sidara* cap, on condition that the other plate was returned. Both the King and the photographer were thus satisfied. But that night an evening paper carried the headline: 'King Faisal insults the Bowler.'

While Faisal was in London the ratifications were exchanged of a second Treaty, signed at Baghdad on the 13th January 1926; a third Treaty prior to complete independence, signed in Baghdad on 30th June 1930, was to follow: it must have seemed to Whitehall that the main feature of relations with Iraq was an almost permanent state of negotiation over treaties—with accompanying troubles in Baghdad.

It was not surprising that Faisal felt tired. Not only were there Iraqi politics, but also international Arab politics, to occupy him. There were constant visitors to Baghdad and to the Palace, both tribal and urban, men from over his frontier, from Arabia, Trans-Jordan and Syria. From Arabia they hoped to win Faisal's sympathy by tales about their discontent with Ibn Saud's regime. He kept on his payroll one of the Princes of the Shammar capital, Hail, a rival of Ibn Saud, who once, unfurling his green silk war-flag, went a little way over the border into Arabia. Receiving no support, he came home again to Baghdad and the payroll. The flag, he told me some time later when I enquired about it, had since been made into dresses for his women.

From Syria there were tales against the French and about Arab longing for a joint kingdom, Syrian-Iraqi, under Faisal. At one time it became quite a live issue, in spite of the fact that the Syrians were more advanced than the Iraqis while Iraq was richer than Syria, characteristics which alone made for a difficulty between them in the matter of unity.

Iraqi politics led to the suicide of one Prime Minister, Sir Abdul Muhsin al Saadun, who killed himself on the 13th November 1929, worn out by attempts to please the King, the British and the Iraqi political parties and 'as the result of extreme Nationalist pressure and a feeling that the Iraqis were ungrateful for his sincere efforts on their behalf'. The third British High Commissioner, Sir Gilbert Clayton, had died suddenly, a few months earlier, on 11th September. Both had been trying to

E

reconcile Nationalism with reason as a preliminary to independence and the passing of a Treaty.

The Nationalists in the Chamber were so bothersome that from time to time one wondered if British policy was wise. The older British officers would sometimes debate it at their dinner tables.

Though some of them had quarters with the civilians in the new cantonments outside the city, most of them still lived in the maze of the city lanes in order to be near their work in the Citadel. On full-moon nights the way to their houses could be found without much difficulty; otherwise it was customary to send a lantern-bearer to meet a guest. Under the eaves of the latticed windows in the narrow lanes it was dark and it was best to carry arms, though I never heard of them being used, perhaps because it was known that they were carried.

Colonel Eadie of the Military Mission was one who would invite us, and he usually had with him the American Consul-General, the first one to be appointed, an ardent poker-player whose previous posts had been in South and Central America. Sometimes Nuri al Said, the whereabouts of his pistols showing beneath his clothes, would come with an escort of thuggish soldiery. Eadie's cook, whom Eadie said was a convicted murderer on parole, was the best maker of curries in the country. They were so hot that small towels were provided as well as napkins. The furniture, the only kind that had been easily obtainable, came from India and was elaborately carved in blackened wood, and from its journey and the climate it was cracking and had dust in the corners of the carving.

Eadie spoke some thirteen languages, including Amharic and Armenian. He and other officers of the Mission were working from after dawn daily forming the Iraq Army, to which he had been first Chief Adviser. It did not even have a vocabulary. Jaafar al Askari had initiated the use of a huge ledger-like book in the Ministry of Defence where Arabic words approved as the equivalent of English military terms were entered up. Since it seemed unlikely to be published for years, I published at the Hilal Press a short list for everyday use. Even words of command had to be invented and strange and impracticable they seemed at first.

Men such as Eadie remembered the constant fear in Indian Government circles of Czarist Russian advances, though in fact Russia always withdrew whenever she occupied for a time northern Persia. British representatives in Persia were still furnished by the Indian Foreign and Political Department, whose staff was partly recruited from the Army, and even in Turkey, in outlying districts, the British Consuls before the war of 1914–18 were military men, supplementing the civilian Consuls of the Levant Service of the Foreign Office. Thus a number of Consuls and military officers had an unusually good knowledge of the countries and languages of the Near East, as it was then still called.

But in their debates, even if some favoured a republic for Iraq and others preferred the rule of a King and a Council of State, without the modern democratic forms of a parliament, it was nearly always agreed that in general there was nothing much else that could have been done than act as we had done. Once Turkey entered the First World War on the German side it was certain that the Arab provinces would try to break away and that the Allies, in particular Britain, and the Indian Government, would be obliged to show their support. What did astonish them was that there was a new diathesis of the Oriental peoples which no amount of adroitness in handling seemed able to overcome. They put it down mostly to weakness among the Allies after the war, together with President Wilson's unsettling pronouncements implying immediate self-determination. But the truth, looking back on those days, was that the impact of the West upon the Arab East, after a long period without change, had come with startling suddenness, throwing the Arabic-speaking peoples off their balance.

The Arabs believed that empires rose and fell and they now had every reason to believe that the British and the West were beginning to withdraw. They failed to see that the days of individual and supreme empires were over and that a new form of pressure, economic, social, idealogical and above all cosmopolitan, was taking their place and was quite inescapable.

If the British tide was indeed running out, the Western undertow was stronger against it. Far from reaching the imaginary island of their hoped-for independence, breast-stroke valiantly towards it as they might, the Arabs were being whirled about. They would even be caught in another, Russian, eddy. But that condition was not yet reached, and our hard work, hard exercise and the exhausting climate disinclined us from protracted debates at night.

Abdulla al Misfir,[1] an Hijazi follower of the King, had been made an extra Chamberlain to deal with the stream of bedouin visitors to Faisal's Palace. He would talk to me about Arabia and Mecca and excite a fondness for esoteric knowledge by his stories of distant tribes and parts of Arabia forbidden to Europeans.

He asked me one day whether, since I was leaving for Jordan and Egypt, I would be good enough to take with me in the aircraft a trifling present intended for King Faisal's brother, the Emir Abdulla in Amman. I accepted, supposing that it was a bottle or two of rose-water or perhaps essence of sandalwood. It was, in fact, four large packages done up in calico, carefully sewn, that were sent to me. Camel-hair cloaks and postheens, as his letter explained, made in Iraq and unobtainable in Jordan.

The R.A.F. pilot agreed in the end that their weight was not too much for his load. The aircraft lumbered all day across the desert and came down at last—it was a Vickers Victoria bomber —on the small and awkward landing-ground at Amman. The pilot intended to leave for Egypt at ten o'clock precisely the following morning.

Very early the next day I went to the Palace with the bundles. At that hour the Palace, though open, was nearly deserted. A page flitted away and did not return, but he had shown me a door into a drawing-room where soon a suave young courtier appeared.

'His Highness will not be long coming, and tell me, how goes Iraq?' he said, leaning forward confidentially. His questions showed a knowledge of politics, doubtless acquired through having a role in the Palace. Cautious though I was, he picked out from my replies material for more questions. The Arabs are

[1] Died, aged about a hundred and one years old, in 1960. He had entirely missed hearing that there had been a revolution in 1958.

natural diplomatists and, given a position in a Palace, know how to cull from a visitor in the politest way his news from afar. But time was going on. Without, I hoped, his noticing, I stole a look at my watch. His extreme politeness was catching and I did not wish to offend the young man by so rude a gesture as looking at a watch while talking to him. But perhaps he saw, for he reassured me: 'His Highness will really not be long now,' and continued his conversing on topics piquant for their introduction of lively comments by the King on matters of high policy. But by now it was time I left. 'I must go,' I said firmly. He looked disturbed.

'I can assure you, once more, that His Highness is coming, at this very minute. He is most regular in his habits. Exactly half an hour ago, as usual, I trimmed his beard and touched it up a little, you know, and from the moment when I finish him His Highness takes precisely half an hour before appearing. I do therefore assure you——' But at that moment the double doors at the end of the drawing-room were thrown open by two Caucasian guards who, advancing towards us, announced: 'His Highness!' With which the Emir's barber and I rose and bowed. As the Emir talked I found myself admiring his complexion, its pink freshness, and the cut of his beard and its colour. I had, however, to cut short my stay as much as I dared and arrived at the airfield only just in time. The propellors were already turning and the pilot was anxious to be off.

'More of your high politics, I suppose,' he said, tolerantly enough.

Every now and then Abdulla made visits to his relatives in Iraq and I was able to see him for longer than on my first call upon him in Amman. He had a boyish sense of humour, was warm in his manner to strangers, and quickly succeeded in capturing their affection by affability and liveliness. Unlike Faisal, he retained his original Oriental habits and, except on most rare occasions, his Arab dress. His was a simpler and more definable character than Faisal's.

In April 1934 I found myself translating for him and the Chief of the Air Staff from England, who during tea-time harped upon racing. 'The totalisator at Ascot,' he said, 'is twice as large as the façade of this Palace,' in front of which we were sitting.

I gave in over 'totalisator' and asked King Ghazi, who said 'betting machine', which simplication I could have managed myself. I left out the part about the Palace and said 'very big', but Abdulla had understood my embarrassment and later, as we went round the Palace, took my arm, saying: 'Some people, like you, translate better than the original.'

In 1941 he came to see the Regent of Iraq as he went through Trans-Jordan on his way to Baghdad with the help of the British Army. Abdulla took me aside and made a grandiloquent little speech, saying that he relied upon us to do the utmost and speediest to restore the regime.

When, much later, I was writing a book about the Rulers of Mecca, I visited the King, as Abdulla had by then become, to discuss the book and the material for it. There are a number of Arabic accounts of the history of Mecca and there is no doubt that the family was ruling there from about A.D. 480, before the time of the Prophet Muhammad.

While we were talking before luncheon about the history of Mecca, Abdulla spoke about a strange stick or wand which had recently been brought to him from Medina. It had been closed up in the wall of the great mosque there and found during repairs. A friend of the Hashimites had secured it and brought it to him. With it was found a short document saying to which Emir it had belonged and when it was concealed, and the King said he would show me both the wand and the letter after our meal.

He was wearing Arab dress, with the small turban and gold-embroidered centre usual to the Sherifs in Mecca, and was strongly perfumed. For their retention of these habits his brother Faisal had been outspokenly critical of him and his brother Ali, saying it was backward.

Only his personal suite and one of his Ministers were at the luncheon table. Arabs do not speak much among themselves at meals, or did not do so until Western manners began to be adopted. They relied for sociability very largely on quotations and the capping of quotations from poetry, a trial for the knowledge and patience of foreigners, however well known the language might be to them. Our conversation was of that old-fashioned kind.

After luncheon the King invited me to go up to his newly decorated pavilion, on the hillside above the Palace. He would come there, he said, and join me for coffee. It was a pleasing, white-plastered, little building in the old Oriental style, although the interior decorations had garish touches; the emerald-coloured cushions had bunches of conspicuously artificial pink roses sewn to them, so that one feared to lean back and crush them.

A Chamberlain and I stood idly conversing until a fusillade of shots interrupted us. 'It is only His Majesty, I think,' he said. Was he taking an assassination very calmly? Then a soldier arrived, walking at an unhurried pace. 'It is the King trying out one of the new revolvers supplied to his bodyguards on the sparrows. He shoots, as always, very well, and has killed several of them,' he added.

The King, possibly elated by his post-prandial bag, was smiling and happy when he arrived. At once he began to speak of the book and of material for it, and, after a time, remembering his promise to show me the find from Medina, he called a guardsman and told him to fetch his confidante, a reader of the Koran. There was a long pause and the King sent another soldier after the first on the same errand. At last a handsome, bearded bedouin arrived, clearly in a very bad temper, having, I dare say, been roused from a siesta in the warm afternoon or from some other private diversion. He stood in the doorway while Abdulla gave him instructions for finding and bringing the wand and letter, then turned away in silent sulkiness, without the customary words of obedience.

We continued our conversation until, the afternoon heat becoming overpowering, I asked leave to say farewell. Another messenger was sent to hasten the bringing of the stick but, since it did not come and there were no more messengers left in sight, the King expressed the belief that we should not receive it. He said this sadly, then, becoming brighter, told me to come to the Palace in the morning. 'I shall have it by then. I can get it myself.' He said it like one who has had a clever and unexpected thought.

The next day I went to the Palace, taking with me the British archaeologist, Gerald King, and his photographic equipment. The wand was of grey-white wood, with tiny ridges along it and a

crook carved like foliage. There were some very small holes on
the crook that might have held some metal coverings for jewels
or rings. The letter had every appearance of being genuinely of
its very early date, but the statements in it and the titles employed
did not fit with the facts known from the surviving chronicles of
Mecca. We could not think what the wand could have been,
unless it were that known as the Prophet's Wand, lost long
ago.

Abdulla's marksmanship was remarkably confident. He gave
one of many examples of it during the Second World War when
visiting the Third (Mechanized) Regiment of the Arab Legion.
Asked by the British officers to show his prowess, he agreed to
have some tins put out as targets, but wanted two of his slaves
to stand by them in order to signal wides. They stood about ten
yards off the target and the King waved to them to go closer.
The first shots were off the target, which the slaves duly sig-
nalled. He shot standing up, holding the rifle by its magazine, his
shoulder against a tent pole. The slaves then waved to indicate
hits, fortunately on the target, by the King.

Abdulla was, too, a good mimic and storyteller. Sometimes
his stories had a funnier side than he himself knew. One from his
repertoire was about visiting the Opera in Vienna, with St. John
Philby, during a tour of Europe. His staff had preferred to go to
a cabaret and he and Philby sat alone in an otherwise empty box.
'It was ridiculous,' said the King, getting up to prance around,
waving his arms horizontally, imitating the singers and saying
in a sing-song voice: ' "How are you? How are, are, are you,
you, you?" Absurd! Thank heavens you do not have such
childish nonsense in London.'

He had a quick way with tiresome petitioners. A minor
bedouin Shaikh, who asked him to reverse a judge's decision of
imprisonment of one of his men, received his reply in a proverb:
'Women and children think men are capable of anything.'

Another time, bothered by a man for a letter of recommendation to the Head of Police, who was reputed to take bribes, in
order that he would employ him in the Police, the King said: 'In
that case, if you want help, I will not give you a letter, which
will be no good, but another more useful piece of paper,' and he
took out and gave him a five-pound note.

He used to say that his father, Hussain, when asked for money by Faisal, had replied with a phrase from the Koran: 'Spendthrifts were the brothers of the devil and the devil was a traitor to the Lord.'

Abdulla's big failure, though not admitted by him, was being surprised by Ibn Saud's forces at the battle of Taraba, a fight which both Abdulla himself, in his own book, and St. John Philby have described. 'After that,' Ibn Saud used to say, 'I was not afraid of any Sherif any more, except Pockface'—the Sherif Shakir. Ibn Saud soon afterwards put his belief to the test. By 1924 Hussain was forced to abdicate as the forces of Ibn Saud advanced into the Hijaz, and after a year's resistance in the seaport of Jedda, Hussain's eldest son and successor to the throne, Ali, was obliged to surrender and end the rule of the Sherifs in the Hijaz.

After his abdication Hussain had gone to the port of Aqaba and then to Cyprus. In June 1931, after a stroke, at the age of seventy-five, he died in Amman, an embittered but unwavering old man.

His family had wished him to come to Amman so that he might die near them, in an Arab land.

It was late evening when the party of relatives and a doctor sent to Cyprus for him reached his house. There were no lights in the room. Hussain was already partly wandering in his mind, and spoke of one of them as if he were an emissary of Ibn Saud, his enemy, and at first refused to leave.

In Amman all his sons and the family gathered to attend the old patriach's end, exiled from Mecca though in an Arab land.

'Despite his limitations and his defects,' as George Antonius says in *The Arab Awakening*, he had that strength of spirit and that integrity of character that betokens greatness; and, if the standard is that a man's moral worth must signify more than the measure of his failure, then Hussain deserves our admiration.'

His eldest son, King Ali, had gone on a British ship, in December 1925, to Basra and so into exile at the Court of his younger brother, Faisal.

I used to visit him in his rambling palace on the west bank of the river at Baghdad, the very house which his only son, the

Emir Abdulillah, lent to me later. Ali was small and delicate, wonderfully neat and clean, dressed in striped or flowered robes with the small Meccan turban. His gestures and manners were restrained and elegant, and his Arabic clear. Sometimes his son, then a shy, slim boy with large eyes in an oval face—a gazelle-like creature—would flit across the end of the room and be called upon to come back and say 'How do you do?'. His four daughters, Aliya, afterwards Queen of Iraq, Badiya, Abdiya and Jalila and their mother, Nafisa, like all Muslim women of standing, were still secluded and I did not come to know them until much later.

When King Ali came to dine at the Residency I would be asked to dine too, and sometimes I had to translate for him. I did so one day when he had agreed to play chess with Sir Hubert Young, a good player. The King made his moves very quickly. While Sir Hubert pondered his own moves the King would talk quietly aside to me. Soon the result was going in the King's favour. They played again, and again the King won in a seemingly effortless way. 'And would you ask His Majesty,' Sir Hubert said, 'how it comes about that he used the opening move only recently employed for the first time by the new world champion?' 'I learnt it in Mecca as a child and am in the habit of using it,' the King replied. 'My family is rather well known for ability in making the right moves. When our allies adhere to the rules, we win,' he added, smiling.

T. E. Lawrence wrote of him in *The Seven Pillars of Wisdom*:

To Ali himself I took a great fancy. . . . He was bookish, learned in law and religion, and pious almost to fanaticism. He was too conscious of his high heritage to be ambitious; and his nature was too clean to see or suspect interested motives in those about him. Consequently he was much the prey of any constant companion, and too sensitive to advice for a great leader, though his purity of intention and conduct gained him the love of those who came into direct contact with him.

It was he who had sent Lawrence off in secrecy from the Red Sea coast, giving him a disguise for his uniform, in order to meet his brothers Faisal and Abdulla, who were already campaigning against the Turks in the interior of the Hijaz.

Ali had brought with him on the British ship that took him away from the Hijaz, after his defeat by Ibn Saud, an ancient German radio that looked like a child's coffin, made in unusually solid fashion. Radios were rare and the King treasured it, though it was often out of order and almost incomprehensibly hoarse when it was not. Periodically I would bring over an N.C.O. from the Royal Air Force headquarters to try to mend it. They would shake their heads in despondency, but would succeed in obtaining some response for a time.

At last one of them, Corporal Budd, told me that it was now beyond hope except with prolonged attention and some replacements. It would take several days to mend, if, indeed, it could be put right. The King, who had at first been upset, brightened at once. 'Then,' he said, 'the Corporal must stay several days as my guest, until it is right.' It was like him to delight in thus returning kindness by hospitality in a simple, straightforward way, just as he might have pressed some visiting bedouin to stay, and he would have sat with him and delighted in his company and tales of far-off places. The Corporal was willing to stay if he could have his tools and bench, though there was, of course, no likelihood of the R.A.F. headquarters agreeing. I had to think of excuses and make a promise to mend the radio later on in the year, when the wireless experts were to be 'less fully occupied'.

King Ali was out of place and time, like, say, a courteous old rural dean thrust into the hurly-burly of a great city, arousing one's admiration and protective instincts. On the other hand, he liked the boxing by the Royal Air Force and Army. When this penchant became known he was regularly invited and asked to give away the prizes. Once, when perhaps owing to a change in staff he was not asked, he sent for me and diplomatically recalled the practice on former occasions. I was able to arrange for him to go and he was happy again, arriving at the ringside in good time, ready to follow every punch.

When I was saying goodbye to the King on leaving for England, where his son was shortly expected in order to continue his studies, he suddenly raised himself on his toes and, kissing me on the cheeks, said: 'Take special care of Abdulillah.' It was the last time I ever saw him, so that they were his last words to me.

In any event I was at that time unable to help his son, and the boy, who was unhappy where he was placed, in some tutor's house in England, ran away back to the East.

Years later, however, after the King was dead and his son had unexpectedly become Regent of Iraq, I remembered his words and found them poignant. I was made Chargé d'Affaires with him when he was in exile during the 1941 revolt in Iraq, and did indeed have to take especial care to help him. Abdullillah used to send me little personal notes about this and that, some of which have survived with other papers. A mixture of simplicity, attention to detail and quiet assumption of his standing is exemplified in them.

Ali had been given an estate called Naamaniya, south of Baghdad, by Faisal. It was mostly desert, but by means of irrigation pumps and the use of mechanical tractors, then newly imported, it became more valuable, and he and his wife, Nafisa, his daughters and Abdulillah would stay there, seeking to improve it.

Visiting country estates, like that of King Ali, led to meeting the neighbouring farmers, well-established men who, like most of the city merchants, took no active part in politics and wished the politicians at the bottom of the sea. And there were many others, hospitable and civilized, whose only interest in Faisal and politicians was limited to a precautionary desire to keep themselves informed of what was afoot.

Hamid Khan, who lived in Najaf and Baghdad, agent and cousin of the Aga Khan, well read and speaking several languages, carefully perusing *The Times*, was one of them. On returning one day from shooting at Beled Rouz on the farm of Steven Vlasto, a Greek and a resident of Paris, I found a number of messages from Hamid asking me to meet Aly Khan. The Aga had interests in Mesopotamia, property and followers and a family burial ground at Najaf, and Aly, on one of his early tours of the East, made a point of stopping there.

With me at Vlasto's farm, an estate given to his father by the Sultan of Turkey and said to have belonged to Roxane, wife of Alexander the Great, was a representative of another cosmopolitan family in Iraq with whom I shot nearly every Friday—Ghazi Daghestani.

He had recently returned from Woolwich and was a son of Field Marshal Muhammad Fadhil Pasha al Daghestani, a descendant of the rulers of Daghestan in the Eastern Caucasus. One of them, the hero of Tolstoy's story *Hajji Murad*, had resisted the Russians in the Caucasus until, just after the Crimean War, they brought up mountain guns against him. When the Russians took over the country the children of the ruling family had been divided for diplomatic reasons between St. Petersburg and Constantinople. Thus Muhammad Pasha, brought up in Turkey, had become Commander of the Sultan's Caucasian Bodyguard and afterwards Commander-in-Chief in Mesopotamia and Acting Governor of Baghdad. Gertrude Bell described a visit to him, during the heat of an afternoon before the First World War, and told how she found a chained lion, from southern Mesopotamia, asleep on his roof in the Citadel at Baghdad. It must have been one of the last to be seen, though they had been numerous in the previous century.

On nearing his retirement, just before the 1914–18 War, he had been warned by friends that the Sultan, through the malign influence of his Grand Wezir and Court Astrologer, Abdul-Huda, had become suspicious of him and in consequence he had asked leave to buy an estate south of Baghdad and live there.

When the 1914–18 War was declared, he had sent a telegram to the Sultan asking which was more use to His Imperial Majesty —a retired Field Marshal or a reserve Captain. The Sultan understood its meaning and replied: 'You will command our Arab levies and your son Daoud is excused his military service.'

Muhammad Pasha was killed by British shrapnel at the siege of Kut-el-Amara, but shortly before, though about seventy years of age, he had married again, which accounted for about forty years' difference in age between Ghazi, born by the last wife, and his elder brother Daoud Bey. Daoud himself was a devoted countryman and farmer, conservative in habits, wearing a white *kalpak* or tall fur cap, and seldom came to the capital except to see one of his horses race. His salukis were perfectly trained to work with his falcons in the pursuit of gazelle, and he delighted to have guests to accompany him on his hunting expeditions in the desert under the Persian hills.

Ghazi went ahead quickly in his military career, in spite of the coolness that existed at one time between himself and the Regent. He was Military Attaché in London at the time of the Coronation of Queen Elizabeth, became Deputy Chief of Staff and then a General of Division at forty years of age, when, with the other senior officers of the Army, he was arrested and condemned to death at the revolution in 1958. His sentence was not carried out at once and he was still in prison two years later.[1] His sister, married to Najib al Rawi, Iraqi Ambassador in Turkey in 1958, was fortunately out of the country.

There were very few good libraries in the country. One belonged to Raouf Bey al Chadirchi, living, when I first knew him, in an extensive house hidden behind a row of stalls in the bazaar quarter. You entered it by a long, narrow passage to find a very Turkish figure, squat and strongly built with cropped head, in a romantic setting. He had collected many old things— carved woodwork from houses being demolished, brass and silver, carpets, lamps, and books in many languages. His land had come to him from an ancestor who had arrived with Sultan Murad and been rewarded with it for his services in the campaign. He was erudite, kind, generous and witty. As a young officer during the First World War he had been on the Intelligence Staff of Field Marshal von der Goltz, and while with him had caught typhus, the disease which killed the Marshal. Some years afterwards he had been made legal adviser to the Iraq Petroleum Company, and during the Second World War was Iraqi Minister in London, which he did not leave during the bombing. He had the distinction of owning part of Babylon and there, in the palm garden on the bank of the river, had a useful, small house which he would lend to his friends for weekends.

Another good library was that of the legal agent of the Shaikh of Muhammera, who lived in a house on the bank of the Shatt-al-Arab at Basra. Sometimes he entertained in his garden, at night during the summer. The oleanders, vines, pomegranates and orange trees, young palm trees, with bougainvillaeas, grew thickly and close together with only narrow paths between them, hiding the arbour where the tables and chairs were set out, the

[1] Released in 1960.

former laden with fruits, fresh and sugared. His grapes tasted of roses, which he explained was owed to grafting rose trees on to the vines, and there was manna, a sweet made from the down of a wild plant collected near Isfahan. To drink there were sherbets, date-arak and a cordial made from the stamen of the male date-palm. The sound of gentle music from unseen musicians floated through the trees. His servants wore the long-out-of-date Persian dress of high, narrow, pointed hats of black felt, baggy trousers and short coatees of nankeen. He would discourse learnedly on the history of the region, of the Shahs of Persia and of Ottoman conquerors, and tell stories of his late master, famous for his fabulous entertainment in the old style, who had died a prisoner of the Shah in Tehran. He was versed in European history, though he saw it from the East 'as in a glass darkly', and some-times strangely revised for Oriental taste.

Such men were civilized, liberally minded citizens of the world.

The farmers among them were by law obliged to give their tenant workers a fixed percentage of their harvest profits, supply them with seed and pay for maintaining roads and irrigation channels. In many cases they gave more than sixty per cent and, in the far North where in some years there was no flow of water owing to poor rains, the worker tenant received eighty-five per cent.

The picture of 'oppression by feudal landlords grinding down their fellahs', which was drawn later, was largely a false one de-rived from Egypt. The agricultural systems in Iraq in fact worked satisfactorily, from the point of view of both landlord and workers, until the later years of the monarchy, when democracy and bureaucracy, advancing apace and relieving the Shaikhly land-lords of the patriarchal nature of their roles, began to change their characteristics and the attitude to them of their workers.

Among the notables at the larger parties in Baghdad were the poets; and few parties were complete without at least one of them holding the floor with his latest laudatory effort. The chief among them was the bent cripple, Jamil al Zahawi, who would be hoisted on to a chair or a stage to bore us with a sermon-long poem in classical Arabic and be enthusiastically applauded after-wards. Better, from the foreigners' point of view, was Marouf al Risafi, whom some Arabs held to be a better poet and who was a humorist and less long-winded. He made no bones about doting on boys and sometimes introduced allusions to his fancy which would be explained to us. The similes in his poems would often be far-fetched—hoopoes on telegraph wires are not really like 'emeralds strung across the bosom of the earth', but it was the sound of the language which delighted the listeners.

King Faisal was beginning to show marked signs of weariness and he looked forward with evident pleasure to the relief from perpetual audiences and endless political crises which journeying in Europe afforded him.

Sir George Rendel, an unprejudiced observer from the Foreign Office, describing a visit to him in 1932, wrote:

Eric Kennington's portraits have given them [King Faisal, Nuri Pasha and Jaafar Pasha] an artistic immortality. But King Faisal had travelled far since the days of the Revolt in the Desert. He had grown more European—indeed almost dapper—in his appearance, manner and dress. He had become a keen bridge player and preferred to spend an evening in cards than in talk. He was then an ageing, lean and rather melancholy looking man with a neatly trimmed grey beard. He showed a pleasant dignity of manner and considerable charm. In talking with him I felt that he had a penetrating, but perhaps rather unduly subtle and complex mind. My impression was that, like King Boris of Bulgaria and unlike King Ibn Saud of Arabia, he might tend to rely rather too much on manœuvre. But there was no doubt that he was in many ways an outstanding personality and possessed some elements of greatness.[1]

The King had always shown an interest in Western ingenuity and in the winter of 1932–3 he bought a Puss Moth for his private use and sent Squadron Leader Warburton of the Royal Air Force, an instructor with the new Royal Iraq Air Force, to bring it to him from Egypt. I happened to be in the desert on tour when news of his failure to arrive in Iraq began to cause anxiety. As time went on the number of aircraft looking for him, and the rank of the officers in charge of the operation,

[1] *The Sword and the Olive* by Sir George Rendel. John Murray, 1957; page 42.

became higher. Armoured cars from Basra and squadrons of French aircraft from Syria joined in the search. Bedouin Shaikhs were warned and sent off scouts on fast-riding camels. Oil-company officials joined in, using their Buick cars. The area in which he could have come down was 'squared' on maps and each air unit given sections for examination. 'This,' said one of the Operations Staff, 'is a certain means of location. Now we shall find him.' But still they did not do so and when four days had gone by without success it was decided to continue for only one more day and then give up. Warburton was known to have had little water and only about one orange with him.

All the pilots were assembled outside the Rutba fort, halfway across the Syrian desert, for orders on a full and final operation the next day. I went to listen to the instructions being given, but my attention was distracted by a bedouin boy who had sidled up to the group and seemed to want attention. When I spoke to him he felt inside his ragged shirt and brought out a tiny piece of paper, a page from a diary. Warburton had written to describe his position as well as he could. He gave the name of the gully in which he had come down from information gleaned from the boy, Fulayan. Warburton knew little Arabic, but had managed to make them understand enough for his purpose.

I sought to interrupt the Group Captain who was briefing the pilots, but he made it clear with a warning gesture that it was not the moment to do so. When he did understand there was immediate reaction, but it was already late evening and after one attempt we had to abandon all hope of success that night.

The following morning we mounted Fulayan on a box in the pilot's cabin—it was the first time he had been in a mechanical vehicle, car or aircraft—and flew so low that he could recognize the ground features. At last we found the Puss Moth beside two black tents of Haizan ibn Hablan of the Anaza tribe.

When offered a reward for befriending Warburton who, having lost his way, fortunately saw the tents just as he ran out of petrol, the bedouin asked for 'gold, not paper'. His comment when we sat him in his King's aircraft was: 'By God—what Royal comfort to the behind.'

Some months later he came to call on me in Baghdad and

F

saw the King, who thanked him and gave him gold as he had wished.[1]

Faisal's overriding passion was still independence for Iraq; and with the third Treaty, in 1930, and the end of the Mandate, which the British promised to sponsor and recommend at the League of Nations, his success was in sight.

As a consequence of the Treaty, there was one particularly closely guarded secret in British official circles which I only learnt by deduction. Quite often, sometimes for several mornings running, the Air Vice-Marshal would send for me to accompany him upon mysterious flights. They were mysterious because all that he, a busy commander, did was to come down in out-of-the way places and, taking out his binoculars, bird-watch, and then, through me, ask the wandering Arabs about the climate and mosquitoes. They were enjoyable, these early-morning flights by small, open aircraft, into the cool upper air, clear of the dust that made a haze at midday. As the aircraft rose the capital diminished into a khaki jigsaw on the desert, land cut in two by the sweep of a gleaming sabre, the Tigris, its hilt the dark palm gardens in which the golden domes and cerulean-blue tiles of Kadhimain shone and twinkled in the slanting rays of the early-morning sun.

The wrangling of men, their political disputes, diminished in importance with the dwindling of the earth and in the rarefied, keen dry air thought came more clearly than in the heat below.

A compromise had been found between the Iraqi desire for complete independence, with the removal of all British Forces from Iraqi soil, and the British official stand, which the King had been obliged to admit was well founded, for the retention of the Forces for security. Under the compromise the Royal Air Force establishments were to be out of urban sight, west of the Euphrates, and the levies were to be kept only as guards for its camps.

The Air Marshal's frequent morning flights were in reconnaissance for a new camp, in the end chosen at Sinn al-Dhibban, or 'ridge of flies', below Lake Habbaniya on the edge of the Syrian desert. It took long to build, was under Iraqi fire in 1941 and was given up twenty years after occupation.

[1] *The Spectator*, 2nd March 1934—'Iraqi Encounter', by 'Nemo' (the author).

The coming metamorphosis under King Faisal was shown in other ways. As a country about to be independent, good relations would have be to established with the three independent neighbours, all of them geographically larger than Iraq. Two of the three invaded Iraq—Turkey in 1922, until repelled by the British, and Saudi Arabia between 1926 and 1929, when stopped by the British. The incursions into Iraq from Saudi Arabia had been made by fanatical Wahhabis, mostly of the Mutair tribe under their Shaikh, Faisal al Dawish. Since raids continued throughout 1927 on a seriously large scale, the raiders killing or seizing sheep and camels and mutilating their Iraqi owners, the Royal Air Force moved some units to the south of Iraq, where the Iraq Army also increased its strength and the Police built a line of blockhouses on the nearer desert walls. The raids continued nevertheless and when in November 1927 an Iraqi Police post, at Busaiya, was destroyed and all the garrison killed and mutilated by the Saudis, it was clear that a defensive role was useless. Deliberate attacks continuing throughout 1928, it was beyond dispute that a serious effort was required if order were to be re-established on the frontier.

Royal Air Force units moved into forward positions from which to take the initiative. British ships later anchored off Kuwait and finally British marines and sailors were landed to garrison its towers and walls.

At the same time, it was brought home to Ibn Saud that he must either control his tribes or fall out with the British Government. Since he was not prepared to do the latter he was driven into the position of admitting that Faisal al Dawish was a rebel, who might in consequence be rounded up by the British. And so armoured cars went far into the desert, to the wells from which he made his raids.

On their way the R.A.F. crews passed the rotting corpses of Arabs and their sheep. Some were of old men, and there were even bodies of women, little heaps of bloody rags and bone, alone on the clean, open desert. Beside one recently killed shepherd-boy, drenched in his own blood, I remember seeing a double reed-pipe, the plaintive and simple instrument with which they console their watchful hours.

Move by move, al Dawish was checkmated and cut off from

watering-places in his line of retreat, until he was only able to save his men and their mounts by entering Kuwait territory. Prevented from attacking the city itself by the Royal Navy garrison, they came within a mile or two of the city walls, slaughtering tribesmen on their way in the name of religion. All who were not of their Wahhabi sect were meet for death and looting. The greater part of the shepherds kept inside or very near the walls of Kuwait, or the villages on the coast, but there were still a few who were obliged to search farther afield for grazing for their animals lest they die. Their tales were pathetic in the extreme, and their gratitude deep for such protection as could be given them.

At last, near Jahrah, in Kuwait territory, at the end of 1929, al Dawish was captured, surrendering his sword to the senior British Royal Air Force officer. Handed over to Ibn Saud, he was imprisoned in irons and died soon afterwards.

Following the defeat of the Wahhabis a meeting was arranged, by Sir Francis Humphrys, the British High Commissioner, between Ibn Saud and King Faisal, on a British warship, H.M.S. *Lupin*, in the Persian Gulf in 1930. It was a remarkable feat to have brought the two enemies together; and Faisal, whose family had been driven out of Mecca by Ibn Saud after ruling there for many hundreds of years and whose new kingdom had since been constantly attacked by Ibn Saud's men, was of the two the more to be praised for sinking his very strong personal feelings for the sake of future relations between the two countries. Out of their somewhat prickly conversations grew a bon-voisinage agreement and in time ordinary diplomatic exchanges.

Faisal went to Turkey the following year and paid a State visit to Persia in 1932, from which followed the Saadabad Pact, signed only after his death.

Thus Iraq began, through Faisal's successful personal efforts, her foreign relations, and formed her independent Foreign Service, without any British advisers, though with some preliminary organizing, administratively, by a British expert.

Faisal's asset in his foreign relations was his obvious sincerity in desiring that they should be good. His principles were, firstly, Anglo-Arab friendship, 'without sacrificing Arab rights', and in order to obtain British support in the process of liberating other

Arab countries; secondly, good-neighbour relations with the Middle East countries; thirdly, obligations towards the Arabs of Syria and Palestine. If he was not able to do much for them, he tried to create sympathy for them and pleaded ardently on their behalf. Lastly, he hoped for a union between Iraq and Syria, once the independence of both countries had been obtained.

The raging attacks of the Mutair tribe and the Wahhabis in general were not confined to the Iraqi border. There were similar outbreaks on the Trans-Jordan frontier where, too, they were brought to an end by the Royal Air Force. At first, as in Iraq, small raids, they grew in size and ferocity. As the local Police were unable to deal with them adequately, the Air Force was gradually obliged to take a larger part in defence. It was by good fortune that a sergeant-pilot on routine patrol saw, well in time before it reached its prey, the largest party yet taking the field, the Arabians having been encouraged by former almost scatheless incursions. Thanks to early warning by the pilot, the armoured-car unit of the Royal Air Force destroyed them utterly in one battle. The deaths of several hundred Wahhabis brought to an abrupt end the sorties from Arabia of the puritans and it was to be for all time that such attacks were halted. Tribesmen with rifles from that day onwards knew that they were no match for modern forces.

There was a significance in their outbreaks beyond the obvious desire for enrichment by raiding and apart from religious zeal.

A little over a century earlier there had been similar attacks by Wahhabi puritans from Arabia against Mesopotamia and the Hijaz. In each case the Ruler of Najd, head of the Saudi family, had at first encouraged them and then found that they were beyond his control. There was something in the make-up of the Arab which lent itself to these bloodthirsty outbreaks, to a kind of catharsis by killing until they themselves were destroyed.

In the nineteenth century, as in the 'twenties of the twentieth century, the Hashimites, then ruling in Mecca, had suffered from them; but that was coincidental. In the first case the Saudi Emir claimed, as did King Abdul Aziz Ibn Saud constantly until his death, that he was 'surrounded and hemmed in'. His men were attacking the urban and shepherd peoples on their borders because they represented something they could not tolerate, which they, rightly from their point of view, resented deeply. It was the last of the old nomad world's response to new civilization. The 'impact of West upon East' is a phrase that for many people has come to lose anything except a vague, almost abstract, meaning; but on the borders of Arabia, up to the 'thirties, it was seen as a simple issue, with the surrounding countries acting as cushioned buffers for the West, Abdullah and Faisal and their peoples being 'Westerners' to the central Arabians.

The Mandate was finally brought to an end, to Faisal's great joy and pride, in October 1932. A State visit by him to King George the Fifth was to mark the new status and the term of all his efforts. The tiredness which had showed in Faisal's face and manner in the last years seemed to be leaving him.

He had always had a penchant, since his first visit, for spending his leisure in Europe—at one time using the incognito title of Prince Usama—and for the company there of Oriental or Western friends, including women friends, which it was not easy for him to enjoy freely in the East. Following the State visit, he would have a renewed opportunity for these indulgences. At last he could relax in Europe, his aims achieved.

He was in almost boisterous mood, making little jokes about incidents on the journey. Sinderson Pasha, his doctor, says that one day on the ship, when a fellow passenger, a European converted to be a Muslim, appeared on deck smoking a cigar, Faisal said gaily: 'Quick, get your camera and take the strict Muslim.'

He joked about the way he ought to wear the cocked hats and full-dress white uniforms to be worn for the first time on arrival in England. The State visit was a great success and went, as such visits do, like clockwork, and Faisal enjoyed the stay in Scotland afterwards.

But in Iraq matters were far from well. When complete independence had become an active issue, and had been brought up before the League, some authorities had asked pertinent questions about the safety of minorities, and in particular of Christians such as the Assyrians, and had made gloomy prophecies about the future. Within a few months of the end of the Mandate, for which Faisal had striven unremittingly for ten years, these fears were to be proved right and the British sponsors to have been over-optimistic.

The immediate cause of this first serious trouble in independent Iraq was an Iraqi officer, Bakr Sidqi. The first time I saw him was just for a few minutes. I had been waiting one evening in the little New Maude Hotel, by the main bridge in Baghdad, for an officer of the Air Intelligence Staff. Turning from the terrace above the river, where the sunlight was still overbright, into a cool, half-underground room, I saw a singularly unattractive middle-aged Iraqi sitting alone drinking whisky. The back of the head was flat, the neck thick, the lips sensuous, the face and expression vulgarly brutal. It was the face of a man born to be criminal. The impression was so strong that when my friend arrived I told him of it and whispered an enquiry. He knew little about him except that he was a senior officer of the Iraq Army called Bakr Sidqi and that he was said to be liked and seen often by Prince Ghazi.

The attitude of the Army to the Assyrians was partly accounted for by their recent arrival in the country after a terrible adventure. Before the 1914–18 War the Assyrian mountaineers had lived in Hakkiari, a roadless district of Turkey, in the corner between present-day Iraq and Persia, where the summits of the mountains reach fourteen thousand feet. Some Assyrian plainsmen lived to the west of Lake Van and a third section lived among the Kurdish tribes in hilly country south of Hakkiari, inside what is now Iraq. It was believed that the Assyrians had migrated from Mesopotamia after the fall of Ur about 2,000 B.C. They speak Syriac, a language derived from Aramaic, the language which Christ spoke and which is still used in their church services, and their Paramount Chief is an ecclesiastic called the Mar or Bishop Shimon, a celibate, the succession going usually from uncle to nephew. The Mar Shimon is Patriarch of the East and head of the Nestorian Church.

Little was known about the Assyrians until 1886, when a mission was sent among them by the Archbishop of Canterbury in order 'to strengthen and illuminate the ancient Church . . . and not to draw anyone from the flock of your Church', as his letter to the then Mar Shimon stated.

When the 1914–18 War began the Assyrians found themselves wooed by both sides. In the end the Assyrians boldly declared war on Turkey, but the Cossacks sent as help never reached them owing to ambushes by Kurds. At last, realizing that Russian assistance would never come, the Assyrians decided to make their way down to join them near Lake Urmiya, being with their families, some forty thousand strong.

But early in 1917 the Russian revolution brought the collapse of the Russian front, and encouraged by the unpromising news from other Allied fronts the Persians demanded surrender of the Assyrians' arms. An officer of the Royal Air Force succeeded in reaching them at Lake Urmiya after a daring flight, and worked out with them a plan which, although at first successful, ended in a retreat to join the British Forces in Persia. During their passage through the territory of their Kurdish enemies they lost more than a third of their numbers.

They wished to fight for the Allies, but it was already late in the war and in the end there was nothing left for them to do but collect at the great refugee camp established for them at Baquba in Iraq.

Countries outside Iraq, some within the Commonwealth, which were invited to receive them, did not welcome the idea, nor were most of the Assyrians desirous of going to some unknown land. The British High Commissioner could only do his best to settle them on the northern frontier of the Mosul Province where there were deserted lands, and some of them were employed to maintain order in the Kurdish areas as levies in British pay.

Like most refugees, they were a difficult people to help, but it was calculated that no more than three hundred Assyrian families would remain unsettled by the time the Mandate ended. As the levies were being gradually disbanded, the men left to become agriculturalists, railway employees, shopkeepers, or to join the Iraq Army or Police. On the whole the settlement had worked fairly well, though neither the Assyrians nor the Iraqi Government were easy in their minds or unsuspicious of each other.

In 1931, when the Permanent Mandates Commission had qualms about the safety of minorities in Iraq after the end of the

Mandate, Sir Francis Humphrys, the British High Commissioner, attended its meetings in person.

'Was it,' he was asked, 'sufficient for a country to present externally the appearance of an organized State to conclude from it that it had attained political maturity?' In reply he said that as regards tolerance, realizing the heavy responsibility which lay upon him, he could assure the Commission that, in his thirty years of experience of Mohammedan countries, he had never found such tolerance of other races and religions as in Iraq. He attributed this partly to the fact that Moslems, Jews and Christians had been used to living amicably together in the same villages for centuries. His Majesty's Government, he declared, fully realized its responsibilities in recommending that Iraq should be admitted to the League, which was, in his view, the only legal way of terminating the Mandate. Should Iraq prove herself unworthy of the confidence which had been placed in her, the moral responsibility must rest with His Majesty's Government, which would not attempt to transfer it to the Mandates Commission.

This was the background when, in 1933, while Faisal was in Europe, three hundred Assyrians were massacred by troops commanded by General Bakr Sidqi at the village of Simel in the Mosul Province of northern Iraq. Whoever fired the first shot in a brush on the Syrian frontier on the 4th August, there could be no justification for the shooting down by the Iraq Army of numbers of Assyrians in villages far away, on the 7th August onwards, culminating in the massacre at Simel on the 11th August. For the 13th an even worse massacre was planned by the Army to take place at Alqush. The people killed were entirely innocent. It was enough for them to be Assyrians to be shot. The Assyrians in Dohuk were taken away in batches of eight or ten for a short distance from the village in lorries and there turned out and machine-gunned.

On the 1st August the Minister of the Interior, Hikmat Bey Sulaiman, arrived in Mosul, having been flown up in an R.A.F. machine. He was more Turk than Arab, a tall, thin man, who was to be frequently in opposition and joined later with Bakr Sidqi in a coup d'état. He was a brother of the well-known Mahmoud Shawkat Beg, one of the leaders of the Committee of Union and

Progress at Constantinople in 1908, and was himself an ambitious man.

Sir Francis Humphrys was fishing in Scandinavia and could not immediately be traced.

King Faisal was in Switzerland following his successful State visit to England. During his stay he had been disquieted by telegrams from Iraq and now, much as he needed a rest, he had to hurry back to Baghdad in the very worst of its midsummer heat. It was believed by the Baghdad mob and politicians that the British would stand by their protégés, the Assyrians, and there was a wave of feeling against the British and against the King, held to be their tool. He was a very worried man and could not sleep, seeking to console himself by drinking coffee and smoking cigarettes. It was said that he wished to abdicate and he was only with difficulty persuaded to remain in the country until Sir Francis Humphrys returned to it. The Arabic Press was outrageous in its anti-Christian virulence. Hikmat Sulaiman found himself raised to the status of a great national hero who had broken the influence of the British.

Sir Francis Humphrys, when he returned on the 23rd August, made it clear that the British would still support the Iraqis in the maintenance of their independence, and the tension began to lessen. The Mar Shimon, leader of the Assyrians, was removed for his own safety to live in Cyprus and his family were given a small pension. Meanwhile the Arab tribes, out for loot, closed in on the Assyrians, but it was the Iraqi Army, disciplined troops under direct command of their officers, mostly of the motor machine-gun detachments, which had been responsible for nearly all the killing.

Bakr Sidqi himself was acclaimed by the mob as a conquering hero—and, what was even worse, was later decorated and promoted by the Iraqi Government.

Every effort was made by Hikmat Sulaiman to hush up what had happened, but eventually the Iraqi delegate to Geneva had to admit that 'excesses had been committed by the Iraq Army'.

Faisal was clearly ill and his condition was worsened by a sense of unpopularity. Hardly a cheer had been raised for him in Baghdad. One of the last British officials to see the King before his return to Europe was the Commander of the Royal Air Force.

Faisal thanked him anew for all that had been done by his Command in securing the kingdom. He left the capital almost unnoticed on the 2nd of September, to return to Switzerland, where he died five days later of a coronary thrombosis. Because the only long-distance radio was that of the British Services, I was the first person in Baghdad to hear of the death of King Faisal. The officer on night duty at the Royal Air Force camp at Hinaidi, seven miles from the city, rang with a request that the Embassy be told of the King's sudden death from heart failure in Berne.

The body was carried by British ship to the Levant and onwards in a Royal Air Force aircraft, and long before the hour of arrival the streets were lined by inhabitants, the great majority crying without restraint. The women, covered in their usual black veils and cloaks, lined the balconies and roof-edges, where they rocked and moaned and shrieked in unison and were but little less subdued than their men.

When the aircraft arrived at the airport and taxied towards the waiting officials and soldiers, the crowd behind them began to wail in earnest and their cries echoed through the city in a great and continuous sound of emotion. Meanwhile the front of the aircraft was removed by airmen and the coffin was eased out on to the shoulders of eight senior Iraqi officers. It had not been foreseen that the British Consular authorities and Swiss undertakers would be at pains to provide a coffin, richly appropriate to a King, one of the heaviest kind. The pall-bearers were coffin-bearers, for coffin-bearers there were none. As the portly Arab Generals began to sag, the young British airmen ran forward to lend a shoulder and were able to support the coffin sufficiently for it to reach the gun-carriage on which it was to be carried through the city to the Royal mausoleum, seven miles away.

While the procession slowly made its way through the city, to the accompaniment of the sound of a grief-ridden populace, the crowds in the street joined the procession and pressed upon it so that its order was soon lost. Many of the senior Iraqi and British officials and foreign representatives, having lost their position, were jostled severely and altogether forced out of the procession. Some of them took to their beds afterwards and were several days recovering. Disorder being concomitant with mourning, it was hardly to be expected otherwise.

To take part in a funeral in the Orient is judged an honourable thing to do. In the case of small funerals, when the coffin is carried through city lanes, and perhaps the bazaar, on its way to the cemetery, those who knew the deceased person, belong to his guild, or wish to fulfil pious obligations, join the mourners and lend a shoulder to the coffin for a part of the way. As they do so they mutter the conventionally acceptable phrases about a departed one and his resting-place. It was this old custom that suggested a practical joke to some young sparks of Baghdad of a less conservative turn of mind. Filling a coffin with stones, and dressing themselves suitably, they carried it to the bazaar and one by one permitted themselves to be replaced by pious onlookers, so that after a time there were only sanctimonious persons carrying the weighty 'body' onwards. When a junction in the lanes was reached they began to ask one another which road they should take. It became only too clear to them that of true mourners there were none.

It is said by some people that the Arabs are materialistic and quite unsentimental, but opinions vary about the meaning of such words as sentimentality. 'A tendency to be swayed by feeling rather than reason' and 'nursing of the emotions' are the usual explanations of the word, and the Arabs are often swayed by feeling rather than reason and they certainly nurse their emotions. Arab behaviour at the time of a death and afterwards, and sometimes on its approach too, is to others bizarre.

Before the death of a member of the Royal family, if its approach has been foreseen, women of high position at Arabian Courts habitually appear unhinged in the extravagance of their gloomy prophecies and when death has come then all reason seems to leave them. Tearing their clothes and hair, beating themselves, moaning and wailing, they vie with each other, and when one is exhausted before the others her sister-mourners take her up and throw her down again and bang her head on a chair-leg or any convenient object. By this standard the men are only partly deranged. They usually come prepared for the scene, with handkerchiefs or, nowadays, a box of Kleenex or some such article; but it is correct to be, or seem to be, quite incapable of giving the simplest of directions to the staff of the Palace or office. All must be in utter disorder, like the minds of the mourners. Nevertheless, these same men and women, of the highest standing in Arabia, conform to European manners when in European houses, and it is difficult to believe that they are one and the same people.

When the whole people of a city or countryside are mourners, as was the case at the death of King Faisal and later at the death of King Ghazi, then the scene is to Europeans truly eccentric.

3

Youth in a Hurry

It was already clear that if ever the only authoritative hand not involved in these uneasy intrigues should be removed—that of the King—there would be opportunity, or almost inevitability, for some other power to intervene with decision, a part which in the event was to be that of the Army.

Iraq, 1900 to 1950

S. LONGRIGG

A FEW days before his accession Ghazi, the new King, had swung into popularity on the emotions roused by Bakr Sidqi's massacre of the Assyrians.

On the 27th August Ghazi had gone to Mosul for a tour of inspection, accompanied by the Prime Minister, Rashid Ali Gailani, and Hikmat Sulaiman, Minster of the Interior. Emotion was still at boiling point in the northern capital and the slightest incident might have led to a general massacre of Christians. The lessening of tension following the return of Sir Francis Humphrys to Baghdad had not had time to reach Mosul.

As the Crown Prince entered the city for his reception, he was met with prolonged cheering and sustained shouts of 'Down with the British' and 'Down with the Colonizers'. At the review of the troops, the enthusiasm for them and for the Prince had been equally great, but the name of his father had not once been heard. Bakr Sidqi and the 'victorious' colours of the troops were solemnly decorated by the Crown Prince. Among the notable spectators was the Shaikh Ajil of the Shammar, whose men had a few days earlier been brought in to continue the looting of the Assyrian villages begun by the Army.

Though it was not intentional, the visit of Ghazi did in fact have the effect of letting off a dangerously strong head of steam. Within the week he was King, at twenty-one years old and still a bachelor.

Ghazi was courageous and had charm, and also a good head for heights, both politically and physically. I had already had proof of the latter qualification on climbing with him the un-repaired and dangerously narrow path to the top of the minaret at Samarra. Before its narrowest point, very near the summit, I pressed him repeatedly to stop, but he refused to halt and sidled round the last turn of the tower, climbing out on the very top. It was perilous for anyone without an exceptionally good head and certainly not to be recommended to a Prince who was an unmarried only son. Had he fallen, the lot of an Englishman with him would doubtless have been short and unenviable.

The view from the summit was romantic. The Tigris wound through the desert, gleaming silver between steep banks in the plain, past the small, walled city with its domes and minarets. Immediately below was the vast, ruined court of the mosque for a city, once, for a few years, capital of the Caliph Mutasim, a move dictated by the constant threats to the Caliphs from the military rabble and mob in Baghdad.

The boy was avid for sensations. To be alone on the great tower at Samarra with the impetuous Prince conjured up recollections of weird episodes in William Beckford's eighteenth-century fantasy, *Vathek*. I half expected an announcement of their beginning from the Queen's brother, who had struggled up the tower behind us. In the end it was not the people of Samarra, or a Caliph's courtiers, that the wayward Prince teased, but Royal Air Force pilots, at a picnic luncheon in the court of the ruined mosque, and the only magic was flying with them back to Baghdad.

In the decade since the beginning of the monarchy there had been great changes in the capital and its people. The youth were now convinced that they were 'modern' and educated. It was education that seemed important to them.

When Ghazi's father arrived in Baghdad writing was still a

mystery to most of his people, and scribes ready for the public squatted in rows outside the government offices. In those days the word for school conjured up for most people the picture of a cluster of very small, cross-legged boys learning the Koran by heart—nothing more; for though there had been good Turkish-run and Christian schools in Baghdad they were the exception.

By Ghazi's day it was quite different. The word for school meant a gaunt new building or a bungalow, one of many, where youths—so far few girls—studiously pursued the usual subjects. They took it all very seriously, brooding on their future, and occasionally shot their masters when they were failed in examin-ations. The same thing occurred in the Army. One of the nicest and best staff officers, the blue-eyed Colonel Muhammad Sebti, was killed by a young officer whom he had failed in an examination at the Iraqi Staff College. The murderer used a hand-grenade which blew them both to bits.

The Law School had far too many pupils who would never be able to find sufficient vacancies as lawyers. History books, produced for use in schools, were written as political and ultra-patriotic tracts, with little attention to fact, and classical Arabic was culled for old roots that might be used to replace foreign words and to decorate everyday texts.

'My God, it was a splendid article; so well written that even I understood very little of it,' said one ardent student.

'School' and 'school vacancies' were words brought up by visitor after visitor to persons in authority. Vacancies for sons and nephews or for children of dependants were what they wanted. Schooling was the new craze, the latest panacea, the way to power and success. After the Law School, the Military College was the next most popular, though the physical efforts required of cadets were in some cases a deterrent.

Arab clothes had quite gone out of fashion among the citizens of the capital and countrymen and Shaikhs were almost comically conspicuous for wearing them.

Much building and road-making was under way. The plan to keep the façades of the houses similar, with deep arches for shade in the main street, had been dropped. Instead there were shops with glass fronts, something new in a land where shops hitherto had been stalls in which the owner sat cross-legged.

There were cinemas and cabarets in place of the old Arab theatres that had been confined to one quarter of the city. The use of Turkish baths was largely replaced by ordinary, modern baths installed in private houses.

New roads went through and round the city and outside into new suburbs. The old city ramparts and its gates had been pulled down.

These many changes in a decade had an exhilarating effect on youth. What was new and young was good. Ghazi was the new King and young, therefore he must be good. He was cheered wherever he went.

Longrigg says of Ghazi that he was 'active, warmly patriotic and not unamiable; he was popular with the public, and with the young Iraqi officers with whom, after an unsuccessful period at Harrow, he had been educated; but his lack of intellectual equipment and of interest in public affairs, and his devotion to pleasure and to sport, forbade the hope that he would prove adequate to the Royal functions in Iraq'.

Within six weeks of his accession the young King, advised by Ali Jaudat, head of the Royal Diwan, had rebuffed members of his Government and so brought about its resignation as a whole.

In the winter following his accession he married Aliya, his first cousin, daughter of ex-King Ali of the Hijaz, a remarkably sensible girl.

When the new Cabinet in turn fell, it was to Ali Jaudat, as the head of the Diwan, that the Premiership went—as he, Ali Jaudat, had doubtless intended. The new Chamber of Deputies was packed with his own nominees. Ali Jaudat, a small man with receding hair and dark round eyes, was Ottoman-trained and came from Mosul, where his father had been in the Police. He graduated into the new professionally political class along with men like Nuri al Said and Jaafar al Askari, unlike the members of the Saadun, the Gailani and older families who had more to lose and less to gain in politics.

Trouble, brought about by maladministration, had been brewing in the South, on the Middle Euphrates, and talk of an early introduction of conscription increased the disaffection, both there and in the towns. Ali Jaudat ineffectually tried to keep

G

order by censorship and suppression of meetings and newspapers; but the ferment in the South was not so easily cooled.
Since the King's support of Ali Jaudat was bringing him criticism he was obliged to change the Government again, at first to
one under Jamil Madfai and then to another under Yassin al
Hashimi, both Ottoman-trained Nationalist followers of King
Faisal. Jamil had been involved in the murder of two British
officers at Tel Afar in the north of Iraq in 1920 and British
influence had for a long time prevented his advancement.

At this time of changes and uncertainty the inexperienced
King allowed Sir Kinahan Cornwallis, the Adviser to his father,
to end his long career in the Iraq Government's service.

In June 1936 one of the many tribal disturbances on the
Euphrates, following upon Ali Jaudat's handling of affairs, was
brutally suppressed by Bakr Sidqi, Army Commander in the
district. Even so, the area remained far from tranquil and conscription was finally introduced, and the Iraq Air Force increased
to three squadrons, both the Army and Air Force being used
for keeping order.

Conscription had been to the fore in the Nationalists' programme because a large army provided a convincing answer to
questions about readiness for independence. It would, it was
said, guarantee national defence and security. In the event,
although independence was reached without national conscription, the issue was soon afterwards brought up in Parliament,
largely because of the alarm felt over the tribal risings then being
encouraged by Hikmat Sulaiman and the opposition. Apart from
the reasons given officially and in the Chamber of Deputies, there
were other aspects of it which came up in conversations with
Baghdadis.

I asked a Minister about it at a party, rather late in the night,
and he said that it was an excellent thing. The Jews would be the
first to be called to the Colours and they would all pay for
exemption to the tune, he reckoned, of some five hundred
thousand pounds; so conscription would pay for itself and even
save the country money.

An army officer said it was a good thing without giving
reasons. I asked him if he expected promotion and he said: 'Yes,
two ranks at least.' I asked the head of the British Military

Mission and he offered to show me his file on the subject, which contained a letter thirty-seven pages long with references to Staff College papers, the practice in Italy, Germany and elsewhere, the findings of the Disarmament Conference, his personal experience and much else, with opportunity for any conclusion desired at the end of it.

I asked a Shaikh of a tribe, who said his men hated it, but I noticed that he voted and spoke in favour of it in the Chamber of Deputies the next day, when the King watched the proceedings.

My barber, aged about twenty-eight, was in favour of it. He said that some of his young rivals who captured his customers—though they were far less expert barbers—would have to go into the Army.

The National Conscription Law, passed in 1934 during the premiership of Madfai, was finally enforced the following year.

The King's popularity continued to grow with the younger generation until it reached the point of adoration. Young officers carried a photograph of him and even preserved one in their pocket-books twenty years afterwards.

On the other hand, among tribal Shaikhs and serious persons in the cities, he was losing ground owing to his shortcomings and to the flight of his sister, Azza, with a servant from a hotel on the Island of Rhodes and her alleged conversion to Christianity. The Government itself, under Yassin al Hashimi, seemed stable and the last thing it expected was a military coup d'état.

In October 1936 the Chief of the General Staff went to visit Turkey, leaving Bakr Sidqi to act for him. Autumn manœuvres in the Diyala district gave an opportunity to concentrate almost all the Armed Forces outside the capital. The plot conceived by Bakr Sidqi and the opposition leader, Hikmat Sulaiman, was only known to a few officers, the chief among them being the General commanding a division at Qaraghan, near the Persian frontier. The two Generals drafted a letter to the King demanding a new Ministry under Hikmat and handed it to the latter to deliver. The Air Force, under Muhammad Ali Jawad, a close friend of Bakr, was also concentrated at Qaraghan and was furnished with leaflets to scatter over Baghdad at the right moment. On the 28th October the Army began marching on Baghdad.

The British Royal Air Force headquarters at Hinaidi had

suspected that something unusual was happening when the Iraqi
Air Force took off without warning for a destination unknown.
The Commander, Air Vice-Marshal Mitchell, ordered a state of
alertness and sent a staff officer to the Ministry of Defence in
Baghdad to make enquiries.

The head of the Military Mission told him that there was no
cause for alarm since Jaafar Pasha al Askari, Minister of Defence,
had gone in person to meet Bakr Sidqi and bring him to reason.
Involuntarily the airman said: 'How stupid. We won't see poor
Jaafar alive again.' Since the British General had been in favour
of Jaafar's mission there was a moment of silence, which was
broken by the sound of aircraft overhead, followed by four
explosions nearby.

'Twenty-pounders,' said the Air Force officer, 'and it would
be safer on the ground floor.'

The effect of these four small bombs was remarkable. There
was a rush to get out of the Ministry of Defence, the target. Some
officers took refuge under the old arches of a vaulted building
opposite, but hurriedly moved on when they found that it was
the magazine. Any plans to meet the threat came to an end
abruptly because the personnel engaged on them melted away.
Since the telephones were cut the R.A.F. officer began his return
journey to Hinaidi in order to inform the Air Vice-Marshal, but
it took him a long time and was made with many detours to
avoid the exodus of people from the city.

Jaafar Pasha had met the Army halfway between Baquba and
Baghdad and was at once slaughtered. Baqr Sidqi made an un-
opposed entry into the city and was acclaimed with King Ghazi's
enthusiastic support as a national hero. Nuri al Said, Foreign
Minister, sought refuge in the British Embassy and many others
went into hiding. The Embassy was faced with the problem of
getting Nuri away from there and through the city to Hinaidi
camp so that he might leave the country in a Royal Air Force
aircraft. He insisted, moreover, upon not leaving without his
son, Sabah, who, threatened with death, had taken refuge in the
Egyptian Embassy—like the British Embassy, closely watched.

In mid-afternoon Bakr's watchers must have thought that
the British Embassy car, leaving with one passenger, contained
only an Embassy official, with despatch cases and documents,

probably one en route for a conference at Air Headquarters. Without opening the door they could not have seen Nuri lying on the floor at the back of the car, covered with a rug. The Egyptian Embassy was in the suburbs of Baghdad on the Hinaidi side of the city. Messengers were sent there to Sabah telling him to follow instructions to the very second. At five minutes to five o'clock he and his wife Ismet were to be behind the closed door of the Embassy and ready to step into a slow-moving car, without any luggage. Watches were synchronized by telephone. A few minutes before the hour an inconspicuous old Ford car, driven by a British civilian, went slowly into the Embassy grounds, as if bringing an afternoon caller. The timing worked out well. The car did not stop. Sabah and his courageous wife jumped into it. When the car reached the picket outside the gates the men saw to their astonishment that the driver was now wearing an R.A.F. officer's cap. The passengers in the back were recognized but, as had been hoped, there was a moment of indecision by the soldiery when faced by an R.A.F. officer which permitted the car to gather speed and turn the corner. The old Ford was worked up to its maximum speed and luckily had a clear run towards Hinaidi. An Iraq Army patrol car came in full pursuit after it, but it was still three hundred yards behind when the Ford passed the guard-post at the camp and the barrier came down behind it.

Nuri, who had been depressed, at once became cheerful again and soon was talking of plans to oust Bakr and return to power; but meanwhile, that night, he was flown out for Egypt, with Sabah and Ismet. The Prime Minister, Yassin al Hashimi, and the unpopular Rashid Ali Gailani went under escort to Syria.

The new Prime Minister failed signally at everything except criticism of the past order. Group after group came into opposition against him. 'The ferment of self-seeking and vengeful faction which was the normal life of the Euphrates Shaikhly and religious circles refused to cool at his bidding,' as Longrigg says in his book. The new Chamber of Deputies was uneasy and unpopular. The People's Reform League was suppressed and prominent Communists, real or alleged, were arrested or fled the country. The Army clearly dominated and almost alone supported the Prime Minister, and Bakr Sidqi and his cronies, corrupted by power, lost the respect of all the better elements by their drunkenness and arrogance, Bakr marrying a Viennese dancing girl. Meanwhile Yassin al Hashimi died in Syria, Jaafar's brother committed suicide and a Baghdad notable was murdered by a Kurd whom Bakr protected.

After less than nine months of uneasy life the Ministry came to an end as suddenly as it had come into being. On the 8th August 1937 Bakr was waiting on the Mosul airport on his way for a visit to Turkish manœuvres when he was shot dead at point-blank range by an Iraqi soldier, a company storeman. His companion, Muhammad Ali Jawad, Chief of the R.I.A.F., lived only a few minutes longer.

There was a month of indecision, when for a time it looked as though there would be civil war, until the Army Commander at Baghdad West, Said Takriti, siding with the Military Commander at Mosul, Amin al Umari, and the elements of the Army opposed to the Bakr faction, issued a proclamation of loyalty to the King in which he called for no reprisals and promised abstention of the Army from politics.

Hikmat Sulaiman was left powerless and was forced to resign by a second military coup. The company storeman who had shot Bakr was rewarded with a well-paid post as Chief Gardener to the Ministry of Defence, which had no garden other than a few beds of zinnias.

As if in disgust at his unsatisfactory flirtation with ambitious Generals, the King increasingly diverted himself with light aircraft, radios, fast cars and companions far lower in the military and social scale.

Ghazi's father had approved the building of a palace in which he never lived, dying before it was built. Like a French villa, with pepper-pot turrets and balustraded outside steps, it was beyond the city on the western side and called Qasr al Zuhur (or Palace of the Blossoms). It was furnished in the style recommended and provided by a big furnishing store in London, with plenty of chintzes, heavy flounces, large tassels and pink silk shades. Someone had daringly and unhappily introduced a large white and only partly draped female figure carrying a torch, which stood in the hall. Parts of the building were not solid enough to withstand the climate. A few years later a car backing before the Palace and touching lightly the corner of the last step broke it in pieces, to the astonishment and delight of the foreign Royal visitor in the car.

Ghazi, when he came to live in it, merely added to Faisal's design some extra garage room. He built for himself and liked using a small pavilion on top of a knoll near the main road still farther westwards out of Baghdad.[1] There he often spent the night. It had a built-in bar, considered most unusual in a private house in Iraq, and it was somewhere he could relax unobserved by the public and undisturbed by Ministers and Court officials. He found official and formal life irksome and did his best to avoid it.

A man was killed and a pilot was seriously harmed in one of his escapades from the humdrum. A negro servant from the Palace, loudly mouthing his fear of air travel, gave Ghazi an idea. He ordered the man to go up at once. The blackamoor's rolling eyes and his struggles as he was forced into the machine were found highly amusing. But when, in mid-air, he clutched wildly about him, seizing the control wires and leaving the airman powerless, the machine came crashing to the ground. The negro was killed and the pilot, Sabah, the son of Nuri al Said, spent months in hospital in England with a cracked skull, broken leg and damaged hand and arm.

Another prank by the King was the painting of a servant's face with luminous paint which almost skinned him, so that he spent painful days bandaged up and under medical attention. Another trick which amused him was to attach electric batteries to various everyday objects in the Palace, so that visitors and servants received a shock when picking them up. And when, knowing about this, they became more wary, he much enjoyed asking them to pass him something which was no longer wired but which still might be, for all they knew.

He became hypochondriacal about the condition of his heart, which was in fact quite sound. After long nights of gaiety he would feel tired and send for a doctor. 'My heart, here,' putting his hand on it, 'is weak.' It was a fear that came perhaps from the memory of his father's death and what the doctors had said then.

[1] It was called Tel al Milh, or Salt Dome.

He usually wore very dark glasses and sometimes carried two revolvers, one on either thigh. But his charm and freshness survived it all and conquered most people who came in contact with him.

Sir Maurice Peterson, the British Ambassador, however, wrote afterwards in his book, *Both Sides of the Curtain*,[1] that

he was weak and unstable as water and his intemperate habits, combined with his choice of companions from among the wildest of the young army officers and even his own servants at the Palace, made him impossible to control, difficult to influence, and dangerous to all, especially to himself. His one intelligent and healthy interest was aviation. . . . He possessed several planes of his own at his private aerodrome . . . and was able and anxious to fly them himself. . . . He was very averse to appearing in public and did so only on the rarest occasions. . . .

The King's interest in radio took an extravagant turn. He acquired a private radio broadcasting station on which he spoke himself and put out programmes to bemuse the conservative public and upset foreigners. In the end the broadcasts took on a political form, attacking Kuwait repeatedly.

Kuwait had long lived on pearl-fishing and smuggling, which was made easier and more profitable by the high tariffs at Basra and none at Kuwait. And since Kuwait was under British aegis, attacks on it had the additional piquancy of being an heroic 'coat-trailing' before the powerful British. Iraqi youth listened, entranced by its King. To heighten the effect, Iraqi troops were ordered to Zubair, near the Kuwait frontier, and the Iraqi Police were encouraged to encroach upon its territory. They pulled up frontier notice-boards in the desert and moved them some miles nearer the Kuwait bay, they cruised inside Kuwait territory, shooting on sight and forcing hunting parties into Iraqi territory.

Kuwait's Ruler was 'feudal and useless' and 'Kuwait must join Iraq' were the cries of the King's private radio, cries which were redoubled when oil was found in Kuwait territory.

Sir Maurice Peterson was the right man to deal with such bizarre irregularities of behaviour and he succeeded in achieving better results than could have been expected, though the wireless

[1] Published by Constable, 1950.

behaviourism did not altogether cease; from attacking Kuwait, Ghazi turned to attacks upon his uncle Abdulla in Jordan.

Queen Aliya, who had borne Ghazi a son in 1935, also had some restraining influence on him. The boy Prince, who was called Faisal after his grandfather, had been brought into the world by Dr. Sinderson and Miss Borland, a British nurse, who had first been with the Afghan Royal family and then stayed with the Iraqi Royal family until Faisal's death. The boy was very small, but otherwise a promising child. The Queen's brother, Abdulillah—a shy young man the same age as the King, the son of King Ali of the Hijaz—spent more time in the Palace than hitherto, in order to be with the Queen, his eldest sister. He and Aliya had always been very close friends, and with the King's peculiarities and the baby's progress to discuss they were more than ever drawn together.

Abdulillah had established himself soon after his father's death in a house of his own near the Royal Palace. It began by being no more than an inornate villa built of the local yellow brick, standing in the open fields, a creek draining into the Tigris on one side of it. The Prince called the house the Qasr al Rihab or Welcome Palace. It was in front of its main door that he was shot by revolutionaries twenty years later.

From time to time he proudly made additions to his villa: more rooms, garages, stables, guard-houses, aviaries and kennels, quarters for serving men: and it was given a fountain and a pool, thus making a circular entrance-way between the iron gates and the steps leading up to a platform before the front door. To the right of the fountain facing the Palace was a space for the cars of callers, and to the left a lawn. The garden, with certain types of trees, bushes and grass, which grew very quickly in the Iraq climate, soon improved.

The large drawing-room later contained a number of portraits of the men of the family, painted by a Polish artist called Norblin. The older generation had been portrayed from photographs, some unsatisfactorily, but those of the younger members, including Abdulillah himself and the King, by Norblin and Anthony Devas, were pleasing portraits from life. Presentation photographs in silver frames stood about. Those of the English Sovereigns were in the place of honour above the fireplace.

At the outset simply furnished, the rooms had later received a number of trophies of journeys in Europe—clocks, mantel decoration, small boxes—which, being well-enough chosen, had not upset their essentially 'private' appearance. There was nothing of that garish mixture of styles which was the fashion in the Levant and Egypt and known, in a mixed phrase, as 'Moda Luigi Khamstasher' (Louis XV style). In an upstairs hall were glass, lighted show-cases containing illuminated Korans, gold swords and daggers and the decorations which had belonged to the older generation.

It was this house that King Faisal the Second later shared with him, the King maintaining the nearby Royal Palace, the Qasr al Zuhur, but not sleeping in it. In it, too, lived the Emir's mother, Queen Nafisa. Of his sisters, at first living with him, only one remained unmarried until the end, Abdiya, who, reading much, became in some ways the best informed of them. Badiya, the prettiest, married the Sherif Hussain bin Ali, son of a former Ruler of Mecca and a member of her clan, who had been resident in Egypt. Another sister, Jalila, twice tried to commit suicide, succeeding the second time in December 1955 by throwing over herself the lighted fuel of a primus stove. She was subject to fits of depression and had married the Sherif Hazim, another member of the Hashimite clan. Aliya, the eldest daughter, who married King Ghazi, was considered by her sisters the wisest of them.

Queen Nafisa continued to be rigid in her ways. She never made up and all her life kept alive old customs, including divination of the best day for a journey. When the time came for it, she would go round the Palace writing phrases from the Koran on the wall, and on the eve of departure she wrote one of them on a paper, dividing it in two halves, one being taken by the traveller and the other remaining with her to ensure his safe return. At the moment of departure there was an important ceremony: water was always thrown by a servant over the wheels of the vehicle. These customs were never omitted.

Abdulillah and his mother were happy in their new house. The Arab in general is pragmatic and no treasurer of relics of the past. An Arabian visitor in England, invited to spend a little time seeing a fine old house, replied, astonished: 'Why ever should I see a house three hundred years old? I wish to see only the newest houses.'

Abdulillah's arrangement of his house was unusual in Baghdad for its display of portraits and of objects that had no immediate and practical use, but were decorative. The representation of the human form is forbidden to Muslims out of fear of a renewal of idolatry, and statues and portraits are looked at askance by ultra-strict Muslims to this day. It was therefore surprising that a statue in bronze of King Faisal the First, mounted and in Arab dress, was erected to his memory and placed in the middle of the city (there was already one of General Maude, the British conqueror of Mesopotamia, in front of the British Embassy gates).[1] It was also astonishing that, early in Ghazi's reign, relics of King Faisal the First were put together and housed in a small museum at the South Gate of the city. There were photographs of him, there was one of his early cars, his clothes, uniforms and other objects belonging to him. Most of them were later removed, presumably to the Palace. What happened to his diaries—including those covering the time of the Versailles Peace Conference, which he had shown to George Antonius when he was writing his book *The Arab Awakening*—is not known. They may have been in the Qasr al Zuhur. At the revolution, documents brought from the Hijaz by ex-King Ali disappeared from the Qasr al Rihab.

In the summer of 1937 there was a new development in the foreign relations of Iraq. Immediately following agreement with Persia over the hitherto disputed frontier, she signed with Afghanistan, Persia and Turkey a non-aggression pact at Saadabad in Persia. There were never any meetings of the Council, except the first one, and within two years the pact was a dead letter, but at least there was an attempt at regional solidarity, the first since the country's independence.

The third Army coup d'état in Iraq took place on Christmas Day 1938, following a lenient government under Jamil Madfai. A policy of forgetting the past had allowed seven politically

---

[1] Both statues were destroyed in the revolution. Both were excellent work, like that of the third statue in Baghdad to the Prime Minister, Abdul Muhsin al Saadun, who committed suicide.

minded senior officers to form a dominant clique. Their discontent was increased when a new Minister of Defence, himself a former army officer, treated them high-handedly and let it be known that he could break their power. They decided to act first.

Three of them conducted secret negotiations with Nuri al Said and came to a tacit understanding to use force to compel Madfai to resign. They would be relieved of the enmity of the Minister of Defence and enhance their power by carrying out another coup. Colonel Salah-ad-Din Sabbagh placed the troops on the alert and called his supporters together on Christmas Eve. One of them tried to see the King, but the Chief of the Royal Household, unaware of the seriousness of the crisis, refused to permit them to do so without authority from the Minister.

The Prime Minister, warned by one of the conspirators, called a Cabinet and resigned forthwith.

King Ghazi sent for the Chief of Staff, who told him of the Army's discontent and demanded a new Cabinet under General Nuri al Said. Madfai's formal tendering of his resignation to the King took place next morning in the presence of the Chief of Staff and the prominent army officers concerned in the coup.

Thus the Army again won. They had overthrown three Cabinets within two years. Nuri al Said, who complained bitterly of the Army's interference in politics, had himself been placed in authority as a result of action by the Army.

On the 4th January he made a speech announcing his policy of reform and admitting mistakes in the past 'owing to our political immaturity'. Saying that there were two forms of government in the West, dictatorial and democratic, he stressed his belief in the second form, which was subscribed to by King Faisal the First and those who had framed the Constitution. It was a statesmanlike speech, in which he announced his intention of reviving party politics, raising the standard of the Press and giving it more freedom, amending the Constitution and the Electoral Law in order to make Parliament more genuinely representative of the people.

He subsequently showed that it was his intention to isolate the Army from politics, but he moved cautiously and seemed concerned first to remove Hikmat Sulaiman and his cronies of the dangerous opposition, who had supported Bakr Sidqi and his military junta. In March 1939 a plot against the regime was discovered and Hikmat Sulaiman and others were arrested and condemned to death or hard labour by a military court martial, Hikmat himself receiving the death sentence. 'They have been the cause of all the pernicious and unfortunate events that have befallen the country in recent years,' it was officially announced.

The plot uncovered by the investigations of the court martial was said to have taken the form of a wholesale assassination plan, of some forty persons, at a banquet to be given in the Palace of the Emir Abdulillah, who was then to be placed on the throne. The Emir, having obtained all the information about it from those who got in touch with him, had told the King and Government. Two of the accused confessed. The Emir had acted bravely in keeping the conspirators about him, when they might have discovered that they were being watched and had been given away. The scheme was reminiscent of the Cato Street Conspiracy in London at the beginning of the nineteenth century and might almost have been copied from it; and it had the same abortive result.

Hikmat Sulaiman, whatever his role in this particular plot, was clearly to blame for several past plots, and he was to be responsible for further troubles in the future; for the death sentence was not carried out. The British Ambassador had pressed hard for mercy for him and his sentence was changed to one of five years' imprisonment. Finally all the death sentences were commuted.

While Nuri al Said was engaged on his uphill task of reducing the more turbulent politicians to a humbler mood, and putting into effect his reforms, there was a sudden and totally new turn to events.

King Ghazi was killed on the night of the 4th April 1939.

4

War

RIDING with the Regent early one summer morning after the war, he pointed out to me the closed iron gates of the Zuhur Palace, saying: 'They have been closed ever since the King was killed. We think that it is a house of ill omen'— and he went on to tell how Ghazi died.

The King had invited some friends to supper and drinks. Afterwards he wanted to show them a film which he had left in the little house called al Harthiya, the cottage built for his father near a backwater of the Tigris. The King, taking with him his favourite and chauffeur, Ibrahim, and the supervisor of his Royal broadcasting station, leapt into his open Buick car and, seizing the wheel, drove off at great speed to get the film. The lane leading past the Palace stables to the Harthiya is rather narrow, bordered by trees and bushes, with telegraph poles on the far side of the road from the Palace gates. Just beyond the turning out of the gates on to the lane is a small, humpbacked bridge, surmounting a conduit.

'It was almost, if not quite, the first day he had had the car. As he went over the conduit at high speed, the front wheels must have left the ground, so that, when he tried to bear to the left, he had no control. The car ran hard into a telegraph pole which cracked and fell forward, smashing his head.'

Dr. Sinderson, the Royal physician, was called at once. From the excited way the message was given, he knew that it must be serious and highly urgent. He packed some surgical instruments, though himself a physician, and rang the British Embassy asking that a surgical colleague, Dr. Braham, be told to follow him to the Palace. He found that the King was unconscious, his head so damaged that he was unrecognizable and dying. There was nothing that could be done to save him, but Queen Aliya implored the doctor to give him an injection. There was no reaction. 'He must speak. It is imperative under the Constitution for him to name a Regent before he dies,' she insisted. He gave him another injection and the women, putting their heads down to the King's, said that he had murmured 'Abdulillah'. At forty minutes past midnight on the 4th April 1939 he died.

Later the Queen and the Princess Rajha testified that the King had always wanted Abdulillah, the Queen's brother, to be Regent should anything happen to him before his only child, Faisal, came of age.

The Germans put it about that the King was assassinated by the British Intelligence Service. Within a few hours an infuriated mob surrounded the British Consulate in Mosul and when the Consul, Mr. G. E. Monck-Mason, bravely, but unwisely, went out to try to quieten the people, one of them at once killed him with a single blow from a pick-axe.

Thus Abdulillah, the shy Prince, under thirty years of age, a lover of horses and the countryside, became Regent of Iraq for his four-year-old nephew and held the Regency for fourteen years, until the King came of age, ruling longer than Faisal the First or King Ghazi and in more difficult times.

Ghazi was mourned by the emotional people of Baghdad with great intensity. From early morning processions of people weeping and beating their breasts passed through the main streets and the wail of women gave a macabre note to an unforgettable scene. The life of the city was at a standstill. Mr. Houston-Boswell, the British Chargé d'Affaires, represented the King of England at the interment in the Royal mausoleum.

The Times' leading article and other accounts described Ghazi as a fearless horseman, an enthusiastic airman who piloted his own machines, and an ardent motorist with a passion for speed, 'and his physical courage was beyond doubt', but they hinted that his popularity had been waning among the older people.

Dying when he did, at the age of twenty-seven, he remained the idol of young Iraqis. But *The Times* was gloomy. There were dangers in a long Regency. The amalgamation of the different elements of the population was still far from complete. The recent military conspiracy was recalled and the impressionable nature of the people stressed.

Nevertheless, all went fairly well at the beginning. Nuri al Said was Premier and Ali Jaudat Minister of Foreign Affairs. At elections in May a large number of Nuri's followers were again elected and he remained in power. The new British Ambassador, to whom the problems of the Middle East were not familiar, had been appointed in March 1939.

The Regent, although the same age as the dead King, was expected—from what little was known of his character by diplomatic and government officials—to be more serious than Ghazi.

Abdulillah had grown taller than any of his family and was fair-skinned, a trait he may have inherited from his Caucasian grandmother and great-grandmothers. 'I wonder just how Arab I am?' he said once, and counted up his forbears of non-Arab blood. Faisal the First had been able to tax his elder brothers with slowness in moving with the times, but the younger generation of the family were not open to the same charge. The Emir Zaid, King Ghazi and Abdulillah had all taken to Western dress and conformed to Western ways. Not unnaturally, it was the youngest of them, Abdullilah, who was the most anxious to excel in that way and who best succeeded.

He began by missing an education in Europe, which the others had had in some degree, but he learnt what he could at Victoria College, Alexandria, a public school run on English lines under the headmastership of Mr. Reid. He was a man whom all the boys loved and revered—and who had influence over them even after they had left him and grown up. The good headmaster's private talks with him had made a permanent impression on Abdulillah, which, joined to his background, gave him a strong sense of responsibility and of pride in his family's role in the Arab world. While a very young man, it had only showed itself in a rather sad acceptance of his standing and a markedly shy dignity of manner. His chief hobby then was breeding horses, and he had taken an interest in racing and farming, which kept

him away from politicians and intrigue in the capital. It was his
very timidity and self-questioning that educated him most.

Sometimes he talked to me about his boyhood, recalling his
early days in Mecca. He remembered how he had been taken
hurriedly, without at the time understanding why, carried pick-
a-back by a negro slave, from his father's house in Mecca to a
higher part of the city, going there without the lanterns that he
knew were customarily carried after dark. It had been a secretive
flitting of all the women and children of the family to a place of
greater safety, on that night in 1916 when his grandfather had
declared revolt against the Turks.

He remembered the Mahmal coming from Egypt at the time
of the annual pilgrimage and the excitement that would attend
its arrival: the decorated camels that carried it and the glittering
escort for that precious load, the black-and-gold-thread carpet
for the Kaaba, the Holy of Holies, and the devoted and distinguished pilgrims who came with it. He remembered the other
annual pilgrim ceremonies, the donning of ritual dress, the seven
circuits of the Kaaba, the sacrifice on Mount Ararat, the stoning
of the Devil. He recalled the stately progresses of his grandfather
and the great State umbrella carried immediately behind him,
whether he were on horse or foot, by a gigantic negro, and a
State carriage, seldom used, in which the umbrella could be fixed.

In those days Nawabs from India, Emirs from Afghanistan,
Rulers and Princes, Shaikhs and Holy Men from all the Muslim
world would come in turn with companies of followers, bringing
with them great sums to spend in Mecca. As he grew up, he saw
and accepted that there was a role in the world for such men as
his grandfather and his Hashimite forbears, father-kings of their
people. He knew that had it not been for Ibn Saud, the Emir of
central Arabia, who had climbed to power on the fanatic strength
of the puritans and captured the Hijaz, he would have succeeded
his father in the rule of Mecca.

When they had come to Iraq, pride for long forbade him and
his father from giving up their claim to the Hijaz and their status
as natives of Arabia. But, after all, Iraq was a country with a
stronger position in the world and a more agreeable climate than
the Hijaz; and there were practical considerations which in the
end helped him to make up his mind to become an Iraqi subject.

H

His mother, Nafisa, had at first found it hard to bear her new position in Iraq, as a person of comparatively small importance, with little money, ranking after the women of her husband's younger brother. When her daughter married Ghazi she had been pleased, still more pleased when Aliya gave him a son—her grandson. When her own son became Regent she was frankly happy. The position of the women of Faisal the First's family no longer irked her. She and her widowed daughter, the King's mother, were the leading women in Iraq.

At the time he accepted the Regency, Abdulillah was twenty-seven years old. Hardly had he assumed his position than he became aware that there would almost certainly be a second world war, brought about by Germany.

Dr. Grobba, the German Minister in Baghdad, was able and indefatigable. His forte was covering up his ability with a bland and reassuring hospitality. Although a typical German in build and appearance—with his large frame and rugged looks he might have been any North German business man—he conveyed to the British his disapproval of the regime which circumstances had forced him to serve. Whatever his inmost thoughts, he played the German game successfully, and his wife was indefatigable in helping him and particularly in making friends with the British colony.

Another German often in Baghdad was an archaeologist. Such a man, with great knowledge of the past, steeped in the histories of ancient empires, grey-haired, slim and slightly bent from scholarly application, might well wish to disregard modern party politics. He succeeded in convincing his British acquaintances that he did so. And when, during the war, secret German organization in Iraq was uncovered, he was found to have been at the heart of it.

They played up fear of Zionism and distributed German propaganda which made their country seem so powerful that she must win any war. They gave many promises of aid in money and arms. They organized sympathizers, thus created, into a secret league and paid a corps of agents and informers of high and low degree.

Within five months of Abdulillah becoming Regent of Iraq, the Second World War was declared.

King Faisal the First, by
Augustus John

King Faisal the First,
from a presentation
photograph

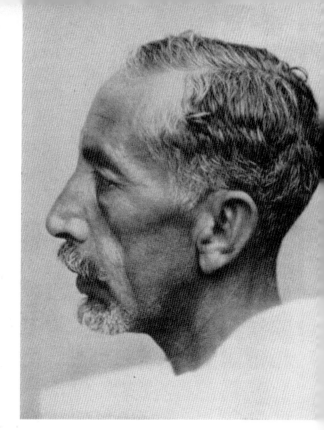

King Faisal the First, from a photograph in the possession of Mr. P. Metcalfe, c.v.o. who designed the Iraqi coinage

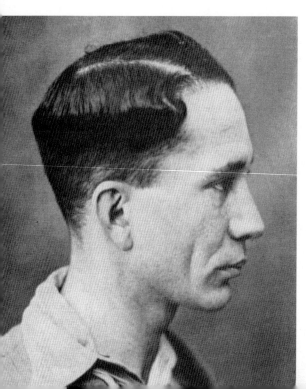

King Ghazi, from a photograph in the possession of Mr. Metcalfe

King Ghazi, from a
photograph taken in
Iraq

The Regent of Iraq,
by Norblin

King Faisal the Second, by Anthony Devas

King Ali of the Hijaz, last Grand Sherif of Mecca

King Abdulla of Jordan

The Regent of Iraq with the President of Turkey and the Author

King Faisal the Second on his Accession Day,
from a photograph in the possession of Dr. R. Dixon Firth

Iraq did not hesitate. Diplomatic relations with Germany
were broken off and Dr. Grobba left the country. Nuri envisaged
close relations and even joint action with the Allies. He pressed
hard, later on in the war, to be allowed to furnish an Iraqi Legion
to fight with the British Army.

It was not until January 1940 that German intrigue, which
had been maturing underground, came to the surface with the
murder by an ex-police officer with German sympathies of the
Minister of Finance, Rustam Haidar, Faisal the First's friend and
adviser and the most generally reliable and experienced member
of the Government. Rustam was a Shiah and Nuri al Said found
himself in a dilemma over the trial of the murderer, Hussain
Fauzi Ibrahim, who, after first denying accomplices, later confessed to support by a number of leading politicians. The Shiahs
wanted trial by immediate court martial of everyone concerned.
The remainder of the Cabinet and the Sunnis in general wanted
the ordinary criminal procedure. So Nuri resigned, in February.
Some senior army officers were active in pressing Nuri's opponent, the head of the Royal Diwan, Rashid Ali al Gailani, to
accept office. Other Generals supported Nuri and both parties
stood their troops to arms. The young Regent faced his first
crisis.

Rashid Ali al Gailani refused to accept office, appreciating
the strength of the opposition against him, and Nuri once more
came into power, without direct military intervention. The
murderer was tried by court martial and hanged. One of his
accomplices was imprisoned for a year; the others were released
for lack of evidence.

Rashid Ali, in his position as head of the Diwan, next advised the Regent to form a Coalition which would avoid Army
pressure. Nuri agreed and proposed Rashid Ali as Premier,
himself taking Foreign Affairs. It all seemed amiably settled and
correct. But success of the German armies and German propaganda were having their effect. Iraq not having broken off relations with Italy, the Italian representatives were in a position
to act comparatively freely against the interests of the Allies and
made the most of their liberty to do so. By the end of 1940 Nuri
was losing ground and those opposed to him, backed by a
number of senior army officers, were gaining strength. The

cleavage in public and Cabinet opinion was clear. At first the Regent attempted to manœuvre Rashid Ali out of office, but he was obliged in the end, after a deadlock, to keep him, while having the field cleared by the resignation of Nuri al Said and a Cabinet opponent simultaneously.

Rashid's new Ministers were two extremists and he began to show increasing confidence as his relations with the Iraqi Generals became closer. When a number of his other Ministers decided to resign, in order to force his own resignation, the Generals intervened and the Regent was obliged to retain him in office, with still more extremist Ministers.

To gain time, and to escape the duress of the Generals, the Regent left Baghdad to lodge with the loyal Commander of the Fourth Division, Ibrahim al Rawi, at Diwaniya on the Euphrates. There he summoned elder statesmen and managed to form a new government under one Taha al Hashimi, a former General, the only politician whom the serving Generals would accept as an alternative to Rashid Ali. The Regent was able to return to the capital. It was the 1st February 1941. Nevertheless, in spite of the Regent's return, the situation was deteriorating and a number of the leading members of the British colony got up a petition to the authorities asking for the appointment of Cornwallis as Ambassador. They felt that he was their only hope and took steps to lobby for his appointment.

Meanwhile, the splendidly enthusiastic Colonel 'Fighting Bill' Donovan, of the United States O.S.S., at this time visited Baghdad in passing. He asked to see the ex-Mufti, or chief religious of Jerusalem, Hajji Amin al Hussaini, and his followers among the politicians. The Mufti, a refugee in Iraq, who was behind the scenes in all the pro-German party's manœuvres, rather reluctantly came to see him at the American Legation, but was alone, having concealed from his companions the invitation extended to them. Donovan explained to the Mufti that America, though she had not yet declared war, was already behind Britain and would resent the activities of persons working against her. The Mufti should look ahead and understand the consequences of actions which, being against the interest of Britain, were therefore against the interests of America herself. He asked him to explain the position to his friends. The Mufti agreed, but never, it is believed, did so. On the contrary, he continued his intrigues against the authorities and his dangerous plots. 'Wherever the Mufti is,' said Nuri al Said to me with a grim smile, at the end of the war, 'there is trouble.' He had been in Germany, as Nuri knew, at the collapse of that country. The Mufti of Jerusalem, whose appointment had been approved by a British Governor, was, like Bakr Sidqi, a man whose very appearance was enough to alert anyone used to summing up the characters of other men. How he had ever received any British backing at all it is difficult to understand. He had been an Ottoman officer and somehow one seemed to see a uniform beneath his Mufti's robe, it did so little to conceal his aggressive character. He had watery, pale-blue eyes, a red beard and tight lips, with a cunning expression, hence was nicknamed Red Fox. He knew the agents of the Communists and had his own gang of gunmen. 'The end justifies the means,' the Mufti would reiterate. He was generally accepted as having approved and organized several murders including, later, that of King Abdulla of Jordan in the mosque of Jerusalem.

Two British High Commissioners in Palestine had in the past seemingly thought him worthy; the first, Sir Herbert Samuel, had approved his appointment as Mufti, even though it was scarcely in order according to the ancient Ottoman election regulations and Muslim practice. In the end, about to be arrested, he had escaped, with beard shaved and disguised as a woman, to Syria and from there to Iraq. The Iraqi authorities had regretfully allowed him to stay.

The American Minister, the American Special Envoy and Mr. Anthony Eden, who had seen Tawfiq al Suwaidi, the Iraqi Foreign Minister, in Cairo, all tried to deflect the increasingly pro-German sentiment of the Gailani faction. It already deeply resented the moderation of the Regent and Nuri and their pro-British attitude, though Rashid Ali himself professed a certain degree of neutrality as cover to his true feelings. The Regent decided to break the power of the four leading Generals, the 'Golden Square' as they were nicknamed in British circles, and began by ordering one of them away from Baghdad, but the command was ignored.

In spite of this defiance, a senior British administrative official with the Iraqi Government was inclined to believe in Rashid

Ali's protestations of his ability to control the Generals and advised patience.

On the night of the 1st April the four Generals seized power, bringing their troops into the capital to guard important points and the Palace.

The British Air Liaison Officer was stopped at bayonet point when on his way to the R.A.F. headquarters at Habbaniya. Obliged to return, he went to the Embassy and found there a disbelief in the seriousness of the situation. He started off a second time, crossing the river by the boat bridge at Kadhimain, and, obtaining a tribal guide, eventually reached Habbaniya through the desert and via a ferry over the Euphrates at Ramadi. He was thus able to give the R.A.F. headquarters immediate warning of the beginning of the coup d'état.

The Regent decided to leave the capital, for the second time, only when the Palace cook brought him a copy of a certificate of his death from a heart attack, signed and dated for that night. The doctor, who had signed it under duress, had sought out the cook and despatched it with him to the Palace. Whether it had been planted, so that it would be taken to the Regent and frighten him out of the city, is uncertain. He was firmly of the opinion that it was not so, and that his death was planned, and events seemed to confirm that he was right. He drove away at once, by car, to the house of the Sherifa Salha, an aunt, who lived in an old building on the east bank of the river. 'Troops were already on either side of the road between my house, the Qasr al Rihab, and the airport, but they were sitting about or standing at ease, apparently waiting for orders not yet arrived. I hoped I would not be stopped.' Meanwhile, one of the family in the Palace, as so often when in trouble, had rung for Dr. Sinderson.

She gave no name. All the voice said was: 'Please go to my aunt's house at once. It is urgent.' Sinderson understood that it was the Princess Abdiya, the Regent's sister, speaking and that she was in fear. At Salha's house it was decided that the Regent should be properly dressed in women's clothes and make his way, in a horse cab, to the American Legation—not to the British Embassy. To go to the British Embassy, the doctor said, would be unwise, for that was just where he would be expected to go.

So the Regent made himself up with the help of Princess Salha, borrowing a woman's cloak, dress and shoes from the family.

Arrived at the United States Legation, he had momentary difficulty in obtaining admittance, in the role of an unknown woman of Baghdad, to the presence of the Minister, but managed to convince one of the staff that he must see the Minister's wife, Mrs. Knabenshue. So he was received and looked after while waiting for a British representative and Dr. Sinderson to arrive and discuss the next move. Sinderson had spoken with Adrian Holman, the British Counsellor of Embassy, and two R.A.F. staff cars with two officers' uniforms were sent to a rendezvous near the American Legation, a club. In the end they were not used by the Regent, but by his A.D.C., Ubaid bin Abdulla, who was given uniform, dark glasses and a copy of *The Times*, to hold up in front of his face. The Knabenshues were soon due to leave Baghdad for the R.A.F. air station at Habbaniya, to welcome the new British Ambassador, Sir Kinahan Cornwallis, arriving, as he himself said, 'Damned late in the day,' too late to avert the coup. The journey to Habbaniya provided a means of getting the Regent to safety. It had already been arranged for him to be flown to Basra, if, that is, he were able to reach Habbaniya. Once in Basra he could, if need be, board a British warship.

The Regent was concealed in the Ambassador's car, beneath a rug and between the feet of Knabenshue and his wife. The R.A.F. cars with his A.D.C. were to go ahead, cross the bridge and wait, and then follow the U.S. Legation car.

At the bridge over the river an officer peered into the car. Mrs. Knabenshue saw the end of the Regent's automatic pistol projecting from the rug, but the officer stood back and allowed the car to pass. The flag of the United States of America on the bonnet of the car provided a sufficient passport elsewhere on the road to safety with the Royal Air Force, in their camp beyond the bridge over the Euphrates at Faluja. The new Ambassador was able only to see the Ruler of the country in this camp, as he was on his way out of the country. He himself only reached his Embassy in time to be imprisoned in it by the rebellious Army.

The Queen and the remainder of the Royal family in the Palace were cut off by telephone and visitors were prevented from reaching them. Servants were still allowed to come and go and schemes were devised for rescuing the baby King, but none seemed safe and practical.

In order to discuss these plans, the Queen and her sister Abdiya did manage to break out for a time one afternoon. They put on old cloaks and hired a succession of cabs, changing from one to another until they reached Dr. Sinderson's house and could speak with his Pakistani servant.

'There are two ladies dressed in ragged cloaks to see you. They say they are important persons and they do speak as if they were so. They won't give their names.'

In the end the family stayed together in the Palace until removed 'under house arrest' to Kurdistan, where they remained until the interregnum was ended.

Some jewels, orders, including the Gold Chain of the Hashimi and Victorian Orders, together with, strangely, a silver-plated pistol presented to Ghazi by Hitler, and documents, were handed to the Royal Air Force for sending to Kuwait where the Regent had gone in a British man-o'-war. The aircraft, with the jewels in the keeping of the Chief Intelligence Officer, Wing Commander Jope-Slade, came down in the Persian Gulf, the pilot having lost direction and failed to find either Shaiba or Kuwait landing-grounds before coming to the end of his petrol. The journey had been undertaken at night for greater safety while taking off, since the aerodrome was under sniping fire. The pilot and Jope-Slade swam for a long time, and it was only a number of minutes after Jope-Slade, though a practised swimmer, said that he must give in, that a water-boat, bound from Basra to Kuwait, came upon the scene and picked up the pilot. Several efforts to find the aircraft and its freight failed. The jewels, the Iraqi and British documents, and a large sum in notes from the Intelligence chest in Iraq, remained lost beneath the sea off Bubiyan Island, an extensive sandbank only notable for a mention in *The Shape of Things to Come* by H. G. Wells.[1]

Meanwhile, Nuri Pasha had been taken by night to Habbaniya in an R.A.F. car by the Air Liaison Officer, Squadron Leader P. Domvile. They were stopped at the Faluja bridge by an Iraq Army guard, but with civilian hats pulled down over their eyes

---

[1] The Chain of the Victorian Order was replaced by a duplicate by order of King George the Sixth, after the war.

they managed to convince the guard that they were a couple of officers returning from a weekend's leave in Baghdad.

The Regent was taken to Jordan and on to Palestine by the Royal Air Force and the party that gathered there in the King David Hotel was Nuri al Said and his son, Sabah, who had been flown over by the R.A.F.; Daud Pasha al Haidari; Ali Jaudat, a former Prime Minister; Jamil Madfai, also a former Prime Minister; Ubaid bin Abdulla of the Royal bodyguard, an A.D.C., son of my friend the bedouin Chamberlain to King Faisal the First; and the Sherif Hussain, brother of Faisal's Queen. I joined them, coming via Basra from Tehran, a few days after their arrival.

The first four were politicians. Ubaid, who had been the first Iraqi to go to Sandhurst, was a horseman before all else. The Sherif Hussain had never had the least pretensions to political life and was not well known outside the court circle. The 'Government-in-exile', if it were to be so called, therefore had no more than four members. A quorum for the Iraqi Cabinet was six persons. When telegrams from London began to come, pressing the Regent to form a government,' he was reluctant to do so, not only because there was not a quorum unless the Sherif and his A.D.C. were made Cabinet Ministers, but because he felt that waverers in Iraq could be much put off if they knew that Nuri was Prime Minister again. Furthermore, Nuri, Jamil Madfai and Ali Jaudat were eyeing each other quizzically. If the Regent showed, or seemed to show, favour to one of them, the others sulked. When I came down to the hall of the hotel in the mornings there would usually be one missing. 'Where,' I would ask the Regent, 'is So-and-So?' The missing ex-Minister would be behind a newspaper in a distant corner. When I later went to talk to him he would plead a headache or some other indisposition. Each day it would be one of them in turn who was hipped and alone.

Moreover, as the Regent knew, it would be a mistake to make Nuri al Said his Prime Minister at a moment when he was so unpopular in the country—though he did not want that given as his reason—and he resisted all my attempts to persuade him to form a 'government'. Failure to create one more 'government-in-exile', according to pattern, was doubtless viewed askance in London.

All the Iraqis in exile would constantly ask for news of their departure for Iraq. They seemed to think that the British Army were the slowest coaches they had ever known. The units, which had been charged with taking Rutba fort in mid-desert before the main column advanced beyond it, were indeed rather slow about it, being understandably wary of a frontal attack since the garrison was known to have a number of machine-guns. At long last, after support from the air, the fort fell to the R.A.F. No. 2 Armoured Car Company, and the next move began. Nuri and the others were agog when they were given transport and money and told that they were about to leave. In the end we travelled by air to Habbaniya. The baggage, except for one suitcase each for the Regent and myself, went by road with a small party of Iraqis, volunteers who had been in Jordan or elsewhere when the revolt began. The Iraqi transport party was told to take orders from the British commander of the convoy. Elated when they arrived near the Euphrates, they refused to halt and drove on to Ramadi, still in rebel hands, and were never seen again. Thus, after a few days, the politicians were anxious for a change of clothes and implored me to obtain permission for them to shop in the canteen at Habbaniya. It was incorrect for them to do so, but an exception was made. For a time the dignified, and some of them portly, politicians appeared in the khaki shorts and white, short-sleeved shirts worn by airmen off duty.

They were given tents in a palm grove outside the camp so that an air of independence might be better maintained. It was there that they were machine-gunned from a Messerschmitt. As they slowly picked themselves up afterwards, looking far from happy, the Regent said lightly: 'Who wants to go back to the King David—and who wants to go on to Baghdad with me?' He was brave. But the next morning I found them gone, not to Jerusalem, but to a building on the shores of Lake Habbaniya, used by Imperial Airways and since looted by the rebels. They preferred the shelter of walls to the cover of trees. They and the volunteers were cleaning it up, removing the quantity of broken glass, every single window having been deliberately smashed by the rebel Army, and making it habitable again.

The Regent was busy interviewing 'prisoners', men captured

by the British column and volunteers, who had come to 'surrender' with a view to joining him. Those thought to be genuinely loyal were armed and formed into a guard which might soon, it was hoped, be large enough to form a loyal regiment.

I was encouraged by the British authorities to spend money and was given credit, with which I had obtained vehicles in Jerusalem for the Regent and his party and made contingent payments with a sum which Iraq would later repay.

It was hoped that with the money we could 'raise the tribes' in support of the Crown. 'We have few arms except one—money,' it was said. I felt blameworthy for not spending lavishly. But raising the tribes then was impossible. It must have been a disappointment to those who had conjured up in their minds a picture on the lines of the Lawrence campaign in the Arab Revolt long ago. A churning mass of camelry advancing across the desert, the Regent in their midst, and myself, with chinking bags of sovereigns at my saddle-bow, surrounded by a splendidly accoutred bodyguard—this was how they may have seen it.

The disappointing truth is that it was in any case the wrong time of year for mobilizing in the desert. It takes some weeks to raise tribesmen, and they are reluctant to rise without up-to-date arms, for they have tasted metal—from machine-guns and aircraft—and they know that against well-equipped troops they have no hope of winning a battle. Bedouin can be enlisted and trained as was done in Jordan's Arab Legion, but that takes time and we were all for speed. Even to gather them together for petty raiding of communications at this time of year would have been next to impossible. The bedouin retreat perforce to permanent water in summer; otherwise their animals die for lack of watering. And the Arabian summer was already on us. Those of them who leave their tents must have their own food and water. And the margin of surplus food in the tent households by May is low. They 'shop' and restock at their 'ports', towns on the edge of the desert, in early autumn. As there is little or no grazing in summer, they require bags of food for their mounts as well as for themselves. Again, they like to debate new ideas at length. Sending messages to call together the Shaikhs, who travel reluctantly in days of great heat, would take some days, and their arrival even longer.

Such plans lapsed and instead we had bought in Palestine cars and buses and enlisted drivers and escort guards.

The use of the important riverain tribes of Iraq proper was a different matter. We looked forward to organizing their loyalty, dropped money and sent off messengers to them. None of them rose in support of Rashid Ali.

Meanwhile in London there was warrantable anxiety. Mr. Winston Churchill, beginning a speech in the House of Commons on the war situation on 7th May, referred first to 'a most unfortunate and tiresome thing, that Persia and Mesopotamia, when they changed their names about the same time, did so to names so much alike as Iraq and Iran'. He then went on to say:

Some have pointed to what has happened in Iraq as another instance of the failure of our Intelligence and our diplomacy. My Hon. and gallant friend the Member for Wycombe [Sir A. Knox], though in a perfectly friendly way, has inquired about that. We have been told that the Foreign Office never knows anything that is going on in the world, and that our organization is quite unadapted to meet the present juncture. But we have known only too well what was going on in Iraq, and as long ago as last May, a year ago, the Foreign Office began to ask for troops to be sent there to guard the line of communications. We had not the troops. All that we could send had to go to the Nile Valley. In default of troops it was very difficult to make head against the pronounced pro-Axis intrigues of Rashid Ali, who, eventually, after his removal from power at our instance, staged a coup d'état against the Regent and the lawful Government of the country. Obviously his object was to have everything ready for the Germans as soon as they could reach Iraq according to programme. However, in this case the ill-informed, slothful, kid-gloved British Government, as it has no doubt become since it has been deprived of the abilities of some valuable Members, actually forestalled this plot. Three weeks ago strong British forces, which are continually being reinforced from India, were landed at Basra, and they assumed control of that highly important bridgehead in the East for which we shall, no doubt, have to fight hard and long.[1]

In point of fact the British Embassy was not so fully alive to coming events as they might have been, and Rashid Ali was not 'removed at our instance'. He did do his best right up to

[1] *Hansard*, Vol. 371, cols. 942–3.

the last moment to prevent, or delay, the arrival and passage of our troops in Iraq, though it was fully in accordance with the Treaty of 1930.

The commander of the British troops from India, when they arrived in Basra after the coup d'état, seemed to contemplate, as Mr. Churchill in Parliament mentioned, having to 'fight hard and long', perhaps because it had taken the British and Indian Army three years to reach Baghdad from Basra, through the riverain tribal areas, in the First World War. When I suggested to him at Basra that some of his troops should advance rapidly to Baghdad, through the deserts well west of the rivers, taking each small desert police post and its desert well in turn, the idea was rejected out of hand. I went on to Palestine by a Dutch civil air-craft and was glad that I did. The advance across the desert from Palestine reached Baghdad in a month; and it was made with few casualties, during all which time the troops at Basra had hardly moved.

The heat was great and one of the members of the force from Palestine whom I saw looking really uncomfortable in it was the monkey of the Household Cavalry, who found the hot sand at midday intolerable and, when put down, hopped and bounded wildly towards the shade.

The garrison of Habbaniya, we learnt, had fought bravely. The rebels had at first taken up a stand on the hills commanding the camp, and their aircraft bombed it. There was a seven-mile perimeter to defend, and had the garrison not attacked and driven off the enemy from its gates it would have perished. Two ancient howitzers, 4.5 in., mounted as ornament at a gateway, were re-commissioned as the only artillery of the defenders and their aircraft were a few old training machines. The morale and initiative of the small garrison were their saving. They had bravely made a sortie, retaken the high ground dominating the camp, and, led by Major Alistair Graham of the Royal Dragoons and his company of Assyrians, later stormed and captured the only bridge across the Euphrates and entered the village of Faluja on the farther, eastern bank. They, and the King's Own Regiment, held it and repelled counter-attacks in the same fiery mood. When the force from Palestine arrived at Habbaniya the Regent and Nuri had put forward ideas, using their local knowledge. Very soon a swing bridge thrown across the Euphrates enabled one column to outflank Faluja and the Arab Legion, to deny to the rebels use by day of the road northwards from Baghdad.

The Regent's small Iraqi Force was growing and he hoped to be able to take the field with it. The main British column, under Major-General Clark, immediately began making a necessarily slow advance towards Baghdad through country flooded by the rebels.

The British soldiers who crossed the Euphrates were following in the footsteps of famous armies of the past. Here marched southward, on the left bank towards Babylon, Cyrus and his Persians, with the Ten Thousand Greeks and Xenophon. Close at hand, between Faluja and Musaiyib, 'six marches' south from the narrows above Ramadi, was the site of the battle of Cunaxa, from which the Greeks had turned towards the Black Sea and their homeland. We were on historic ground, and the restoration of order in Iraq could well be an important and historic moment in the war in the East.

The Germans had already been moving aircraft into Iraq via Aleppo and sending official advisers to the rebels. One of them, Axel von Blomberg, a distinguished airman, son of the Field Marshal, was to be met at the Baghdad airport by senior rebels on the 12th May. As the aircraft came in to land, someone, unknown to the pilot and the committee of reception, had fired a shot at it, hitting the passenger in the throat. When the Iraqis hurried forward to shake hands they found only a blood-bespattered body. The morale of the rebel leaders was already low and this incident seemed to mark its turning point. A few days later, as the British column neared Baghdad, the rebel leaders began to slip away, to Persia and, eventually, like Rashid Ali himself, to Germany.

The Royal Air Force had in the first days of the revolt destroyed the rebel air-petrol reserves and they had since been indefatigable in dropping messages to tribal Shaikhs. On one occasion messages were dropped on the Palace in the hope that the Queen would receive them. In fact, the King and the Royal ladies had already been removed to Erbil in Kurdistan by the rebels to make an enforced stay with one of the notables. The

Royal Air Force dropped messages from the Regent to the Mayor and Chief of Police and the people of Baghdad.

The rebels were not receiving all the immediate help they expected from Germany. So Rashid Ali sent his Foreign Secretary, Naji al Suwaidi, to see King Ibn Saud, in the hope that he might aid him. But Ibn Saud was not to be beguiled. 'If I had seen benefit to the Arabs in Rashid Ali's action, I would have been at his side without your coming to ask for my help,' he told Naji.

'Does Rashid Ali wish me, now I am old, to be a traitor to those who helped me when I was young?' he asked.

'Go back and say to your master: "Is it better to take the claw of the eagle in hand or go along with a well-fed lion?"' He turned to his Chamberlain. 'Give him as a present one of the best Buick cars and see that he leaves us speedily.'

By the end of May the British General was still doubtful about early success. The enemy was 'dug in', supported by artillery at Kadhimain. The British column was eight miles west of Baghdad, repairing broken canal bridges and culverts as it advanced. The country lent itself, he said, to 'defence by machine-guns, of which the enemy has plenty'. The rebel broadcasts, however, showed a rapidly dropping morale, and Nuri and Daud al Haidari wrote out with flowing enthusiasm the text of papers, dropped by the Royal Air Force, exhorting the people to throw out the rebels and support the Regent. On 30th May a cable from Persia told us that Rashid Ali had crossed the frontier and a little later a wireless signal was received, the first from the British Embassy in Baghdad after its long silence, saying that Iraqi emissaries would come to the Iron Bridge over the Khirr Canal west of Baghdad at 2 a.m.

I went to meet them, accompanied by Major Spence, a Yeomanry officer, Ali Jaudat and Sabah al Said. They were late at the rendezvous and did not arrive until 4 a.m. When they at last turned up I found that one of them was my old friend, Ghazi Daghestani.

We said first that we must see the Ambassador and so we went to the Embassy, making its first contact with the outside world. Terms with the rebels could not be made without the Ambassador, and, since the General could not leave his troops, Sir Kinahan came back with us to the head of the column.

There it was that he expressed strongly his view that there need be no military safeguards and the Iraqi Army, many of them deceived by their leaders and not in fact disloyal, must be allowed to march away with their arms. It was this wise decision, though it dismayed the Chiefs of Staff in England at the time, that for long afterwards made relations better than could have been expected, and I believe it still has some effect even today. In later troubles, at the height of emotion, hardly a single Britisher has been deliberately hurt, though some have suffered great inconvenience.

The Emir of Trans-Jordan sent a congratulatory telegram to the British Government, praising 'the spirit of friendship which exists between the Arabs and the British' and the 'co-operation which has been maintained between H.R.H. the Regent and his followers, the great personalities of Iraq, and the responsible British authorities who were by his side, and the considerate policy which was followed by the British commanders on land and in the air'.

The Regent was welcomed enthusiastically by the notables of Baghdad, led out to meet him by the Head of the Senators, Sayid Muhammad al Sadr, in his great black turban and dark robes, and by the dapper little Lord Mayor.

The Regent insisted on waiving the ceremonious reception which the Lord Mayor proposed, and a few hours later he drove into Baghdad, straight to the Palace, where his first concern was to get in touch with the King by telephone. He held the receiver so that I, too, could hear the boy's voice, squeaky with excitement at speaking again to his uncle.

The Mayor and the Chief of Police assured the Regent that order would be kept, but suddenly, when the mob realized that the Army was marching away and that the British Army had not entered the city—their commander had refused to do so on the grounds of danger to his troops in narrow streets, quoting, as an example well known to military men, Amritsar—it set out to loot the Christian and Jewish shops in the main street, some of whose owners had had the temerity to fly British flags and banter the defeated Muslims. The resultant disturbances were soon put down, but representations in London led to the good names of the Regent and those with him being blackened. Joy at return was spoilt for him. It was said incorrectly that, had there been formed a government-in-exile to take over in Baghdad on entry, no one would have suffered, but Ministers could have done no more or acted no faster than did the city authorities, who took immediate measures to quell the trouble.

The Regent, however, showed his gratitude to those who had been loyal and who had signally helped him in 1941. When Mr. Knabenshue, the courageous American Minister, died of blood poisoning soon after the events of 1941, the Regent gave his wife a house and assistance to live in Baghdad, until after the war, so that she would not have to face the long journey through dangerous seas to her homeland.

To others he gave Iraqi orders or appointments in Iraq. In November 1943 a London evening paper reported that 'an unusual event had an hotel setting last night—an investiture. Held in the suite which the Regent of Iraq is occupying at Claridges, it was an expression of the youthful Prince's gratitude to those members of the British Forces who, in the stormy days of 1941, helped him to flee the country—eventually to return to guide it to the side of the United Nations.'

On the other side of the picture, he was determined that the men who had led the rebellion should be fully punished. Those condemned to death were hanged at the time or as soon as they were secured.

Rashid Ali had gone over to the enemy and when, after the war, he had to leave Germany, he fled to Saudi Arabia where King Ibn Saud gave him sanctuary. On returning to Baghdad after the revolution in 1958 he was not free for long, and by 1959 was in confinement in a barred cell in Baghdad.

The ex-Mufti of Jerusalem had escaped from Baghdad to Persia. When the British Army entered Persia in the summer of 1941 his leading gunman was captured, but the Mufti, helped by the Italians, took a place, with beard shaved, among the crew of a small Italian vessel who were being repatriated by air.

While the war continued he stayed in Italy and Germany, entering Switzerland in May 1945 from where he was at once deported to France. There he was kept under police surveillance, at Louveciennes near Paris, until he escaped from Orly, in a U.S. aircraft of Transcontinental Airlines, in May 1946, to Cairo.

I

Thus he was able, after the war, to continue his campaign in the Middle East with Russian support against Britain and her friends.

The Regent was always careful to support his diminutive nephew, the King, in public. If they appeared walking abreast at some inspection it was noticeable from the side that the Regent was always just half a pace back. Few men in his position have not succumbed to some desire to supplant their wards and many in the Orient, and Europe, too, in the past, have actively intrigued against them. The Prince allowed no such thoughts to gain their way in his mind.

His official position did not lead him into giving up entirely his informal life, nor did he lose his sense of humour, kindness and enjoyment of small things. Whenever he could he gave small private dinner parties and would invite leading Iraqis and British officers into the Palace. One British officer of the Military Mission in Iraq, hailed by the Prince while out riding and asked in for a drink, told him that he would be going to Kurdistan on duty in two days' time. 'It looks,' he said, 'as if I'll be spending my birthday next week on a Kurdish mountain-top.' Two days later the Prince's A.D.C. telephoned the officer with a message bidding him to a dinner on the date of his birthday. 'And should you be ordered north at that time, would you please ask the General to postpone your departure so that you can attend.'

When the Regent was in London in July 1945, on his way back from visiting President Truman and the Governor-General of Canada, he was invited to lunch at Buckingham Palace. He was still a shy man and he asked if it were possible to find out who the other guests would be. 'I like to know who I am to meet and have to talk with—it will be easier for me if I know beforehand.'

On his return he was radiant. He had been alone with the King, the Queen and Princess Elizabeth.

The Government suggested that he might like to visit the British Army in Germany. He and Nuri al Said were flown over and made a quick tour, seeing the troops under Sir Brian Horrocks and some of the devastated cities. In rubble at the centre of Hanover, he and Nuri were told that they were at the railway station. A battered station lamp was the only clue. Here

and there wretched creatures could be seen emerging from
burrows, homes they had made for themselves in the remains of
basements, dugouts or bomb-shelters, there being nowhere else
for them to live. Both the Regent and Nuri were deeply depressed
by the results of aerial bombing.

The Regent asked whether it would be possible for him to
return by car—he had bought two large ones—through occupied Europe and go on by boat to Turkey, where he had been
invited by the President with a view to talks on their relations
and the possibility of a new Middle East pact. Since there were
no liners sailing regularly he was offered passage in a British
warship. In France and Italy he could stay with the British
Army.

The party left London for Dover early on the morning of
25th August 1945, the Regent insisting on driving himself the
whole way from Calais to Naples. In towns and villages along
the Italian Riviera he and Nuri were struck by the happier
appearance of the Italians as compared with that of the people
of Germany and France.

Along the Italian Riviera were hundreds of young workmen,
dressed only in shorts made from camouflage material, working
on the shell-damaged roads. The car was directed round one
sharp corner of the corniche road by a young Hercules with a
pick-axe, standing statuesquely on a pile of broken rocks. 'Why,'
asked the Prince, 'did he say "I want you"?' He said, I explained,
'Avanti'. From Milan he was taken to lunch on the shores of
Lake Como and by launch to see in the distance the house where
Mussolini was killed. 'Did you notice,' he asked, 'that Nuri
would not look at it?'

The Regent and Nuri spent their time in Venice quietly.
Freya Stark came down from Asolo to help in his entertainment.
He usually went on the Grand Canal after dinner, gondoliers in
accompanying gondolas on either side singing across him strophes
from Ariosto.

Of all the cities he visited in Continental Europe, Venice was
the least changed by war. Except for the presence of men of the
Allied Forces and the absence of pigeons in the Piazza S. Marco,
said to have been shot and eaten by the Venetians, there seemed
little difference, and he and Nuri often mentioned afterwards the

pleasure they had had in being there for a few days at the end of the war.

The party left Rome for Naples on 10th September, General Infante coming from the Palace to say farewell on behalf of the then Lieutenant of the Realm, whom the Regent had visited and liked. On the way a stop was made at Monte Cassino for a description of the battles.

At Caserta, Field Marshal Alexander presented him with a gift for the King of Iraq, a scale model of an anti-tank gun, pair to a miniature tank presented during his visit to the Western Desert in 1942.

The party visited Pompeii and Sorrento, crossing by a British M.T.B., ably manœuvred by a very smart crew, to Capri.

On the quayside, since Capri was an American rest camp, he was met by an American Lieutenant and Sergeant with two jeeps. The Lieutenant introduced the Sergeant, who said: 'Pleased to meet you, Regent.' The jeeps went at a tremendous pace through the lanes to Gracie Fields' villa and then the party sipped drinks on the terrace above the Piccola Marina. Below us were steps and platforms of rock, on each of which lay a beauty with an American of field rank, every officer in bathing dress with a drink beside him. 'Well, Regent, if you wish to see the Blue Grotto I guess we had better scram,' said the Lieutenant.

The Regent sailed from Naples in H.M.S. *Ajax* on the 12th September, bound for Turkey.

It was the first visit of an Arab Ruler there since the break-up of the Ottoman Empire, and the first visit of a British warship to Istanbul since the beginning of the Second World War.

The captain and officers and crew were in consequence on their mettle and the Arab party unusually stirred. Before the city was in sight very early in the morning the Regent and the Pashas were on deck. None of them had seen it for many years. Nuri Pasha and Daud Pasha al Haidari had been educated there. The Regent's grandmother still lived in the house long belonging to the family at Emirgaun, on the narrows of the Bosphorus, above the city.

The Arab party all spoke Turkish, though without the latest turns of phrase and new words introduced under Kemal Ataturk.

They spoke in the more courtly, old-world speech, of the Ottomans. Nuri broke into Turkish and moved from side to side of
the ship, calling to Daud to see the places they remembered,
recalling the names of companions of long ago, some of them
killed in war. As the ship passed beneath the walls of the old city,
and the guns began to fire a royal salute, Nuri stood gripping the
rail of the ship, and I saw tears of emotion in his eyes. He was
entering the capital of the empire against which he had revolted
thirty years earlier.

When the A.D.C. to President Inönü came aboard, he
brought with him a programme of the visit for approval. It
included a dinner on the Presidential yacht and a naval ball
for the first night. 'Istanbul not sleep tonight,' he said with a
happy smile.

The Regent stayed in the Old Imperial Palace of Dolme
Bagche in the very rooms used by Sultan Abdul Aziz in the
middle of the nineteenth century.

The banquet on the yacht was 'private', for the party and
those attached to it for the visit. The chairs were placed on one
side of the table only and at its ends, but there were empty seats
ranged against the opposite walls of the salon. At the end of the
meal it became clear what this portended. A string of musicians
and singers filed into their places in front of the table. The instruments were the old-fashioned Arab and Turkish kind. It was a
compliment and a pleasant surprise, intended in particular for
Nuri Pasha, who was known to be a lover of the old Arabic way
of playing. He bore it for what seemed like many hours, nibbling
sweetmeats and drinking araq in the intervals between songs. At
long last the Pashas were satisfied and the players more or less
exhausted. 'Now,' the A.D.C. said brightly, 'we change into
"smokings" for the naval ball.' It was already past midnight.

The visit to Istanbul was short and more or less informal, for
the President was in the capital. During it the Regent took me
with him to see his grandmother at Emirgaun. It was an enchanting, rather tumbledown house on the Bosphorus, north of the
city. Fine Persian carpets, giant Bohemian glass chandeliers and
elaborate Italian fountains in alabaster gave the motif in the
sitting-rooms. We were received in an upstairs room looking
over the water through latticed windows. The old lady asked me

if I smoked. I said that I did, expecting her to offer me a cigarette or to pray me to smoke my own. She replied, however: 'So do I—like a chimney,' and, calling for her hubble-bubble, began at once. The Regent translated for me since she spoke Turkish and little or no Arabic. She was handsome, even in old age, and had a pleasing expression. It was not known exactly where she had been born, but she was from the Caucasus. One of the last of the harem-living women of old Turkey, she spoke intelligently of many things and places, and even now in her old age had a brightness in her look and a vivacity of mind that would outdo that of many of her contemporaries of equal standing in the surrounding countries.

The Regent spoke to me of the matters he would mention to the President. He intended to ask for the surrender of one of the four Generals who had taken a leading part in the 1941 revolt in Iraq against the regime of the Hashimite monarchy and the Allies. He spoke with rancour of the rebels and was quite determined to obtain the man for execution, his trial having already taken place *in absentia*. The President, I foresaw, might find it awkward to hand over a man who was living in exile in Turkey, as though he were subject to an extradition agreement which did not exist between Turkey and Iraq.

Changing his mood the Regent asked me if I thought that he could ask the President, when presents were mentioned, for an Angora cat. It would be embarrassing? I asked why it should be so. Surely the request was an easy one? Doubtless that is what he intended me to ask. 'You see, the President is deaf and has a discoloured eye too, like the cats.' I learnt for the first time that Angora cats are sometimes deaf and often have a squint, with one eye blue and the other green.

In the end the Regent obtained both the cat and the man. The latter, however, caused him concern. The Turks, unable to hand over the man officially, arranged for him to be sent to the Syrian frontier, 'where your friends the British can arrange to collect him and it will be no business of ours what happens once he is beyond the frontier'.

The British security officers did arrange to board the train as it entered Syria and the General was duly arrested. That evening, however, he asked his escort, a British Sergeant of the Security

Intelligence Force Unit, if he might go to the station lavatory. Once there he climbed very easily through its window. He had a ten-minute start, of which he made good use. The Regent was furious when he heard of it and sent for me to go to the Palace in Baghdad to talk about it. 'How could they be so inefficient?' He took it very badly. The Embassy sent a forthright message on the urgent need to recapture the man. After forty-eight hours he was found hiding in a village, some twenty miles off. This time he was more closely guarded and despatched to Baghdad where he was executed.

During the whole of the Regent's visit to the Turkish Government relations could not have been better, and out of the talks grew the Treaty signed the following year and approved in 1947, from which in time was developed the Baghdad Pact.

The last time I had reached Turkey was in the autumn of 1940, and then I went from Tehran dirty, tired and hungry, through Tabriz and along the Russian border past Mount Ararat and Erzeroum. The rains had just begun falling and because of the need for passing the gullies before they were in flood, and since the only stopping-places were huts already over-full of persons halted by the rain, I pressed on without stopping for meals or sleep except in the car for the three days between Tabriz and Erzeroum. My two journeys in Turkey were in complete contrast.

5

Peace Disturbed

*There is more pleasure in building castles in the
air than on the ground.*

Decline and Fall of
the Roman Empire

GIBBON

IRAQI Arab travellers reaching the Turkish and Persian
frontier districts have varied feelings on sighting mountains.
Their natural pleasure is tempered by well-rooted fear. From
the mountains came invaders and from them come floods
endangering life on the plain.

Every ten years or so the floods would be serious.

'Baghdad by flood [will be destroyed] and Basra by fire' is
an Iraqi saying, and in the middle of March 1946 the first part
of the saying looked like becoming a fact. The main street of the
city was eight feet below the level of the water, which was only
just being held back by the embankments along the Tigris.
Water was already seeping into the city through the brick-lined
sides of the river.

Ordinarily, in flood-time, when there was sufficient warning,
an embankment some twenty miles above the city would be cut,
allowing the waters to escape over farmland to rejoin the Tigris
below the city by entering one of its tributaries, the Diyala. In
1946 there had been hardly any warning.

The melting of the snows had been quickly followed by
heavy rains; the main river and its tributaries were all in flood
together. And just as the peak of it reached the city there was a
strong south wind to delay the flow and pile up the waters still
more.

The bank of the Tigris was hastily cut, only four miles above the city, so that the water, instead of sweeping across country into the Diyala, ran against the embankment protecting the Iraqi Army camp south of the city. And the Army had not spent enough time and money maintaining it. The bank broke, and the water pouring through it threatened, from the inside, the bank on its western side, one that alone stood between it and the nearest part of the city.

Thousands of soldiers tried vainly to fill up the spoil pit and prevent the undermining of this last defence. It soon became obvious that they were not succeeding. More men were brought. More and more encouragement was given, in food, threats and promises of money rewards. They worked stripped to the waist, sweating and swearing. Long strings of the inhabitants, male and female, supplied them with earth in baskets.

Every few minutes there was a mournfully loud rumbling as houses and barracks inside the camp collapsed and fell one after another into the water. The skies were grey with coming rain.

The Baghdad panic was beginning and even the more taciturn inhabitants and Europeans were starting to leave. The nine-year-old boy King Faisal was taken among the soldiers, and made the gesture of working alongside and encouraging them by his presence, but it was all of little use.

There were clearly only a very few hours left before disaster came when a British official of the Irrigation Department collected and brought up through wet country, overnight, carry-all scrapers, some tractors and bulldozers borrowed from the R.A.F. and a contractor. It was only just in time that they were put to work, so that within a day or two danger was past.

The building of a great dam at Samarra, by which flood-waters can be diverted into the Wadi Tharthar depression, has since prevented such flood dangers to Baghdad, though the second part of the Development Board Scheme, to bring the water back into the Tigris, has not been completed owing to the revolution in 1958.

Before the Victory March in London, which King Faisal the Second and the Regent were both invited to attend, the Prince was present at the Conference in Cairo of Arab Rulers, and on his way to Cairo he went to his uncle's, Emir Abdulla's, 'coronation' as King of Trans-Jordan. The Prince returned to Baghdad for a few days and had time to give me some of his impressions.

I was sitting alone with him on the lawn beside the Palace at dusk when a soldier called Shanaishil came up, in his uniform of the bodyguard, very neat and clean, and interrupted us. He was black, with huge lips, six feet tall, and lusty. The Prince asked him why he had come without taking leave to do so. The expression in the man's eyes was that of a faithful, fawning spaniel. 'But just one word,' he said, holding up two fingers towards his lips, the back of his hand turned to the front, the gesture of affection and supplication. He kissed the Prince's hand and tried to do the same to me. I withdrew mine hastily, which is considered becomingly modest, so that he was reduced to kissing his own fingers, as a sign that he would kiss mine if he could. The Prince, because of his rank, had permitted his hand to be kissed. 'Take care to ask leave when you come to me,' repeated the Prince to him. 'But, but——' he said, with a dog-like look and pleading air. 'Take leave, I say! Go now.' The Prince's voice was rising. The soldier went. 'His name,' I said, 'was once upon a time Gayeed Razooki. He used to be in my company twenty years ago, and he danced well. He was the same then as now. I never succeeded in disciplining him like the others; but his loyalty was unquestioned.'

The Prince repeated my words softly, as if savouring their exact significance: 'Undisciplined but loyal? It is better than disciplined and disloyal.' He gave a little shiver of disgust and called across the lawn to a servant to fetch the Officer of the Guard and have Gayeed's request examined.

Speaking of his visit to Cairo, and of the Conference at Inshass on the 29th May and its resolutions, he told me how he had found Saud, son of King Abdul Aziz Ibn Saud, whom he had not met before, noticeably grave and slow in answering questions. He spoke of him with no disapproval, but as one who had taken his measure and was not dismayed by it. He asked if I had noticed the same mannerism. I had indeed remarked it, but also that he spoke up when he felt strongly, or wished to convince one, with his father's rapidity of speech, though less lavish of phrases from the Koran and bedouin proverbs.

The Prince had sent for Arshad al Umari, of a Mosul family and several times Mayor of Baghdad, to form a Cabinet. As soon as it was in order he wished to leave for London via Cairo, and I was able to confirm next day from the British Embassy that a Lodestar of the Airways Corporation would be ready to take him to London on the 2nd June, via Lydda, Cairo, Malta, Naples and Marseilles. He had wished to travel in his new British aircraft as far as Cairo, but a defect was found in it.

Nuri al Said and I travelled with the Prince and he had in his suite Captain Jassam Muhammad, a pilot of the I.R.A.F., who stayed with him until 1958, and two military A.D.C.s, Halim and Abdul Qadir. A new A.D.C. was an Artillery officer and a poet, Ibrahim ibn Abdul Rahnan, a man of singular charm and unmilitary temperament. Nuri al Said thought highly of his talents as a poet and had recommended him, and every now and then he would speak out his verses to the Court, to everyone's delight. They would listen for a long time, without distaste or impatience, to his epic poems.

The Iraqi Chargé d'Affaires in London, Shakir al Wadi, who had come from England to meet the King—who was himself travelling by a yacht, already in harbour—met us at the airport at Marseilles and said that he had taken a house, Grove Lodge, at Bracknell, near Windsor, for the family.

It was the very first time the Arab ladies of the family had been beyond the Muslim world.

The Prince did not wish the Queen of Iraq to lunch at the Palace on Victory Day if there were publicity given to it or photographs published of her; and for the same reason the Queen of Iraq would be unable to be with the Queen of England during the march past, since the Muslim world was critical of the appearance in public of Muslim women.

The Hashimite ladies, nevertheless, went to the Queen's dressmaker as soon as possible, while the boy King went to Selfridges for his own shopping and then to see Grove Lodge. The King had had a streaming cold, but it stopped suddenly while he was there.

On the 8th June the King and the Regent went to the saluting base and were in the Royal stand with the British Royal family. Queen Nafisa, the Queen Mother, and the Princess from

Iraq, fearful of the effect of publicity, were placed, as they had wished, opposite to, and not in, the Royal stand. The King of Iraq conversed with Princess Alexandra and counted stretcher cases with animation. The Regent, the King and the Queen Mother lunched at the Palace and the King, who interpreted for his mother, was greatly elated on his return.

The ladies were wearing hats for the first time in their lives. In the evening they dined in public in the main dining-room at Claridges Hotel. On the yacht coming to England, Dr. Sinderson, the British physician and the King's tutor, had dined with them, but it was the first very time that they had eaten a meal in public.

After dinner the Regent, Captain Hugh Cruddas of the Iraq Military Mission, to whom the Prince had given a lift, Mr. Harwood from New Scotland Yard and I walked across the parks to the Horseguards, passing Buckingham Palace in order to see the illuminations and the fireworks. Just as we reached the Palace the Royal family came out on to the balcony in answer to repeated cries for them. The crowd in the Mall was very great and Hugh Cruddas, the Regent, Harwood and I linked arms to avoid being separated. Others were doing the same—soldiers, sailors, airmen, civilians. And everyone, of course, was in the greatest good humour. In the middle of this scene of democratic jubilation we were held up by a lady making a very low curtsy in front of us. It was Lady (Charlotte) Bonham-Carter, accompanied by Harold Freese-Pennefather, of the Foreign Office, who bowed. As they did so they brought to a halt a line of sailors, arms linked, whose faces wore the most comical expressions as they looked at the scene just in front of them.

The Prince never forgot this day and was proud of being present. He also never forgot seeing Mr. Winston Churchill as he came out of a private dining-room at Claridges, seemingly undisturbed on the very night of his parliamentary defeat following victory in war, or his stopping to come and exchange civilities with him.

It was while the King was at Bracknell that an Englishman visiting the house on a summer day was astonished by an incident as he waited in the doorway into a corridor running through the house to the garden; a woman, bent double and walking backwards, turned out of a room and came towards him. He coughed, and when she straightened up and turned round he found that it was the King's nanny. 'I am looking,' she said, 'for His Majesty's caterpillar which he has somehow mislaid.'

The King landed at Beirut for his return journey through Syria to Baghdad by train.

When he was in England the asthma from which he had long suffered became much better, and the Queen told me how happy she was to think that perhaps he was growing out of it at last.

There were the usual courtesies in Syria, including an alfresco luncheon party given by the President of Syria at Shtoura, in the valley between the Lebanon and anti-Lebanon mountains. The table was laid by a small river, under trees which partly shaded it from the bright sunlight. The President made a touching little speech. Lebanese youth had already shown surprising warmth in welcoming the King, both at the ship's side and in the streets, and now Syria did the same through her officials.

The war was over. We looked to the future optimistically and the boy King seemed to typify our hopes and the hopes of Arab youth.

The train was waiting at a station north of Damascus, and we did not expect to see the President again, but at a wayside halt the train was stopped without warning and he came aboard to say goodbye, having motored a long way to do so.

As we neared the Iraqi frontier an A.D.C. came to remind the Queen that there would be a guard of honour for the King to inspect at the frontier. He was romping with us, coatless, and was now tidied up, his obedience shadowed by natural reluctance.

When he climbed aboard again his asthma was once more beginning. A few hours later there was another guard of honour, at Mosul, and before we reached Baghdad he was ill with a bad attack of asthma. A concourse and troops were waiting for him and with difficulty he was able to go through his paces and he could only bring up a pathetic smile.

The asthma, it seemed, came from dust. It was particularly brought on by dust in horses' coats and the hair of cats, and hard as experts tried to find a cure it persisted, though rather less violent in form, when he was grown up.

He had behaved very well at all the functions and meetings which he had had to undertake as a King although still a child. Sometimes he had behaved almost too well. On the way to Europe he had been good-heartedly invited by the Ambassador, Lord Killearn, to a tea party. Orders were given for a special spread suited to a young boy, but His Majesty, self-possessed— or perhaps because he was not so—ate guardedly. In the end it was the Ambassador, not the King, who let himself go on cream buns.

The Emir Abdulillah was married three times, firstly to a beautiful Egyptian girl, Malik Faidhi. She bore him no children and he subsequently divorced her, the letter of notice from the Emir being given to her without warning by Nuri al Said in an aircraft on its way to Egypt. She afterwards married an Egyptian officer and bore him children.

The second marriage, of short duration, was also to an Egyptian, Faizi al Taraboulsi. The third marriage was to Huyam, daughter of the Emir Rabia. The Emir is by descent Paramount head of the Anaza Confederation, tribes whom Charles Doughty, in *Arabia Deserta*, called a 'nation' because they were so numerous. The Emir Rabia is by tribal lore overlord of Ibn Saud. Hospitable and distinguished, he was settled on the Tigris, near Kut-al-Amara, at Hussainiya, where he farmed on a grand scale, having been one of the very first to introduce the use of tractors and mechanical farm equipment. After the revolution, when his mansion at al Hussainiya was looted by the armed mob, he sold everything there, and now in his old age lives in his town house in Baghdad with Huyam to look after him.

There were no children of any of the three marriages of the Regent.

At the end of his visit at the time, he proposed to a beautiful English girl, but it came to nothing. He later asked the Ambassador from a Latin country in London for the hand of one of his daughters. This proposal, anyway, ran into difficulty over religion, the girl being a Roman Catholic in a family of high standing. The father, diplomatically, had expressed pleasure at the honour, but stressed the need to consult Rome and the proposal came to nothing.

The Regent was still extremely sensitive, but inquisitiveness and a desire to learn had overcome his reserve. With people, as with his taste in objects, he gradually became more sophisticated. Later, when he met, in London, Emerald Lady Cunard and, in Paris, Elsie Mendel, confident American hostesses of international repute, I thought that he would not be able to find common ground with them or wish to see them again, but he did so. To my astonishment, a week after his meeting with Lady Cunard, I found him with her on a Sunday afternoon, apparently quite at home in a group of her callers, all highly intelligent cosmopolitans. He had called on his own, unescorted, and was, I think, finding her sophisticated ingenuousness refreshing.

'And tell me, Regent,' she was piping in her thin voice, as I came into the room, 'do you have palm trees in your country?'

In spite of a Western way of life, a number of old family customs were retained. The Regent's father, King Ali, had twice received me while in bed and he received others whom he trusted in the same way. Abdulillah, when slightly indisposed in Baghdad in 1947, received me with Colonel Neil MacLean, M.P., while in bed, to the latter's astonishment. It was considered a form of compliment to do so.

The Regent would notice the finer points of English or cosmopolitan manners and customs and quietly adopt them. He liked driving his own cars, but never did so too fast or when it was proper to have a chauffeur. Sometimes he would drive some very small car about the streets of London or Baghdad, and would enjoy confusing a waiting, unofficial host who would be looking only for a Rolls or some big car and would perhaps wave on the small car whose driver was trying to park before his door.

He very much enjoyed shopping in London and after lunching at his hotel he would saunter down Bond Street, alone or with his A.D.C., and drop into various shops where he was soon well known and liked. It was plain that he regarded such visits to the 'bazaar' as a delicious indulgence which circumstances forbade him in Baghdad. Presents in number were bought for his family on each return from London and they nearly always included birds for his mother.

He sought to improve the shooting in Kurdistan by importing pheasants, not unknown in similar countries in the East, which he held to be their ultimate place of origin. Hawks and small wild animals kept reducing their numbers, but a few survived and may possibly develop into a breed which future experts may rediscover some day. Swans from the Thames were taken out, also dogs and some other animals.

He was, in short, a collector, but collected without great extravagance. Whatever may have been said by the critical new Iraqi intelligentsia, he did no more than was to be expected of a man in his position, with an establishment that was new and with very few possessions brought from his homeland, the Hijaz.

He was well aware of the importance of education being developed on the right lines for the youth of the country. He took a special interest in technical schools and caused Nuri al Said to put a check to the large numbers of boys going into the Law School—at one time there were a thousand students in it—for whom there would never be enough openings in the profession. For a time no entries were accepted and afterwards the pupils were reduced to a number suited to the opportunities for them when trained.

He was anxious to see athletics taken up, and encouraged the educational authorities to develop them, having visions of Iraqis one day competing in international events. Not only did he encourage the educational authorities by his enquiries, but when he could he took more practical steps, such as arranging with the Army that horses should be available for boys to learn to ride, giving prizes for subjects and events for which there were none, and taking the boy King with him at school inspections.

It was the Emir Abdulillah who later promoted the establishment of television in Baghdad. It was first suggested to him, half jokingly, at a party in London by Lord Bessborough. He at once turned to me, asking me if I did not consider it an excellent idea. 'Our people think through their eyes, as you know.' He called over Tahsin al Qadri, his Chamberlain, and there and then arranged a meeting to discuss it and learn about costs. 'It could

be used for training the Army, social welfare and education'—
all subjects he held to be important, and not for entertainment
only. It would be good if the people could see the King speaking
to them, and the Prime Minister, too, could use it for explaining
his policy to them. Films from London would have to be selected
by someone who knew the requirements of the country. He set
about guiding a plan for its introduction and for its maintenance
on the right lines.

Baghdad had television before any other Oriental city, owing
to the Regent's quick understanding of its potential value,
though he and Nuri al Said failed to use it for political ends as
much as they might have done. Nor did they use sound radio
as well as it could have been used. King Faisal the Second
did occasionally make broadcasts, from London and Baghdad,
but Nuri al Said used it seldom.

On the other hand, the Regent was careful to have sent off by
airmail to the Press in Baghdad accounts of his visits to establishments in Europe whenever these seemed to be of use or interest
to Iraq.

But the dominant matter in the Prince Regent's mind was
always the welfare and education of his nephew, the King. No
father could have loved his boy more, or been more concerned
about his education. Visiting Field Marshal Lord Alexander in
Naples after the war he asked him if he could find a young officer
to be tutor.

The qualifications for a tutor, said the Regent, were simple.
'The King does not have to pass examinations. He is not becoming a Civil Servant or a business man. He must be trained as
a King and therefore, in particular, learn good manners, the
management of men, history, English and other languages.
Shooting, riding and swimming are sports enough for him.' He
wanted a tutor who had been a brave officer and was of good up-
bringing. The Generals promised to look for such a man. The
Whitehall offices sent round some of their own men, selecting
them in civilian circles. In the end the Regent, since he was
leaving London, decided to form a small committee to choose a
tutor. As chairman of the committee he secured Sir Louis Greig,
who had been with King George the Sixth most of his life. He
recommended enthusiastically Julian Pitt-Rivers, later a Doctor

K

of Philosophy, who came out to Baghdad to spend some years with the King and prepared him, very successfully, for Sandroyd and Harrow.

The King was a quiet boy, very small, with fine bones, like most of his family. In complexion he was very light, with the dark eyes and hair of his race. He was quick-witted, an admirable pupil whom Pitt-Rivers found easy to teach. At the age of twelve he went to Sandroyd Preparatory School and at thirteen passed into Harrow, his mother, Queen Aliya, moving to Stanwell Place, Staines, in order to be near him. The house was rather close to the airport, but when I found it for them and at the same time told the Regent how noisy it was, he said: 'We are very near the airport at Baghdad and are used to it. And if we really were in the country, it might be too quiet.' It was a dignified, small country house hidden in its own grounds, and, since it had been owned by an engineer director who had retired there after building dams in Egypt it must, I felt, be in sterling order; and so the surveyors pronounced it to be. It was bought, the Prince told me, jointly by the King and himself.

After the Second World War the Iraq Army had been in a deplorable condition. For eight years it had done no training, though it had taken part in four coups d'état and a revolution. It was still controlled by Ottoman-trained officers who seldom left their offices in the capital. Its boots were mostly unfit for wear in marching, its supply of clothes short, its leave long overdue, its pay meagre and its rations had been reduced to a figure a thousand calories below the minimum considered necessary by European medical men for Eastern troops. Money for repair of barracks and camps had been stopped. The Police were forbidden to assist in tracing or arresting deserters and by the summer of 1943, out of an established strength of thirty thousand men, twenty thousand were deserters. To be an officer was often to hold only a sinecure appointment; and in spite of the poor condition of the Army as a military instrument, many of them were content.

Both the Regent and Nuri al Said, and in particular the latter, had had no wish to make the Army strong, after what had occurred in 1941, and as a matter of policy Nuri wished it kept 'short of oats'. In his last hours, in 1958, he must have bitterly regretted any change from that policy.

As the British troops were withdrawn from Iraq following the end of the war, and, as a consequence of the easy defeat of some Iraq troops by Kurdish rebels in the autumn of 1943, it naturally occurred to military men in England that the Army of the Ally ought to be made more efficient. Major-General George Bromilow, who had been old enough to have a command of Indian cavalry in Mesopotamia in the First World War, while still a fit and handsome man, devoted to polo and pig-sticking— the very picture of a cavalryman of the old school—retired as head of the British Military Mission and was replaced in the spring of 1944 by a former commander of armour in the Western Desert, Major-General Malcolm Renton, of the Rifle Brigade. He had lost an arm in France in the First World War, had later been the senior staff officer of the Iraq levies, and knew the country.

He at once determined on a purge of a hundred and twenty senior officers; upon a general reorganization and better field training; on an increase in the ration issue; the establishment of canteens and welfare centres; and on the provision of leave with pay and travel warrants for the troops. The difficulty he encountered in introducing these reforms came mostly from the Chief of Staff and senior officers, but the young officers, too, were not happy at being often away from their families on manœuvres, or at being stationed out of Baghdad. To be far from Baghdad had always been felt, by civilian officials as well as by officers, to be not only a financial disadvantage, but to have a stigma, proving lack of influence, that could not fail to be noticed and deplored by an individual's family and underlings.

The Regent, though he had some forebodings, supported Renton in his undertakings for reform. 'I must keep well in touch with the young officers. We must never have the 1941 trouble again.' In consequence he went out frequently on manœuvres and inspections.

For the same reason he arranged for officers in Baghdad to have leave for hunting, which, as in the old days in the British Services, was regarded as if it were a parade or duty. He went out himself and between runs would move his horse alongside a young Lieutenant's or Captain's and talk to him; in this way and others he could come to know many of his officers in an informal fashion.

Since the Regent harped upon the need for knowing and encouraging the officers, Renton, who did not hunt owing to the loss of his arm, used to arrange dinner parties—at his own expense, for he was fortunately well enough off to do so—at which the Regent and he could meet especially promising soldiers. There would be after-dinner games and the Iraqis, some of whom had been under training with the Army in England, seemed to enjoy them as much as the British. Whether or not they really did so, at least the purpose in view appeared to be achieved, and nearly all the best of them were considered sufficiently loyal to the regime to be arrested at the revolution of 1958.

Though the Army was rapidly becoming more efficient, and something like the *esprit de corps* expected of an army was coming into being, arms were short. Lists of requirements sent to England had not met with the prompt response which Iraq had hoped to receive. When a purchasing commission was sent it achieved better results. Although completely new equipment could not be provided in every case, all requirements would, it was said, be met in one way or another.

Renton had particularly asked that the Minister of Defence might accompany the purchasing commission so that there would be full powers to make decisions on purchases. And the Regent was to be in England at the same time.

Ten days after the arrival of the mission a telegram came from the Prime Minister, Salih Jabr, saying that no firm orders were to be placed for any equipment until after the commission had returned to Baghdad and obtained the sanction of the Council of Ministers for each item. His telegram was resented by the Regent, the Minister and the commission. On return to Baghdad every detail had to be fought through the Council of Ministers. After six weeks all orders were approved, except one, on which the Prime Minister was adamant. He refused to allow an order for five hundred four-wheel drive, three-ton lorries, urgently required for second-line transport, to be placed in England, but insisted that they should be American two-wheel drive vehicles, to be ordered from America through a contractor in Baghdad. His action, when it became known, infuriated the Army.

Furthermore, at this time, the early autumn of 1947, the Prime Minister was becoming unpopular because of the generally poor economic state of the country. When I returned from England with the Regent I was at once visited by Daud Pasha al Haidari, who urged me to go immediately to the Regent and explain to him the deplorable state of the country, owing to the poor harvest. 'The people have no bread—and you know how much they eat—they depend upon it.' The Government seemed quite unconcerned, and he added many details. I went to see the Regent as he asked and found that he too had already been hearing much the same story from his Palace servants and how the corn was being sent to Syria.

When, after some delay and seeming reluctance, the Prime Minister agreed to an order forbidding the export of the harvest to Syria or elsewhere, it was only to give, immediately afterwards, a special permit to one of his merchant cronies for the export of a very large quantity to Syria. When this became known the people were still further incensed.

Meanwhile there had been, for some time, high-level discussions about the revision of the 1930 Treaty with Great Britain, particularly in regard to its main military clauses. The Regent had first suggested that a high-ranking officer known to him should come out, on the excuse of shooting with him. In the autumn of 1946 he suggested that Field Marshal Lord Wilson might care to come. Thus talks could go on without it being obvious to the man in the street or to the opposition. The winter of 1946-7 went by and it was too late for such an arrangement, but in November 1947 Air Vice-Marshal Robert Foster, who knew and liked Iraq from his tours of duty there in the past as the Special Service Officer in Baghdad, arrived for further talks in continuation of the negotiations which had already made some progress in Baghdad and London. Great secrecy was to be maintained. The British Chargé d'Affairs in Baghdad took this instruction *au pied de la lettre*, not consulting the chief British Adviser to the Iraq Government, nor telling the head of the Military Mission of progress until later.

It was at a dinner party at Renton's house that the Regent

arrived in a most happy mood and, beaming, said to the Chargé d'Affaires: 'I have some bad news for you. Salih Jabr has resigned.' The Chargé was much upset and told Renton that he must speak to the Regent alone after dinner.

From time to time we eyed them in the corner. At last they rose. The Regent had most reluctantly given way and Salih Jabr remained in office.

Recent negotiations with Egypt having broken down, it was understandably considered most desirable by the British Foreign Secretary, Mr. Ernest Bevin, that the agreement with Iraq should be put through successfully and quickly. It would have an encouraging effect and be a feather in the cap of those concerned to have carried it out so expeditiously.

During the weeks following the opening of the Iraq Parliament on the 1st December 1947, all was ready, or so it must have seemed to the British Embassy, for signature of the new Treaty; not only its principles but most of the text had been agreed upon by Salih Jabr. The leaders of the political parties had not been consulted by him, though, at the Regent's insistence, a certain number of elder statesmen were called to a meeting at the Rihab Palace at which the Treaty was discussed in a general way. Asked at the meeting whether there was a draft Treaty, the Prime Minister had replied: 'No.'

The Regent, by now anxious about the general condition of the country, insisted that two elder statesmen out of office, Nuri al Said and Tawfiq al Suwaidi, should accompany the Prime Minister. The delegation, led by him, left Baghdad on 5th January for London, the full terms having been secretly agreed upon by the British and Iraq Foreign Offices. Mr. Bevin was spending a holiday near Portsmouth and since the Iraqi delegation were being taken there to see some defence establishments, it was agreed that the Treaty should be signed at Portsmouth on the 15th January.

The British Chargé d'Affaires also went to England, handing over to the Commercial Attaché charge in Baghdad.

The main articles covered the taking over of the R.A.F. bases at Habbaniya and Shaiba by Iraq, with a provision for limited British personnel to stay in them at British expense; the British Military Mission, as had been recommended by Renton, was to disappear; a mixed Anglo-Iraqi Council would undertake the development of strategic plans; and standardization of equipment between the British and Iraq armies was to be assured. Help would be given by the R.A.F. in the training of the Iraq R.A.F. abroad, and arms of the latest pattern would be made available to Iraq.

The Treaty as such was an excellent one and was welcomed in Britain and by the Regent, who hastened to exchange warm congratulatory cables with King George VI. The Iraqi delegation in England, highly satisfied, determined to spend a few days' holiday there. It was a proud moment for a Prime Minister who could look back on the day when he had been only an office orderly to a British political officer in southern Iraq.

Meanwhile, in Iraq, the Press very reasonably asked for the Arabic of the Treaty, having so far only received some of the heads of agreement in English. It seems incredibly casual, but none had been made. It existed only in English.

This neglect of established custom and of the interests of the Press was the turning point. The opposition, led by Hikmat Sulaiman, had not been consulted or informed. To anger gratuitously both the opposition and the Press—at a time which was, in any case, owing to nearly famine conditions, aggravated by exports to Syria, completely inappropriate—was to make certain of serious trouble. It came within a matter of hours.

From the 16th to the 21st January agitations and demonstrations by the people of Baghdad and students continued in spite of all efforts by the Police to stop them. Law and engineering students staged a strike; the National Democratic, Independent, Liberal and Communist parties held demonstrations impressive in their size and fervour. Strikes were called in offices and workshops and an attack was made on the premises of the *Iraq Times*. Marches and counter-marches with ugly clashes with the Police filled the streets of the capital. Demonstrations which earlier firmness might have controlled were soon beyond discipline and the mob, including the always volatile *charawiya* element of the al Karkh quarter on the west bank, joined in, its enthusiasm sharpened by hunger. The communiqués of the acting Prime Minister and his now frightened Ministers were disregarded.

Police action in opening fire to restore order was both unsuccessful and savagely resented. The number killed will never be known, but it was probably in the neighbourhood of a hundred, with four times that number hurt. Numerous bodies floated down the river, many others were buried without official registration by the authorities or in the hospitals. The morale of the Police, execrated as they were by the people, began to fall rapidly. The restoration of order could only be undertaken, if at all, by the Army, and the Ministers and the Regent found it imprudent to use the Army.

In London, Salih Jabr was still glowingly confident. On the 22nd January he made a statement in which he denounced his political opponents as 'destructive elements' who had 'exploited some innocent students and succeeded in creating disorders'. He added: 'On our return to Iraq we shall explain the intentions of the new Treaty to the Parliament and people. We are confident that it will be found that the national aspirations of the country are fully realized in this Treaty and that the overwhelming majority of the country will support it. It is with this belief that my colleagues and I signed the Treaty.'

The Counsellor of the British Embassy, the former Chargé d'Affaires, was in London with the parties who had signed the Treaty so very secretly prepared. The new Chargé d'Affaires in Baghdad to my astonishment came to call upon me, to ask my opinion on events. He had, I knew, been in Basra at the Consulate there when he had first heard news of the disturbances in Baghdad. I told him that if Salih Jabr returned there would, in my belief, be three times as many people killed as hitherto. He should certainly not return at present. The Chargé replied that in any case he would be coming and that if what I had told him were true 'it would be just too bad'. I assumed that he meant that it was a matter for the Iraq Government and not one in which he could interfere.

The difficulty in Iraq at this stage of our relations was that there was no clear line of demarcation between justifiable and unjustifiable 'interference' between when advice should be given and taken and when not. Our long experience of governing and the education of our representatives might surely have justified some tactful giving of advice over the steps leading to the signing of a new Treaty, and better selection of the moment and way of doing it; but this would have depended on obtaining and acting on good information.

The main reason for the failure and for the death, incidental to it, of several hundred Iraqis was the absence of proper negotiations with a representative government. As in the case of Egypt, attempts to put through a Treaty with an unrepresentative government had only led to failure. The two successful Treaties made with Middle Eastern governments in the preceding twenty-five years had been with fully representative ones —those of Egypt in 1936 and Iraq in 1930. In 1930, in Iraq, the negotiating government under Yassin Pasha included every prominent politician in the country; the Treaty with Egypt was with the Wafd, then by far the largest and most popular party in that country. An attempt to negotiate when a country was in a deplorable condition economically would have been dangerous in any case, giving dissatisfied leaders an easy opening for making capital out of it. When, as in the case of Iraq at this time, the situation in Palestine was also beginning to have alarming repercussions, the likelihood of a successful issue was nil from the beginning, and the last outside chance was gone from the moment when the Regent was made to seem to support the rightly unpopular Prime Minister, Salih Jabr.

In the event, within a week of signature, on the 21st January, the Regent, faced with almost complete disorder, was obliged to convene a Crown Council and after five hours' debate disclaim the Treaty.

He issued a statement to say that the Treaty 'was found not to realize the national aspiration of Iraq or consolidate the friendship between the two countries' and that he would not 'ratify any agreement which failed to secure for the country all its objectives'.

In spite of this sharp volte-face, wild demonstrations continued. Immense crowds gathered to follow the coffins of students killed in the rioting, subsequently storming through the streets. The Prime Minister, when he arrived—still convinced that he only had to return in order that good would be restored—was faced with even more serious riots than the earlier ones. The Press and people, unchecked by rifle-fire and some arrests of fire-brands, continued to rage against him. His house was full of police and even so he had to seek refuge in another, also guarded. By the 27th January the disorder was reaching a climax that even he was obliged to assume was not in his power to subdue. The crowds were fired upon, the deaths and injuries totalling several hundred, but they were not deterred from marching to the Palace, there to demand the death of the Prime Minister. Once more bodies floated down the river. One was caught up in the roots of a mulberry tree near my house, the Qasr al Melik Ali, and had to be freed for its onward course by the fisher-boys who served us. 'Mulberries,' they said, 'improve the eating, not bodies.'

At long last the Prime Minister resigned and fled for his life to his early home on the lower Euphrates. A hundred thousand people followed the funeral of the latest 'martyrs'. Mass meetings and marches continued. Banners demanded 'Death to all Enemies', 'Free Lands for All' and 'Destruction to all Foreigners'. Farouche parties from the provinces and from Kurdistan came to join in and add to the fears of the Ministers. Business and social life was quite at an end. Policemen were hardly seen. Looting and incendiarism began. Yet it was noticeable that no foreigners were hurt and foreign property was hardly touched. Two Englishmen in a car who met a demonstration were unharmed, though one of the car windows was broken—seemingly the only damage to British property following the riots after Salih Jabr's return.

The Regent sent for the elderly Shiah senator, Muhammad al Sadr, to form a Cabinet. Avoiding all party leaders, he chose elderly and well-known men like himself, a team strong in experience and personality. It was announced by them that the Treaty would not be ratified and Parliament was dissolved on the ground of being unrepresentative. New elections were ordered. Gradually the city became a little quieter.

On the British side, lack of continuity and of good information may be held mostly responsible for the failure of the Treaty. They, in turn, can be laid to the account of the machine of governing, and not against individuals. The wheels of administration turn come what may and in this case their rhythm was off beat with events. Owing to the illness of the British Ambassador, and his consequent absence for some ten months, the

burden of conducting the negotiations with the Iraqis and inter-
preting them to the Foreign Office had fallen on a Counsellor, as
Chargé d'Affairs, but this officer had had little or no previous
experience of the Arab world and did not have an intimate
acquaintanceship with the leading personalities in Baghdad. The
Oriental Counsellor had been sent as Colonial Secretary to
Barbados. He was replaced by a man who was an archaeologist
of distinction and a genuine Arab scholar with knowledge of
tribes. Unfortunately this officer had no friends or even acquaintances among either Government or opposition leaders in
Baghdad. The Assistant Oriental Secretary was sent to the
Foreign Office and was twice replaced in six months. The Head
of Chancery was recalled to London. The Third Secretary,
holding only a temporary appointment, also left the country. In
London the Foreign Office department conducting the negotiations went through almost similar changes. A senior official who
had visited Baghdad to make the acquaintance of the leading
personalities was sent as Ambassador to Rio de Janeiro. The
head of the Eastern Department was sent as Minister to Iceland.
The distinguished official who was in charge of the actual negotiations and who even came out to Baghdad to assist in conducting them in November was posted to the Berlin Control
Commission in December. Even the junior official in charge of
the Iraq Section was sent as Head of Chancery to Rangoon. The
Political Intelligence Service in Baghdad also underwent changes
and a senior police officer from Lahore was put in charge. All
these changes occurred during the ten months of the negotiations.
Moreover, the Englishmen left in the country who really did
know Iraq and the Iraqis and who knew well and of old the
leaders of both the Government and the opposition were not
taken into the confidence of the Embassy, probably owing to
well-meant orders intended to preserve secrecy.

It may be that it was during these days of rioting that the
more malevolent opposition and mob leaders first felt the nature
of their power and realized the weakness of the Iraqi throne and
of British authority. They had forced ajar a door that might
another time be opened farther; or so it may have seemed to
them.

The Regent, aghast at the failure of the proceedings of which he had anyway been mistrustful, sent me to London to explain to his friends, official and unofficial, in an informal way, as his personal representative, the reasons for the failure and for his enforced denial of the Treaty.

At last a new Ambassador, a bright and lively Irishman, Sir Henry Mack, arrived. By his initiative an Australian grain-ship was diverted to Basra and its urgently needed cargo distributed. It was nevertheless an uneasy and frequently changing Government with which he had to deal. The fever allowed to develop in the previous winter took a long time to die down and before it did so the war in Palestine gave the Regent and his Government other problems.

Some guerillas had already been recruited from Iraq to serve under Fawzi al Qawuqchi, a Nationalist soldier of fortune, a man who in somewhat different circumstances might have achieved greater fame.[1] Red-headed, strongly and well built, a soldier first and foremost, he could have been in the line of succession to the soldiers of fortune under the Ottomans, many of them Albanians, who carved out kingdoms for themselves. Though Arab Nationalism gave him opportunities, he was no fanatic. I had been friendly with him in the past and he gave me what were then rare and valuable photographs taken by himself, when he was with the Saudi Arab Army, of the interior of the Shrine of Mecca and of the Saudi Princes on horseback ritually stoning the Devil during the pilgrimage.

Fawzi's force was too weak and ill-provided to do much good. In the face of the resolute Jewish Forces, the Arab League was obliged to decide upon intervention by its regular armies. The Regent, whose leadership and vitality did much to restore his popularity, visited Amman and Cairo with the Ministers, and his Government, bowing to mounting pressure from the people, had no alternative but to sanction large-scale intervention. The Iraq Army crossed into Palestine on the 15th May, immediately after the State of Israel had been declared.

The Regent went to the front and, extraordinary as it seemed at first, the ladies of his household took the field with the canteens

---

[1] Field Marshal Sir William Slim: *Unofficial History*, p. 157, says that he led the most formidable of the gangs organized to resist the British in the Syrian desert in 1941 and he had been active in a similar way in 1937 in Palestine.

and Red Crescent units. The troops, the Regent told me, were greatly touched and the wounded were heartened by their presence and attention. So no doubt they were, but also dumbfounded, for Muslim women of high degree had never been unveiled in Iraq. To be seen in public, and on a battlefield, was something unknown since the beginnings of Islam and the days of paganism.[1]

I had repeatedly asked the Regent if I might accompany him in some capacity as, for example, liaison for the foreign Press, which I rightly foresaw would be needed. Equally rightly, for political reasons, he felt obliged to refuse me.

The organization of the Arab armies was sketchy and uninspired. General Salih Saib, who had been made co-ordinating Chief of Staff for the Arab armies, received no daily reports except from the Iraq Army. The Regent told me how he had found him sitting at an empty desk, complaining of complete lack of interest in co-ordination by the Egyptian and other forces.

The result is well known.

When the Army was about to return to Baghdad across the desert a coup d'état took place in Syria, by officers who at first seemed distraught at their own success. In view of accusations made later against Nuri, and the Regent too, that Iraq intended to occupy Syria, it should be said that, very easy as entry to Damascas would have been and clear as it was that the Army would have been welcomed on arrival there, both of them refused to consider marching to Baghdad 'via Damascus'. The arguments against such action having been demolished one by one, Nuri fell back on a military excuse: 'The Army has no maps.' The true reason was doubtless a general one arising from his political insight. If there was to be a change it was to be an entirely voluntary one.

Later, when there was another military coup in Syria in 1949, Nuri did try to make progress over unification of the two countries. An officer was sent ahead of him to take soundings, and perhaps because he was a military man rumours were set afloat that the Iraqi Army was concentrated on the borders.

[1] Though in certain tribes in Arabia its prettiest girl customarily taunted men advancing in affrays up to about 1930.

When Nuri arrived he was met only with hostility and soon afterwards Syria was turning towards Egypt.

The Regent had given me his father's house on the Tigris in which to live, and while there I wrote a book on his family, the Rulers of Mecca.

The life of the river-bank was largely unchanged from the past. In the summer people came to plant water-melons as the water went down and in a very short time they would have a splendid crop. Islands appeared and arbours would be put up in which, come July and August, young people would spend the summer nights for the sake of coolness. Bushes would grow in a few days on the islands, making parks, untended and free, where the Baghdadis amused themselves, the fishermen who rowed them over making a handsome living out of it.

Troupes of youths would come to wrestle there and compete for the decorated trousers that were the reward for prowess in exercises and wrestling. They were members of an ancient guild of Persian origins, called Zorkhaneh, where moral precepts and submissiveness were joined to athletic ambition.

There are strange survivals in Baghdad of earlier beliefs and ways. Almost every Thursday evening in summer little slats of wood with lighted candles on them would pass the house, floating on the current. It was not until one year when I was present at a festival which takes place annually on 19th March at a monastery near Mosul, in northern Iraq, that I began to understand their meaning. The monastery of Mar Behnam dates from at least the fourth century and is one of the oldest in the world. It stands beside the village of Khidr Elyas, fifteen miles from Mosul, in the rich cornfields between the Tigris River and its tributary, the Greater Zab, among grassy mounds covering Sassanian or earlier ruins.

The annual festival in the spring at Mar Behnam is known as the anniversary of St. Joseph, the place now following the Syrian Catholic rite, but the church contains several lively representations of St. George slaying the dragon. One of them, the biggest, is in stone, standing about seven feet from the stone floor. As I entered the church some girls, dressed in their brightest and newest festival clothes, were laughingly throwing up their head-kerchiefs at it, in order that they might catch on a nail in the

rump of St. George's horse. There they left them while they
wished—usually for a handsome husband or bouncing children.
Some young seminarists kneeling at the rail turned to look at
the girls and then smilingly glanced at each other before sinking
their heads once again in prayer.

A priest led me with agility, for all his seventy years, into
the depths to the tomb of Mar Behnam, lighting the way with a
small taper.

Besides the tomb, in a dark recess forming one side of the
octagon, were manacles and an iron circlet for the throat in
which are fastened men and boys who have some special wish
for penance or are to be cured of an illness—in particular of
madness; they remain in shackles for a whole night, here in the
darkness. In another corner facing the tomb and the manacles is
a very dark cell with a door some feet from the ground, with
holes where bars might be placed across it.

The shrine was frequented by Muslims and Yezidis as well
as Christians and the 19th March is the day of festival, being the
anniversary of the death of St. Joseph, though it was in fact the
death of winter, and of its representative the dragon, that they
were unwittingly celebrating.

Khidhr Elyas—Khidhr means 'green' in Arabic—is closely
connected with St. George, 'Green George' of England and of
the European countryside. He is to be found throughout
northern Europe, in the Middle East and even in India. Always
his festival, as the successor of Adonis, is in the spring.

In Iraq, Khidhr or Adonis is found in many places other than
Mar Behnam—at Baghdad itself, on the Euphrates, and at the
outlet of the two rivers at the head of the Persian Gulf.

In Kurdistan and in Persia the spring festival of Nauruz, or
New Year, coincides with that of Khidhr and they celebrate then,
some say, the defeat, by a lowly youth named 'Kawa', of an old
tyrant Prince, whose effigy they burn. Sometimes Khidhr is
associated with Alexander of Macedon and the search for eternal
life.

In brief, Khidhr was originally the symbol of a fertility cult
which came to be associated with the prophet Elyas (Elijah), even
with Alexander of Macedon, and finally with St. George.

In Baghdad, on Thursday evenings, when I saw once more

the little slats of wood with lighted candles on them floating down the River Tigris—propitiatory offerings set off from the Mosque of Khidhr at the northern end of the city—I understood that Adonis, under one alias or another, whether Christian or Muslim, whether as the guide to life eternal or as the tyrant winter, to be killed so that summer may come, still lived on in Iraq.

In 1948 the Regent told me that he was worried about the health of his sister, the Queen. She seemed unwell from time to time. Once or twice he had found her lying down in the middle of the day and when he came in she would sit up and say that it was nothing. 'I was just a little tired and now feel better for resting.' But gradually he came to understand that she was in fact suffering and had been too proud to confess it. He wanted her to be thoroughly examined and hoped that it was nothing serious.

When it was discovered a little later, in London, that she had an internal cancer he was desperately unhappy. It was now obvious that he had long derived from her more support than was known. Like the great Ibn Saud, he had discussed nearly every problem with his favourite sister, seeing her daily whenever he could do so, and her advice was always wise. Now he said: 'I cannot do without her. She is essential to my work and position. If she goes I will abdicate.' Operations gave no hope—he began to think of trying other methods. 'Is there not a new kind of cure used in America?' The American surgeons were consulted by cable, but the answer was always the same, and the Queen's condition slowly worsened.

When the end was near, in the autumn of 1950, she was moved from the London Clinic to Baghdad. The King, her son, left Harrow for a term to be with her. Local doctors and other persons preferred their own various ideas of treatment. The British and American doctors' advice and orders were taken for her, but there was naturally a feeling that it was worth trying anything.

The King and the Regent then turned, at the suggestion of Queen Nafisa, to the thought of praying at the Prophet's tomb at Medina in the Hijaz. They were flown there and back in one day.

But the Queen was beginning to sink rapidly and as Christmas approached it was clear that she could last only a few days. She died on the 22nd December 1950. When the end came the orphaned King showed more control than the Regent or other members of his family; a sign, probably, of his Western up-bringing. But the Regent did not abdicate as he had said he might do.

It was only a few months later, on 20th July 1951, that the head of the family, Abdulla of Jordan, was murdered while entering the Great Mosque in Old Jerusalem, by a young Arab member of the Holy War organization, who was at once killed by the bodyguard. Hussain, the sixteen-year-old grandson of the King, only escaped murder by instantly flattening himself against the doorpost of the mosque. The toll of political murders in the Arabic-speaking Middle East was mounting. Abdur Rahman Shahbandar, leader of the pro-Hashimite group in Syria, had been killed earlier, in July 1940. In Syria since the war there had been, among others, the killings of Husni Zaim, the President, and of Dr. Muhsin Barazi on 14th August 1949 and of General Sami Hannawi, shot down in vengeance by a cousin of Dr. Barazi, in Beirut on 30th October 1950.

In the Yemen the eighty-year-old King and three of his sons were assassinated on 17th February 1948 and later other Yemenis involved in their overthrow were killed in turn. The murder of the old King was held to be due to the Egyptian Young Men's Muslim Association. Fakhri al Nashashibi of Jordan was killed in the main street, while visiting Baghdad; and in Amman shortly afterwards, and four days before the murder of King Abdulla, the former Prime Minister of Lebanon, Riadh al Solh, was killed on his way to the airport, after visiting the King, by two young Lebanese and a Palestinian. In Egypt, Ahmad Maher Pasha, the Egyptian Premier, a friend of Britain and a strong opponent of totalitarianism, was shot at point-blank range inside the Parliament buildings by a twenty-six-year-old lawyer, a member of the Young Men's Muslim Association, on 24th February 1945. Nokrashy Pasha was killed on 28th December 1948 in the Ministry of the Interior, Cairo, shot at close range by a student, a member of the Muslim Brotherhood. Amin Osman Pasha, a

L

friend of Britain, who had studied in England and been called to
the English Bar, was murdered on 5th January 1946 by a twenty-
year-old student, who fired three bullets into him at point-blank
range when he was visiting his old school in Opera Square,
Cairo. Shaikh Hassan al Banna, head of the Young Men's Muslim
Association, was shot dead in Cairo on 13th February 1949 by an
assailant who escaped. He was believed to be taking vengeance
for the murder of Ahmad Maher Pasha. And there were other
murders, of less famous men.

Elderly statesmen, whom political expediency had obliged to
be in good relations with Britain, or with the Hashimites, were
the prime targets of the murder-planners, though in turn vengeance for their deaths was the cause of some of the killings.

The aim of the organizers, whose instruments were youths
whom they crazed with Nationalistic balderdash, was to make
treating with Britain or her friends tantamount to a sentence of
death. There were murders of much the same kind elsewhere in
the Muslim East, that of the Prime Minister of Persia, General
Ali Razmara, in October 1951.

The young King of Iraq, still at Harrow, and his uncle, the
Regent, knew that they were in constant danger while they were
in the East.

When Abdulillah returned to England in 1952 from his visit
to the United States with the King, his nephew, he gave me
accounts of what he had found most hospitable though arduous
in the programme arranged for them. He seemed to be relieved
to find someone to whom he could talk about all his experiences
in the United States.

The arrangements made for the Iraqi Royal party in America
had thoughtfully included a journey to see a stable and breeding-
ground for Arab horses.

He was both knowledgeable about and superlatively fond of
horses. One year, at the annual horse-show in Iraq, there was
a black stallion said to be unequalled within living memory. His
shining muscles, his broad chest, the lines of his legs, the curve
of neck and nostrils, the beauty of his head and barrel and the
hollow of his back were unsurpassed.

The judges held their breath and gave the owner, the Syrian

Minister, the prize for the best stallion. The Ruler did not conceal his admiration and envy. The Chamberlain hinted that gold was of no consequence beside such beauty.

The Syrian Minister told me what happened later. His son was ailing and his one joy was 'Emir al Husn'. Every other day, between his feverish dreams, he asked after the horse, and when he was a little better he used to go down to look at him each afternoon. His single love was his father's stallion: so the Minister disobeyed his diplomatic conscience and kept the animal. But the boy soon became better and bought a bicycle and went to school and made friends there and seldom asked about Emir al Husn. So when the Rulers of Trans-Jordan and Syria met at al Deraa, through the mediation of the Ruler of Iraq, the Minister made the occasion one on which to offer his horse to the Regent and it was accepted.

'Your Royal Highness likes horses very much?'

'To tell you the truth, if it were possible I would take them to my room and have them sleep by me,' the smiling Prince replied.

He had, like most of his family, an exceptionally good eye for a horse and in Iraq it was easy to indulge it. The number of horses in proportion to the inhabitants was the highest in the world. Arab horses had been exported from Iraq to India for centuries and were at one time in use for light cavalry in Europe. The Arabs in Iraq had always raced their horses, but not regularly until meetings were organized by order of a British Commander-in-Chief, concerned for his troops' amusement while they waited to go home at the end of the First World War. The race-courses in Baghdad and the racing industry had grown out of that beginning.

Three Englishmen had in turn been very largely responsible for keeping the organization going and the standards were well in line with those in Europe. Racing, hunting and horse-breeding had had a marked effect in binding together a large number of the people, whatever their class, creed or race, by a common interest; and it was noteworthy and almost certainly significant that the new Republican Government ordered all race-courses, in which the Regent had taken much interest, to be closed down immediately after the revolution in 1958.

The Prince was seldom able to spend as long as he would have liked outside Baghdad. He much preferred life in the countryside to being in towns, and he would seek opportunities to shoot. In the North there were many ibex, mouflon and mountain deer, in central Iraq black partridge, bustard and gazelle in large number and sandgrouse in myriads.

Inspections in Basra meant an occasion for hawking in the desert, towards the Saudi Arabian frontier, and wild-fowling in the Hammar Lake by the Euphrates.

Duck-shooting in southern Iraq is among the best in the world, and with the help of an expert guide and shot, Anguli of Basra, he was able to enjoy it to the full and preferred it to other shooting.

The last few miles of a journey into the marshes was made in the marshmen's lightest kind of canoes, poled for speed and paddled for traversing shallows or forcing a way through the giant reeds. The freeboard is only an inch or two when loaded and a fresh wind on open water can upset them. The hides, reached before dawn, were usually two feet deep in chilling water and mud, but there was a reward as the light came, in a view of hundreds of birds; geese getting up first, and, after them, going this way and that, mallard, teal, widgeon, pochard and shoveller, gadwell, pintail, golden-eye, tufted, gargany and shell-duck. In the mid-morning, following a breakfast in one of the tunnel-like reed huts of a Shaikh, there was snipe-shooting on the edge of the marsh, the haunt of cranes, waders, bittern and kingfisher. Above them, flying high, would pass long strings of flamingoes, their undersides pink in the sunlight. In the dusk there came once more squadron upon squadron of geese and duck.

The Prince would speak wistfully of days spent in the countryside. He was hardly ever away for more than a few days before there was a message for him from the city calling him back in order to resolve some new crisis.

'They don't like it when I shoot and always arrange some trouble as soon as I leave,' he would say.

It is not easy to convey the exact relationship between the Regent and Nuri al Said. Any couple and nearly all men working closely together over a long period, and through numerous crises, come to assess each other's defects so well that they are sometimes irritated by them, though they appreciate their good qualities and work together happily and long, bitterly missing the loss of the other if one of them goes. Both the Regent and Nuri in confidence complained about each other, but it would be wrong to stress what were no more than understandable and temporary outbursts.

The Regent arranged for Nuri al Said to travel with him on his journeys to Europe and the New World, and though Nuri al Said feared him he admired the Prince and all he was doing for the dynasty and country. He was, indeed, indefatigable in his attention to his duties, which, as in the days of Faisal the First, included seeing a large number of callers daily. Not only Iraqis and Orientals hoped to see him, but foreigners, including journalists, in ever-increasing numbers. There were, apart from State papers, large numbers of petitions to be read; sometimes they were thrown into his car, or a petitioner would run forward seeking to clasp his knee and kiss his foot while holding up a petition to him in the other hand. He never failed to give them attention. On occasions he would discover for himself some hardship to be rectified, particularly in cases requiring medical aid. Once he found a boy with a damaged eye and burn marks standing beside his car and, calling him up and enquiring, realized that much could be done for him by plastic surgery in Europe. He saw to it that the boy went to England. More than once he sent sufferers to London at his own expense.

Perhaps from a natural inclination for relief from his hard daily work he enjoyed practical jokes. Once he simulated death 'to see how people would take it', a macabre form of amusement. He lay on the floor with blood about him. His negro servants seemed more concerned and quicker about First Aid than some of his A.D.C.s. Another time, when members of the British Embassy were dining in a friend's house to meet him, he staged a bomb-burst during dinner and made a soldier, to be found prostrate outside the front door, cover his head with a nylon stocking, with a hideous and deceiving result. But these were rare jokes and only played in the later years, with the purpose of seeing reactions to his misfortune.

Among the Nubian servants in the Palace one, Hassan, who became the King's valet and accompanied him to England when he

went to live there, was the most liked by the King and members
of the Royal family. He was an exceptionally efficient servant
and always spotlessly clean, his white dress perfectly ironed, even
in the hottest weather. The King would relate how he had discovered Hassan's secret. 'I will ring for him and time him. He
is always just a little longer in arriving than he should be in
coming here from his room. It is because he takes everything off,
irons it and hangs it up and stays without his clothes, only
dressing when I ring for him or when he comes on duty.'
And there were other stories about admirable Hassan the
Nubian.

The King was exceptionally observant. It was one of the
characteristics first noticed about him on arriving at Harrow when
he was thirteen, in May 1949, after a year at Sandroyd Preparatory School. At Harrow he went into Moretons, where the house-
master was the late Mr. O. G. Bowlby. Queen Aliya had said
that she wished him to be treated just like other boys, to have no
special privileges and to take his turn at fagging with the rest.
When the time came for him to be a special fag to one of
the senior boys and they were asked, after about a fortnight,
which of the new boys was proving the best, they all said:
'Faisal.'
The housemaster's wife, the late Mrs. O. G. Bowlby, wrote
afterwards:

He got on well with everyone and was considerate and thought-
ful. But there was a much deeper side to his character which was
probably not guessed by his contemporaries. . . . He talked to me a
great deal about his mother's death, and from a very early age the
welfare of his people and country was his main interest. As time went
on, I know that his hopes centred on being able to raise the standard
of living among his people and provide benefit services and new industries to help his country. With a wisdom unexpected in one so
young, he realized that he would not have the authority to carry out
many of these plans until he was older and a more experienced man.
It is a great sadness to me to feel benefits may be carried out in the
future and claimed by others, which were in fact the very aims
King Faisal had so close to his heart for his people he loved so
well.

He specialized in history and did well, though not brilliantly, in other subjects, reaching the Upper Fifth form. The characteristics first mentioned by masters at Harrow remembering him are: 'kindly—appealing—modest—warm in feelings—quietly dignified'. At first he was given a room to himself, instead of sharing with another boy, but otherwise no difference in treatment was made.

He did not show the least resentment over fagging duties and, on the contrary, was seemingly proud of having fagged, for, preserved long afterwards, among other quite different, more important records at Stanwell House, was found a crumpled sheet of lined paper from a penny notebook on which he had written in his early days at Harrow:

Day boys duties 1949:

To attend the sixth formers after excess [i.e. exercise] in the toshes [i.e. baths].

To let the water out of the toshes.

To take down the sixth formers dressing gowns to toshes.

Run to all boys calls and do them running as quickly as poss. Not stop to talk on way.

Cutting boy calls punished severely.

The King's upbringing had included that of an English nanny, governess, tutor, preparatory school and public school.

He was given Arabic lessons by Iraqi tutors, both in Iraq and England, and naturally his family's influence was strong, but otherwise he was by training as nearly a British product as it is possible for a foreigner to be. He was warm in his feelings about the school and friends that he made there, kept up with them after he had left, and later sent his fiancée to see Harrow. He must have hoped that she would one day become the mother of a boy there. He wrote quite frequently to the headmaster, Dr. James, and occasionally sent pamphlets about development and progress in Iraq to him. He kept up a correspondence with boys there, masters, a matron and others. He showed an attachment to his school which is rare in the Arab world east of Beirut.

Hardly had the eighteenth-birthday and coming-of-age

ceremonies of King Faisal been announced for 2nd May 1953 than the same celebrations were announced for King Hussain for the same day. The turmoil in the diplomatic circle concerned can be imagined. In the end, distinguished visitors like the Duke of Gloucester went to Baghdad first and from there to Amman immediately afterwards.

The same difficulty did not arise for a number of visitors from England to whom an invitation from the Court in Baghdad had been sent. They were all persons who had served in Iraq and were well known to the Royal family and the Government, and with them went four young men who had been at Harrow with King Faisal; Mr. Harwood, the New Scotland Yard representative who had several times been attached to the Iraqi Royal visitors in England and who was much liked by them; and Sir Steven Gibson, Chairman of the Iraq Petroleum Company, which provided the aircraft, and members of his staff.

For the first night in Baghdad there was no official entertainment, and in the late evening I went with Harry Sinderson to see the King and the Emir Abdulillah at the Qasr al Melik Ali. They were spending the evening alone with their A.D.C.s and a few friends in the new, one-storey pavilion on the riverside, which had replaced the rambling palace where King Ali, and then I, had lived. We sat in the garden or leant over the wall immediately above the water to catch a little coolness. It was already the Iraq summer and very hot.

When we suggested leaving we were invited to stay on for supper. Darkness was falling and the lights of Baghdad across the river were coming on. And more than ordinary lighting. Every house, all the hotels and offices were brighter than usual with many-coloured lamps for the celebrations. Everyone was, it seemed, happy and in gay mood. The monotonous sound of Arabic music and singing drifted across the water.

The King and the Regent—who was also the Crown Prince of Iraq, and whose role for fourteen years as Regent would in a few hours be over—were full of smiles and good humour. A long dining table was carried out and the only light when we sat down to it was that which fell on it from the house. The food was in the Oriental taste—mounds of rice covering meats and minced-meat balls, rice wrapped in vine leaves, and afterwards a variety of sugary sweets and puddings. As I was talking to my neighbour on the left hand, who sat between Faisal and myself, a servant filled the large wineglass from a silver-beaked glass jug. The King joined our talk and I raised my glass to him, making a little gesture as if drinking to his health and long life. Sipping before putting it down, I found the taste of the dark liquid strange. I tried it again, furtively. Could it possibly be poisoned? Absurd thought on such a night! I sipped once more. It was Pepsi Cola, His Majesty the King's favourite tipple.

The Duke of Gloucester, representing the Queen of England, arrived next day. Attached to his suite for the occasion was Major-General Renton, who had been head of the Military Mission. Among the representatives of other States was Ibn Saud's son, the Crown Prince of Saudi Arabia.

The end of the Regency and the moment of the King's taking over was marked by the King taking the oath in Parliament, a ceremony broadcast to the people, and by a salute of a hundred and one guns. He and the Regent, both wearing white uniforms and plumed cocked hats, mounted a semi-State landau, bought from Hooper's in St. James's Street, London, with a mounted escort of the bodyguard all looking very fine in red uniforms with white helmets glistening in the morning sun. Ubaid bin Abdullah, commanding the Royal bodyguard, rode proudly at their head. 'Long live our orphan King,' shouted the cheering crowds in the streets. At the moment of departure from Parliament the King and the Prince noticed that old Sayid Muhammad al Sadr, Head of the Senate, and Fadhil al Jamali, Minister of Foreign Affairs,[1] were without their cars and commanded them to ride with them away from the Parliament House.

There were parades of the Army at which Nuri was seen to arrive very early, give directions and take upon himself the role of executive officer rather than that of a mere spectator, standing at the corner of the dais the whole time instead of sitting with the political grandees. There was a procession for the Ministries, each

---

[1] Fadhil al Jamali was well known at the headquarters of the United Nations Organization, having been long representative of Iraq. His work and speeches show his unquestionably patriotic nature.

He and his Canadian-born wife were leaders of the intelligentsia in Iraq. He has been imprisoned in Baghdad since the revolution in 1958, and has been exercising his memory by learning the Koran by heart.

of which had prepared floats denoting their activities. Some were
striking or amusing and all were painstakingly done. A workshop
with a number of boys at work surmounted the float of the
Ministry of Works and Communications; it received particularly
loud cheers as connoting technical progress, something most
modern. The display by the Department of Archaeology received
less cheering, but was memorable—a chariot drawn by Arab
horses of the bodyguard and ridden by men of the bodyguard,
replica of a scene from a frieze representing an Assyrian King and
his spear-bearers, with escorting mounted men of the period. A
Ministry of Education spectacle by students took the form of a
long dragon which constantly raised and lowered its great head
with moving jaws and was most realistic. There were other
scenes, less carefully planned but warmly applauded, all those
with girls, to denote the emancipation of women, being loudly
welcomed.

At night the music from bands, radio loudspeakers, cinemas
and night-clubs filled the city and in the poorer quarters there
was drumming and dancing until near dawn.

The people of Baghdad were in a seventh heaven of happiness
and happiest of all was the Crown Prince, his Regency successfully brought to an end, the barque of State, after long and oft-
times stormy passage, safely in harbour. He was still comparatively young, just over forty, and could look forward to many
happy years ahead.

Every now and then between the ceremonies the King would
break away to see the Harrow boys, and swim and target-shoot
with them or engage in games of the kind they had enjoyed
together in England before he came of age.

Another friend of the King, at Harrow with him, was Barakat,
son of the Prince of Berar, eldest son of the Nizam of Hyderabad,
with whom he practised such things as water-skiing. Once, it
was related, the young King made a bet with him for a bottle of
Cola that he could not drive a thousand miles in twenty-four
hours. Barakat won his bet. The King himself did not share his
liking for excessively fast driving. Other friends were young
Iraqis, such as the sons of Jamil Madfai and Ali Jaudat, and a
member of the Chorbachi family of Baghdad, and his cousin
Raad, of the same age as himself.

His early promise was being borne out. In ordinary and private life he did many things well: was an especially good shot, liked underwater swimming, played chess well, collected the latest modern-music records and had taken up painting successfully. He selected pictures with discrimination and was beginning to have a small, worthwhile number of them.[1] Unlike his father, he had regular habits, usually going to bed at eleven o'clock and reading for two hours, very often books on science. He was interested in photography and colour-filming and had a private cinema. One of his favourite, full-sized films was *The Living Desert* by Disney. He was, in short, an exceptionally able young man, and, above all, at twenty-three, he was shaping well as a Constitutional Monarch and a worthy King with the welfare of his people at heart.

It fell out very well that the accession ceremony for King Faisal the Second was in the same year as the Coronation in England. Within a month the Crown Prince was in London to attend the Coronation of Queen Elizabeth and the reason for his journey when thought of in Iraq somehow seemed to bring the two countries nearer together.

In July 1956 Faisal paid his State visit to Queen Elizabeth. The account by *The Times* reporter of his arrival at Dover and in London was unusually warm in tone.

The weather was wonderful, a bright and sunny day, and everything went off very well and there was a large welcoming crowd to see him. He was accompanied by the Crown Prince, and his suite included Nuri al Said.

The leading article in *The Times* said with satisfaction that Iraq alone of the Arab States was now wholeheartedly with Britain and the Western Powers. 'Baghdad alone of Arab capitals has no diplomatic relations with the Soviet Union . . . and in almost all the Arab countries Communist business, technical and political missions are beginning to operate on a large scale. Iraq alone refuses them admission.' Speaking of reform, of progress and the people's welfare, the article ended: 'Quick results cannot be expected. The problem is vast, but given energy, tact,

---

[1] See Appendix IV for note on some other properties in the Palaces of Baghdad. One of the King's paintings, a portrait of a Shaikh of the Shammar, was exhibited at the Trafford Gallery in London for charity.

enthusiasm and the continued determination to suppress Communism inside Iraq, there is no reason why success should not be achieved.'

At the banquet at Buckingham Palace the Queen said that Iraq had become a model of a modern State and that just over a year earlier it had received new strength 'when we joined together with other friendly nations in the wider alliance of the Baghdad Pact'.

The King visited the City for luncheon with the Lord Mayor at Guildhall.

While waiting for him to do so, being early and inside Buckingham Palace, Nuri al Said drew aside one of the British officers attached to the King's suite and sitting on a sofa alone with him spoke at length of his aims. 'I am getting old as you see, and my life has been a hard one, for seventy years now; moreover I am getting more deaf. I am tired and often think that I would like to retire. Now would be a good moment, at the end of this boy's State visit, but I just cannot do so.' Nuri sighed, then laying his hand on his companion's arm went on: 'You see, the plan for developing the country is a good one and I am the architect in charge and must see it through if I can. By the time the oil dries up we will have our agriculture booming and our new industries in full production; and when we have that kind of prosperity we shall have internal security. In the meantime I am not popular with many of the Iraqis; Nasser is making every difficulty for us that he can. Anything might happen, but it isn't easy to get people over here to realize how hard it is for us to maintain our position. If only we can get through the next five or six years successfully all will be well. I shall have proved that I am right in what we are doing. By then we shall see the results of what we have done for the people and there will be great prosperity. I guarantee that Iraq will be the strongest and most prosperous country in the Middle East. If only we can get through the next few years. . . .' The King and Crown Prince arrived and Nuri ended his talk in order to go with them in state to Guildhall.

There was an evening reception given by the Government at Lancaster House, and the King visited Odiham Air Force Station and Harrow School; he gave a dinner at the Iraqi Embassy for

Queen Elizabeth and attended a dinner of the Anglo-Iraqi Society on one of the days following the official visit.

His visit set a seal upon the long minority of the State and of the King himself. There had been observers in 1933 who held that the State of Iraq was unfit for its independence, and later they could have found facts to bolster their argument in the massacre of the Assyrians and in four coups d'état by the Army, but at last, by 1956, though there were disquieting signs, as Nuri said, the State seemed nearly mature.

6

Murder on a Summer Morning

Parliaments and other trappings of Western democracy were seen to have failed to produce democracy in the East. Arabs came increasingly to feel that they had only facilitated corruption and led to weakness. The 'secret of the West' had not been discovered.

Backdrop to Tragedy

POLK STAMLER and ASFOUR

Beacon Press, Boston, U.S.A. 1957

It is too often forgotten that democracy is not an article of export, and there is no automatic guarantee that, just because the outward symbols of democracy are created in an alien soil, democracy itself will suddenly prevail.

Anglo-Turkish Relations and the Emergence of Arab Nationalism

ZEINE N. ZEINE

Khayats, Beirut, Lebanon, 1958

WHEN the King's coming of age and the end of the Regency was near, the Regent would talk of the future. He would spend only one year with the King, to help him, and then, he said, it would be best to leave him to feel his own way forward. He himself might farm in England and keep some horses, perhaps go in for racing. But he was also Crown Prince, and the King, when the time came and as the general situation worsened, kept putting off the day when he would be alone.

Once, when the Regent was leaving London after some medical treatment, for tonsillitis, and his doctor, Raymond Dixon Firth, tried to persuade him to delay a little longer, he added, after giving as his reason for a speedy return some political trouble: 'Ah, well—I suppose they'll get me in the end.' What was thought to be over-confidence in his later days, by some observers, was no more than a courageous acceptance of fate.

Later, when I asked him about leaving, he said: 'I must stay— the King needs me still.' Had he left he would have been criticized for leaving him in the lurch and failing in his duties as Crown Prince. He would have to stay until the King married, at least. On the other hand, it was largely his staying on at the King's side which accounted for his unpopularity. Everyone who hoped to curry favour with the young King, and they were many, felt their lack of success must be owed to the Regent who did not take much trouble with those who did not appeal to him. Like monarchs and men in great positions in every country, he was apt to have favourites for a time, so that others, not selected for the Royal interest, were jealous, and the favourites, if supplanted, were furious.

Participation in local enterprises and his encouragement of light industry merely led to more trouble for him. It was assumed by the critics that his own financial advantage was the prime reason in every case for his interest.

A scurrilous book called *Furs al Arba*, published in Beirut by the brother of Salah-ad-Din Sabbagh, who had been hanged publicly for his part in the 1941 revolt, and which purported to be Salah-ad-Din's own composition, had a *succès de scandale* and added fuel to a fire already glowing. King Ghazi, its hero, was said in it to have been murdered by Abdulillah and Nuri, and the vitriolic Cairo radio used the book as a source. The King's youth made him a poor target and Nuri and Abdulillah were given the weight of the attacks upon the regime.

And there was an opportunity for a linking of cannon-balls. The British, who had always been under fire by the Iraqi Press, could be associated with the name of the Crown Prince and of the old statesman, both of whom were known to like their Allies and to visit Great Britain frequently. Since, over the years, it had become established in Egyptian and in Iraqi publicity that the 'Imperialists' were the cause of every imperfection imaginable, it was only requisite to join their two names to that of Great Britain to lower their repute. Nuri, 'lackey of the West'. Abdulillah, 'hound of the Imperialists'. Gradually Iraqi youth came to accept the idea that they were both 'tyrants'.

On the other hand, the long-sustained virulence of the attack upon the British in both Press and Parliament was apt to be in one way misleading. *Au fond* the British were not much hated. They were attacked largely because they were an important, though nevertheless safe, target. A politician, known to like and associate much with the English, would astonish his British friends by a violently worded speech against them. He would explain it away as necessary to his career. 'No one believes it; everyone understands.' To attack the Iraqi Government in power needed circumspection. The only irritating thing to Iraqi Pressmen, after a time, was the very safety of the British target. The British never hit back, which seemed to show how low they rated the marksmen. Those who knew the British did not believe in the contents of these diatribes and those who did not know them did not, it was thought, count.

The attacks had at one time even had a certain degree of 'boomerang' effect. If the 'Imperialists' were so constantly 'up to no good', had one not better keep in touch with them, in a discreet way? The failure of the Treaty of Portsmouth, however, began to make people wonder, and the seizure of Abadan by the Persians without any immediate reaction by Great Britain made them wonder more. It was in British interest to protect and preserve oil installations in Persia—partly the property of the British Government itself—as everyone knew. If they did not do so it must be because they could not do so. So the atmosphere changed. Who in the pragmatic Arab East wishes to be associated with or dependent upon a failing Power?

And when the Suez Canal was seized without immediate action the position was startlingly clear to all.

The young King of Iraq had been dining with the British Premier at the very moment when the message telling of the Egyptian seizure of the Canal was handed to him. Sir Anthony

Eden did not conceal from his guests what would be known to all the world in a few hours.

From then onwards Nuri al Said desperately and constantly pressed for action against Egypt. The Crown Prince told me that he did not know if he would be seeing Sir Anthony again before he left England, but he wished it made known in Government circles that it was his strong view that, if immediate military action had been impossible because the British Army had not been ready, then as soon as it were ready some pretext must be found for action. He realized that once public indignation in England and France had died down strong action would present greater difficulty; but surely an incident could be arranged?— perhaps something to do with a ship going through the Canal? I answered that in a few months the Egyptians might once more overstep the mark and thus lead to unavoidable intervention. 'It is not, for us, a matter of months, but of weeks,' he said sharply. He rated high the deplorable results that would follow in Iraq and elsewhere following Nasser's triumph. In the event he was indeed right, though the climax was longer in coming than he thought.

He repeated that if Nasser did not fall within a very short time, less than 'a few weeks', it would be too late. By then the Middle East would be in irremediable disorder and the Baghdad Pact dissolving. The Russians would have reinforced Egypt considerably, with pilots and technicians and otherwise.

He added that it was his view—and not simply because he himself was a member of a Royal family, but as his considered opinion after long thought and in application of the principle that monarchy, with its continuity, is best for the East—that a kingdom should be restored in Egypt. King Farouq, however, should not be allowed to return, nor his direct heir. 'Prince Abdul Munin is the best man,' he said, 'and Ali Maher might be Prime Minister. The mob in Cairo is ultra-volatile and would cheer anything new. The bourgeoisie and much of the Army is against Nasser.' He repeated that every kind of subversive element in Egypt and in the Arab East would be let loose if Nasser did not fall within a very short time.

Night after night the Egyptian Government radio stations attacked the Iraqi Government. The Egyptians did more; they concocted plans with Iraqi malcontents and with Russian agents.

M

For once Nuri al Said was driven by the situation into going on the air from Baghdad in a long and convincing talk to the people.

By 1957 there was evidence of the unholy alliance between Iraq's enemies, part of the 'campaign waged by Cairo, Damascus and Moscow against the present Iraq Government', as *The Times* said in a commentary on Cairo Press articles, published on the 4th January. It expressed the hope that the campaign would not have the effect of discrediting the Iraq Government in England or America and added that Iraq was progressive and prosperous under Nuri's premiership.

The Prince's visits abroad, to London and later to America, and once to Japan and Formosa, or to Pakistan, were frequent, sometimes twice a year. He was criticized for these journeys. It showed how much, said the critics, he was in the hands of the West and of foreigners. They quite forgot that this was the opposite of his intentions. It was his wish to know politicians and persons who might be useful to Iraq and make them understand Iraq's problems and requirements and the point of view of the Middle East. His knowledge of English, his qualities and character made him well adapted to do so.

It was his very ability in this matter that made Egypt envious of his success, so that the Press did its best to decry his visits, likening them to those of 'a playboy, wasting money'. He was ahead of his time among Middle Easterners, in using aircraft in a way that is ordinary and habitual among politicians and business men in the United States of America and in Western Europe.

The Egyptians knew that before long Iraq might surpass Egypt, in wealth and in leadership of the Arab Middle East. Iraq had a large income from oil (nearing a hundred million pounds a year) and more oil was being discovered. It had two great rivers, as opposed to one only in Egypt, with far more fertile land; and irrigation schemes on the grand scale were under way. It had mountains and more rain and a healthier population; and its medical service and training establishments, with Western assistance, were much ahead of Egypt's. The population, unlike that of Egypt, was beginning to rise quickly and could within two decades be rivalling hers in numbers.

The process, begun by Faisal the First, of welding into one a country of diverse elements, had gone far. The Arabic language was known everywhere except in a few remote Kurdish villages. There was no longer any true Kurdish separatist movement and Kurds, like Scotsmen in England, occupied so many important positions in the country that they seemed to have rather more standing than their numbers warranted.

The Jews had nearly all left the country after the Israel War and the Christians had become well assimilated into its life. Among the small communities, the Lurs, who used to come from their home over the Persian frontier to earn a bride by working as porters, had been supplanted by machines. The Sabaeans, the Yezidis and other small minorities had all ceased to be obvious as such, and yet felt that no harm had been done to them as communities. Except for a small maintenance party at Habbaniya air base, there were no British troops in the country.

So the task which Faisal the First had begun was nearing completion. Independence had been preserved and the nation was becoming one; and the good qualities which the Iraqis possessed before his day had not been altered. They were as hospitable as ever, poor and rich alike, according to their means. They were as warm-hearted as in the past and full of that indefinable quality, charm. How often had Western travellers come to Baghdad to stay a week, looked at the streets of the capital and the flat land, experienced its heat and duststorms, and decided to move on as early as possible? And were, nevertheless, still in Baghdad ten days later, longer than they had meant to stay, bewitched by the qualities of the Iraqis.

These characteristics remained, though the way of life of youth was different. Roughly tabulated, in order to give an idea of the extent of the change, which only research and statistics could properly convey, it goes as follows:

	1921	1958
Religion:	Strict Muslim.	Little-practising, except for Ramadhan fast.
Transport:	Paddle-steamer, camel or horse, horse cab, rowing boat or on foot.	Public bus, internal ariway, taxi, private car, bicycle. Railway.

1921	1958

Contact with outside world and remainder of Iraq:

Word of mouth from travellers. One Government-sponsored newspaper.

Fifty Arabic daily newspapers of own and neighbouring countries, numerous broadcasts by radio, television, American and European papers.

Some aspects of leisure and pleasure:

Women's habits strict. Female entertainers very few, mostly Jewesses or Christians, singing and dancing Oriental style. Boy female impersonators in Arab theatres. Players rewarded by money thrown on stage.

Women largely emancipated. Cinemas showing 'Westerns', crime and sexy films. Half Westernized cabarets with European and Egyptian artistes and only female dancers. Alcohol of various kinds. Radios and gramophones. Some Western dancing.

Food:

Staple diet—rice, unleavened bread, dates, milk, araq (date or grape), kababs; eaten at home or in cook-shops.

The same, or irregular meals in café, bar or restaurant. Alcohol.

Means of eating:

Fingers.

Knife, fork and spoon.

Clothes:

Cheap, loose and long, cotton shirt with Arab head-dress, or national cap and suit locally made.

Close-fitting 'European' clothes, comparatively expensive; bareheaded.

Education:

Very little, often no more than Koranic school. Only own language.

Secondary and Technical or Law School. Prejudiced 'history' books. A foreign language, usually English.

Number of wives:

Up to four, living unemancipated lives.

One, emancipated, or none.

Another important change was the obviousness of the difference between the rich or successful and the poor and relatively unsuccessful. Journeys by air, possession of large

American motor-cars, shops full of such articles as highly expensive refrigerators, television sets and washing machines, hotels with expensive meals and drinks—even if many of these amenities of life were often bought on expense accounts—all served to emphasize a difference that had been unremarkable in, say, 1920, between the landlords, officials or traders on the one hand and the labourer, junior official or officer and clerks on the other.

The city itself was enormously altered. Its population had trebled and it was rapidly becoming like any other small capital; with gaunt, functional buildings rising in all directions on a maze of new, wide roads and avenues with roundabouts on which lengthy American cars nosed their way along in traffic blocks. There were new, glass-fronted stores and large cinemas in the main centres, where at night there was a blaze of music from loudspeakers in cafés and bars, where rows of backs turned away from the road showed that television held men's eyes and sound radio their ears. The old slums were mostly gone, replaced by model houses, though new slums were fast created by the influx of countrymen seeking work with contractors for the many great schemes under way. Outside a core of the middle class, of old families, army officers and government officials living in the suburbs, perhaps the dominant note of life in new Baghdad was that of haste made slowly and that was in the streets rather than indoors, except in the siesta hours. Everyone seemed to be out of their offices or place of residence more than they were in them. No Arabic word translating perfectly the English word 'home' was in use.

In its unease, Iraqi youth looked for a tyrant—a scapegoat to blame—and jealous Egypt constantly told it that the tyranny was in the regime itself.

During one of the many periods of political turmoil in Baghdad, near the end of the regime, the Chamberlain, Tahsin al Qadri, when asked about the situation, added to his comments with a sigh: 'If only the people of this country could go to sleep for ten years and then wake up.' He meant that the opposition politicians and the young critics would never leave the Government of the day alone long enough for quick and uninterrupted progress.

The Government was for ever under fire. A raw boy journalist, of whom there were many, would criticize in violent language and in ignorance of the facts, which he did not seek out, the undertakings of the Government and of, say, the Development Board.

At the end of the war the Regent had said that some way must be found of avoiding the lack of continuity owed to constantly changing governments. As a result, Nuri al Said had begun to think about means of co-ordinating Iraq's public-investment programme under an autonomous or semi-autonomous Board as early as 1947, when he first made contact with the International Bank for Reconstruction and Development. A draft law for such a body was prepared in Baghdad before the arrival of the first mission from the Bank in 1949. The final law was passed and the Development Board had had its beginnings, as such, in May 1950, under the premiership of Nuri. He, as Prime Minister, was its Chairman, and a British Secretary-General, an ex-Sudan official with fiscal experience, was appointed. The Board received seventy per cent of oil revenue, the Minister of Finance being an ex-officio member. The International Bank's General Survey Mission that visited Iraq in 1951 made suggestions for improving facilities and the personnel of the Board, and the substance of the development programme; but the conception and the autonomous character of the Board, the use of foreign experts and the attraction to it of seventy per cent of the oil revenues were the results of Nuri's authority and influence and the Regent's initiative.

In 1953 the post of Secretary-General was abolished and a Ministry of Development created. 'Given time,' as Lord Birdwood says in his book *Nuri al-Said*, 'it would have transformed the face of Iraq.' It was far ahead of any comparable plan elsewhere in the East, and much had already been done when, after eight years, its great schemes were curtailed and its income reduced by the revolution, the revenue hitherto allotted it being diverted to other purposes.

In March 1957 a great Development Week was held in Baghdad, opened by the King. Housing was the keynote of the second day. Iraq had begun her plan of building twenty-five thousand houses by 1960 and four hundred thousand in the next twenty-five years. The Crown Prince opened a new power plant, one of a series of projects costing twenty-five million pounds, but the most spectacular feature was the King and the Crown Prince driving through the centre of Baghdad on the first day to open a road bridge at the South Gate. The fifteen-hundred-foot-long bridge had cost over a million and a half pounds. More than a quarter of a million people saw the King perform the ceremony and there were scenes of tremendous enthusiasm. He later opened a second bridge over the Tigris in the northern suburb, the fifth bridge in Baghdad. In days of so much pleasurable excitement there were few who cared to recall the story that Baghdad falls when it has five bridges.

The King himself was enthusiastic too. On the 8th April he wrote to Mr. Malan, who had taught him English at Harrow:

. . . We have been having a very busy time recently, the second Development Week, first of all in Baghdad, opening of two bridges, inaugurating a new housing scheme of a total of nearly six thousand houses for Baghdad alone and laying the foundation stone for the new National Museum. Then we went up to the North to Mosul where we layed the foundation stone for a new sugar factory and opened a textile factory. The next day we went to Sulaimaniya where we opened a new cement factory and layed the foundation stone of the most useful Dukan dam which is on the Lower Zab river, a tributary of the Tigris.

I am enclosing two pamphlets recently published by the Government, one of them gives all the information on the schemes and what is to be done in the future as well as a general outline of the country. The other, I thought Mrs. Malan would be especially interested in, it is a creative and cultural history of Iraq, prepared by the Directorate of Antiquities. . . .

And to Dr. Raymond Dixon Firth on the 15th May he wrote, after apologizing for delay in a reply to a letter about a suggested wedding present for him: 'We have for some time now been busy—what with Development Week and various other important things . . . the arrangements for the Federation are almost finished now—thanks to the continuous work of those concerned.'

The projects opened or inaugurated during the week were

part of the five-hundred-million-pound plan running to 1960—
to include restoration of the irrigation of large areas of fertile soil
which had fallen into disuse since the Mongol invasion seven
hundred years earlier.

In April Nuri opened the nuclear training and research centre
in Baghdad under an expert sent out from Harwell. Apart from
the irrigation works and housing schemes, technical help was
being given by Britain and the United States of America. A large
number of foreign technicians was employed, and with the
employees of the foreign contractors and the oil companies
the total number of Europeans in the country ran into many
thousands and was rising all the time.

But general economic and technical aid had not been supported by the important political gesture of adherence and full
membership of the Baghdad Pact by the United States Government. Moreover, some of her Irish-American representatives, of
whom there seemed to be a high proportion in the East, had
from time to time overstepped the bounds of wisdom in advo-
cating change and decrying Iraq's ally, Britain, oblivious of the
ultimate danger to their own cause.

Nuri, at seventy, showed comparatively small visible signs
of old age, though he made a point of visiting doctors in London
whenever he was there. His slight deafness had increased, yet it
was noticed that when he really wanted to hear he was less deaf
than at other times. His mind was still full of high dreams. He
had brought off the Arab Union between Jordan and Iraq and
he was Prime Minister of the Union. Faisal the First had hoped
that Syria and Iraq would join hands. Maybe the Union could
one day include it.

Nuri regarded paternally the young King who was shaping
so well, though there were moments when he wished that he
could have taken more interest in the Army. His mind must often
have reached back to the days of the boy's grandfather, Faisal,
whom he resembled more than his father, Ghazi, and to memories
of his great-grandfather, the old Emir Hussain of Mecca. Sometimes he thought of his own early days in Ottoman Turkey, of
the Ahad Secret Society, of the Arab Revolt, of Allenby and
Lawrence, of riding into Damascus at the head of Arab troops
on 1st October 1918, and of the great men he had met at the

Versailles Conference after the First World War. He had sat on a sofa with Lord Grey and listened to Lord Curzon, had shaken hands with Lloyd George and President Wilson. He had seen governments and powerful men come and go, and he himself had fled Iraq and returned three times. With Mustafa Nahas of Egypt he had played the leading part in forming the Arab League in 1940, and had survived all the many plots against him. Since the war world power had shifted, and there were great new forces which few in Baghdad fully comprehended except himself. From the new currents came eddies as dangerous to Iraq as those in a mill-race.

The King, at twenty-three years old, as everyone who knew him agreed, had changed and developed wonderfully well in the last two years. His questions, his reasoning, his decisions or advice in reply to questions were the subject of delighted comments. All those about him foresaw a brilliant future for Faisal. Nuri was too much taken up with high policy and local politics to tender advice, which anyway he regarded as the prerogative of the Crown Prince as long as he was in Baghdad. The Chamberlain, Tahsin al Qadri, like Nuri, was becoming understandably inclined to relax after almost continuous service in the Palace since his arrival with the King's grandfather in 1921, and was regarded as half retired. Apart from the Crown Prince, there was no imaginative and experienced man with the King to ponder and suggest regal ventures or persist in proposing visits to the Army and unheralded descents into the market-places, the sports grounds, technical establishments or to the Royal box in Parliament. Such ideas were, if thought of by some courtier, rejected as too risky to propose. If something went wrong . . . In another year or two the King would surely have taken such matters into his own hands and gainsaid trepidation. The Crown Prince, observers near him noticed, was less his old self in the last year or two. He carried a more harassed air than hitherto, being aware of plots against the throne, and, probably as a result, seemed to be growing cynical, less generous and responsive in his treatment of those around him, and less tolerant of well-disposed but simple country visitors and of the wiles of politicians.

One can choose a ship, the pilot and the sailors for a journey, and even let the superstitious women select the day of sailing, but if an overwhelming storm is coming, what then? A kind of hardening fatalism was taking him in its grip.

In May a plot by Egyptian military officers to overthrow simultaneously the thrones of Iraq and Jordan was discovered. The Egyptian Committee of Officers charged with organizing it had as their first and most important duty the strengthening of the relations of the Ba'ath Party with the Communist Party. It had the blessing of the Soviet Union.[1]

But the Egyptians, even if they had setbacks and were given away, persisted in their plans.

There were two plots in Iraq to destroy the King, Nuri and the Regent, both of which miscarried. The first, which was to take place at H.3 Oil Pumping Station, was cancelled because Nuri al Said did not, as expected, go there with the Royal party. The second was ineffective in its prime object. Only a gardener was killed—by an exploding time-bomb placed in the bonnet of a parked car at the Palace door. The Royal party and Nuri al Said had not come out of the Palace at the moment announced and expected. After this no cars were allowed to park inside the Palace gates and any strange car was suspect. The Crown Prince greatly alarmed his mother, who happened to look out of a window and see a new Bentley, as yet without its Palace number-plate, which he had just parked in front of his doors.

In spite of his anxiety over the political situation in the Middle East, and the deteriorating state of morale in Iraq due to the Egyptian attacks through Press and broadcasting propaganda and intrigue, the Crown Prince retained his old good humour. When he came back to London on his way back from the United States, in February 1958, he played on me, as he thought, one of his tricks.

Hardly had he arrived than he met a mutual friend who told me that he was visiting me that evening.

I had anyway intended to ask him, should he arrive in time, but he made our mutual friend promise not to tell me and said he would come uninvited, to give me a surprise. So surprise it had to be, and I acted the part of astonished pleasure when he came in.

On his arrival in England in January, on his way to America,

[1] *The Times*, 13th May 1957: Report from Amman, 12th May.

he had lunched with the British Prime Minister before he set out by B.O.A.C. Stratocruiser. The nose-wheel of the 'plane jammed and it circled for one and a half hours. 'It was a bit of a bore and I think most of the passengers saw enough of Staines Reservoir to last them a lifetime. Each time we went round the circle we had quite a good view of Windsor Castle, which did rather compensate for other things,' said the Prince. But that was not the end of the trouble. It was only at the third attempt that they got away to a clear start. It was a little ominous, it might be thought by the superstitious.

But, in fact, the late spring and early summer in the Iraqi political world had been unusually tranquil. That quietness in itself was thought suspicious by some Iraqis.

In June portentous trouble had been stirred up in the Lebanon, and those who were knowledgeable guessed that it was intended to spread, was likely to become 'a prairie fire', as I wrote to parliamentarian friends at the time.

At the beginning of July prophecies were in some sort fulfilled. Another plot had been brewing, but in Jordan, where twelve army officers were arrested for treason and other steps taken to smash it. King Hussain informed his cousin in Baghdad and, while thus warning him, asked for strong military aid. The troops were required as soon as possible.

Much of the populace of the Arab world, no longer simply and unequivocably Nationalist, but maladjusted and frustrated through its impact with the West, was in an aggressive mood and it was now being encouraged to take action. The dance of fury was quickening in tempo. Its ballet-like spins to draw attention to itself were changing into something more sinister. An intricate impulse was working its will and a dagger was being pressed into its hand.

But there were other things than politics.

The King, who was becoming a discriminating collector of works of art, had not long before made purchases in London, and when there arrived a small one-foot-high figure by Rodin, bought at a bargain price at the end of March, he was very pleased. It was a male torso, without hands or feet, to represent 'movement', which it managed to do very well. As soon as it was

unpacked Faisal had put it up on a television cabinet the better
to admire it. As he did so, and he and his friend, a British physician
to the Royal family, who had helped and encouraged him with
his purchasing of *objets d'art*, were enthusiastically praising it, the
Crown Prince came into the room.

'What is that?'

'A Rodin.'

'What is rodin?'

'A great sculptor. You don't approve?'

'I think it is revolting. I shall never be able to look at television as long as such a horrible thing is there.' He turned away
disapprovingly.

The King and the Prince had both been much occupied with
arrangements for the marriage of the King, in October, to
Fadhilah, daughter of Prince and Princess Mehmet Ali Ibrahim.
Fadhilah, a very beautiful girl, was in England improving her
English until a meeting with her fiancé, fixed for the end of
July, prior to marriage in the early autumn. There were frequent
meetings of the Royal family and with the Chamberlains.
Many letters and invitations were being written. Much remained
to be done.

The Emir Zaid, Iraqi Ambassador in London and the King's
uncle, had very frequently spent summers in Iraq as Regent, but
it was in 1958 for once arranged that the Crown Prince was to
remain in Iraq as Regent for the King during his absence in
Turkey and Europe. The Crown Prince had been feeling far
from well and intended to spend as much of the time as possible
in the small summer Palace in Kurdistan, where it would be
quieter and cooler than in Baghdad. He always had a rather rapid
pulse and high nervous tension, and these characteristics had
lately been somewhat more noticeable to the doctors than was
usual. The Emir Zaid and his wife and son, Raad, went to the
Italian island of Ischia for the summer.

The date chosen for the King's departure by a chartered
aircraft for the Baghdad Pact meeting and meeting of Heads of
State in Turkey was the 9th July, but it was put back and finally
altered to the 14th on Nuri's advice, and because of a delay in
preparing the measures for the setting up of the Union High
Court and the formalities required for a change of status of the

Jordanian Ambassador, both matters consequent upon the new Arab Union. For the same day, the 14th, the move of Iraqi troops, including the Mechanized Brigade, had been ordered. They were to pass through Baghdad on their way to Jordan as requested by Jordan under the arrangements for joint defence of the two countries.

Apart from the known plots, growing uneasiness had been felt by a number of experienced politicians; some of them, Ali Jaudat for one, had mentioned their anxiety to the King, to the Crown Prince or Nuri al Said during the preceding months. The unceasing attacks on Iraq by Nasser's radio, which remained un-jammed, and the activities of his agents in Iraq, together with the troubles in the Lebanon and Jordan, were having an effect which could no longer be regarded as anything but highly dangerous. The people themselves were becoming widely affected. The fall of Lebanon would cut Iraq off from the Mediterranean and lead to the fall of the regime in Iraq.

Nuri al Said had stated firmly and by no means for the first time his anxiety on this score, both in the United States of America and in London in June, when he advised the landing of U.S.A. or United Nations troops in Lebanon and Jordan as soon as possible. For almost the first time he had, too, really welcomed an opportunity of making a lengthy statement to the Press in Britain.

He had become Prime Minister of the Arab Union and should have been happy, but as he left London his sadness was manifest. I had never known him so depressed as he was that last morning. In Turkey he met the Crown Prince whom he warned, even suggesting that he should not go to Baghdad, but they both returned there and Nuri made ready for his early return to Turkey, with the King, for the meeting of the Baghdad Pact Heads of State and Ministers.

A retired police officer in Nuri's confidence told him on his arrival in Baghdad that serious trouble was brewing among the army officers and that Brigadier Abdul Karim Kassim was in-volved. Abdul Karim Kassim was known to Nuri as a moody man who had already been warned by Nuri personally once before for being a member of a junto of officers, one which was broken up by transfers and dismissals. Nevertheless, the Prime

Minister seemed disinclined to regard the old police officer's
warning as one requiring action before his own departure in a
few hours' time for Turkey and Kassim's departure at the same
time for Jordan. Such reports were often false.

A story goes that in a coffee-shop where Kassim habitually
sat, ordering but one cup of coffee, the owner had said loudly,
on hearing of his move to Jordan: 'Thank God, that one won't
be sitting here in future.' He was indeed right. Kassim was to
be in the Prime Minister's chair.

It was most unusual for a march of troops to be permitted
through Baghdad, and never was one permitted with ammunition.
On the 13th a senior Staff Officer was asked if the troops going
through Baghdad might carry ammunition for their weapons.
He replied that, as should be well known, it was contrary to
standing orders and Government instructions. When pressed, on
the grounds that it would save time for them to carry it from the
start of their march, instead of drawing it en route, he said that
no one except the Prime Minister could authorize it. It was later
rumoured that Nuri had agreed. He did not do so, and what little
ammunition the Army carried, about five rounds per man, was
taken up from such places as the Mobile Police Centre at Karra-
dat Miriam in Baghdad and the Infantry Training School, against
orders and without the knowledge of Nuri or the Palace. It was
given out to officers and the troops—in order to allay suspicion
among those of them not in the plot—that there would be a
practice of 'house-to-house fighting' on their way out of the city.

The most significant step of all taken by the persons engaged
in the plot was that the Communists imprisoned at Baquba, an
hour by car from Baghdad, were released overnight and brought
to Baghdad. Group leaders were appointed among them and
given written instructions with placards and flags to be used from
dawn in rousing and management of the mob.

On the night of the 13th July, it is related, Jamil Abdul
Wahab, Minister of Communications in the Government, informed the Crown Prince that he was certain a revolutionary
plot was afoot and that members of the Army who should be
elsewhere were in Baghdad and behaving in a mysterious and
secretive way. The Crown Prince, it is said, replied that the movement of troops to Jordan would account for his information, but

Jamil maintained his certainty that there was cause for alarm and for action.

The Prince may have felt that there was something in Jamil's report, for he spoke, it is also said, to the Royal pilot, Jassam Muhammad, and asked for the flight to be put forward by one hour. Jassam, who, surprisingly, was the following day made Director of Civil Aviation by the Kassim Government, replied that it was too late to warn the crew for an earlier start. After further enquiry, Jamil Abdul Wahab was so certain of impending revolt that he went into hiding in an hotel, and, much later, with the help of one of the servants, disguised himself and got by car to Ali Gharbi, the nearest place to the Persian frontier on the road southwards. From there he walked across the border and out of the country unharmed.

In the Royal Palace, on the evening of the 13th July, while it was still very hot at 5 p.m., there was a conjuring show by a Pakistani magician for five children invited by the King—the three sons of the Sherif Hussain Ali and his wife Badiya, sister of the Crown Prince, together with the son and daughter of a divisional General.

The tricks included smashing a boy's watch, which was found intact in the King's breast-pocket, and there were two trained turtle-doves, one drawing the other in a little cart and both obeying their master in picking up small objects and in fluttering when told. The King himself did a card trick. But because of the early start the conjuring games came to an end by 6 p.m. There was a meal and then the children were sent home by car, their mother and her sister staying behind. The Regent's sister, Abdiya, killed fourteen hours later, asked if the girl might spend the night with her, but it was thought better that she should not remain since the departure was early next morning. So, 'by a hair's breadth', the child, aged thirteen, was saved.

A letter had meanwhile been received by the King, which he had handed to the Crown Prince, whose expression changed to one of annoyance as he read it. It was written in English. He excused himself and went off in a Royal chauffeur-driven car for a time. On his return to the Palace he received a caller, and the King and the remainder of the party waited for him before dining, later than intended, at about 9.30 p.m. The lady who sat next to the Prince found that for once in his life his good manners seemed to have deserted him. He hardly replied to her gambits and was deep in thought. The King and some of the grown-ups went afterwards to see a film in the neighbouring Zuhur Palace, the 'unlucky' Palace. When he returned the King said that it was not at all to their taste. It was *The Pajama Game*. By half past midnight he wished to go to bed and the visitors left the Palace.

The Sherif Hussain Ali and Princess Badiya and their boys, and the children's English nanny, Mrs. Hazeldine, were travelling with the King at His Majesty's suggestion. The summer being already half spent, the Princess Badiya had been rather reluctant to put off their departure, even by a few days, in order to travel more comfortably. They already had their personal belongings packed and a flat bespoken in London.

Soon after six o'clock on the morning of the 14th, the Turkish cook in the Palace was cutting sandwiches, having delivered tea to the Prince, who was already being shaved. Alarmed by the arrival in the Palace grounds of soldiers carrying their arms at the ready, the cook leapt out of the pantry window and made off through the trees, railing under his breath.

Some forty minutes later the Sherif Hussain, whose house was only a few hundred yards from the Palace, heard a noise of firing.

Since it continued in bursts and sounded very near, he went up to the upper floor of the building and saw that buses were crossing the Iron Bridge and vegetable-growers and others were going along the road on their way to market just as usual. When new and heavier firing began he rang the Palace on the private line and spoke to the King, who told him that they were besieged and that according to radio broadcasts there was a revolt. 'If you wish I could send some of my guards to you.' He was maybe thinking of the reserve guards in the Qasr Zuhur, which he must have asked should be sent. He spoke very calmly. The Sherif Hussain, besides being a relative, was one of his closest friends, spending nearly every afternoon with him at the swimming pool on these hot summer days, and they had been swimming together as usual, with Hussain's sons, before the conjuring, on the afternoon of the 13th, and had been together again in the evening.

When Hussain tried to ring again a little later the line was dead.

At a few minutes after six o'clock a commander of the bodyguard and an A.D.C. had arrived to report to the Palace. A young officer on his way in a jeep to a new assignment in the South, full of the thought of his appointment, was puzzled at finding troops near the Palace and made a detour to avoid them. He went on his way, unaware that death was in the air.

The firing at the Palace continued intermittently for rather more than half an hour. Then it ceased. Hussain could see little with his binoculars, except that soldiers still surrounded the Palace. The shutters of Hussain's house were closed and the children were taken downstairs. A little later—no one noted the exact time, but it was early morning, say a quarter past eight o'clock—a loyal officer, dishevelled, shirt open and capless, ran up to their door, crying out to them when it was opened to him in such words as: 'They are dead—they have killed them all—God have mercy on them—go quickly, while you can!'

What happened at the Palace may in time become exactly known. Piecing together the scanty, varying information, it appears that a servant, hearing the radio announcement of a revolution, ran to the King, who had already heard it and was on his way to the Crown Prince, himself still being shaved. Some soldiers had lined up on the earth bank or 'bund' near the Palace, but did not fire at first. Some time later they began desultory small-arms firing.

Colonel Naji Talib, an officer in the 3rd Division, a former Royal A.D.C. and Military Attaché in London, had been mentioned on the radio broadcast as one of the new Ministers of the revolutionary Government. 'Good God,' said the Prince to the King, 'Ghazi Daghestani's division.' Had the Prince known it, General Daghestani, commanding the 3rd Division, was already under arrest by the revolutionaries.

When, ten years earlier, the Prince, as Regent, had taken Naji Talib as his A.D.C., he had noticed my expression of doubt. 'I know what you mean,' he said, 'but you see it is just that kind of young man I want to train, to improve his views. I think that if I have him with us and he sees what really goes on, and all our

N

efforts for the people, he will come to understand and change his ideas.' His attempt at conversion had clearly been useless.

The Palace, at this stage, was not fully surrounded, and the King's chauffeur tried to persuade him to break out, at the side, and leave by car for Diwaniya. The King refused. A little later more troops arrived, a few rounds of shelling by an infantry anti-tank gun began and set off some of the ammunition in the Palace, so that a fire started; and it was then too late to escape.

After the second phase of firing at the Palace, an officer, advancing with a sergeant, shouted to offer safe conduct 'through the rebellious troops', to the Palace cars and out of the country, if the King and all his people would trust him. They must have been doubtful of the offer, but after delay agreed to the man's proposals. Ammunition was plentiful and the guards, a company and a half, were numerous and steady, but the King and Crown Prince declined to fire on their own subjects.

So the family and a number of their servants—the King, the Queen Nafisa, mother of the Crown Prince, the Crown Prince, his sister the Princess Abdiya, his wife Hayam, Lieutenant Thabit, an A.D.C., and those servants who volunteered to go with them, including a small negro page, Abdul Razzaq; some fifteen or twenty persons in all, in a compact party, some holding hands—left the Palace behind the officer and sergeant, who had their sub-machine-guns at the alert position, while the soldiers, most of them in fact dismayed and many of them not disloyal, looked on.

At the top of the steps, in the doorway, the Prince noticed that his wife was wearing only a nightdress beneath her coat. 'You cannot come like that. Run and put something else on,' he said, and she ran away into the building. The rest of the party went slowly out.

Halfway across the court of the Palace, at the foot of the steps before the fountain, the officer turned about and sprayed the party, firing again and again. Thabit, the A.D.C., bravely rushed forward, firing, in an endeavour to protect the King with his only shield—his own body. All were killed immediately except the King, who fell mortally wounded and died without regaining full consciousness.

The Crown Prince's wife, on her way out once more, had staggered when there was a new burst of firing and she was lightly wounded. Above her bullets ricocheted, cracking glass fell and curtains were on fire. Terrified, she lay where she had sunk down. An N.C.O. who knew her family and who was beholden to one of them came upon her and asked her name. Hardly knowing what she said, or why, she gave the name of a cousin. He flung a covering over her and told her to lie quite still. 'Shoot at that one,' yelled two of his officers as they ran into the hall. 'She is dead, but there are others inside.' The N.C.O. managed to get her away to the house of a neighbour known to her, carrying her as if she were a corpse for disposal.

She remained in a state of collapse until the house of her father, the Emir Rabia, at Hussainiya near Kut-el-Amara, was sacked by rebels. The second shock seemed to act as a tonic cure for the first and she began to take practical steps in the care of her aged father.

The King, the women and servants killed were buried by the Army. The Crown Prince's body, feet and hands cut off, was mutilated and dragged through the streets, tied up naked for exhibition and run over by cars until finally, after souvenir hunters had had their way, there remained only a piece of the backbone and its flesh to throw aside.

On the same night Nuri al Said had been more on the *qui vive* than had the Palace. Warned once more, he took serious notice of the alarm others had felt. He sent for his son Sabah and prepared to leave. It is said that he waited overlong for the wilful Sabah, who was at his habitual, late-night roistering in the city. The Army found Sabah next morning and it is reported that he died bravely, with a taunt on his lips and a glass in his hand.

Near dawn, further alarmed by the cutting of his telephone wire and new reports to him, Nuri left his house in his pyjamas and went by river—rowed by a couple of fishermen at the point of his two pistols—to the east bank, hoping to reach the house of Shaikh Muhammad al Araibi.

Muhammad al Araibi, an elderly Senator, Chief of the important marshmen tribes near Amarsh on the Tigris, always had a following of his own men at hand. And the way from Baghdad

to Amara, and thence to Persia through the marsh, is on the same
side of the river as his house. Once there Nuri might be safe in
his hands. But when he approached the east bank he saw that
there were armed citizens running to and fro and greatly excited.
Since it was unsafe for him to land he turned back across the
river to the house of Dr. Salah al Bassam. Dr. Bassam took him
in and they debated the various possibilities. In the end it was
decided to move him, hidden in the boot of the doctor's car, to
the house of al Hajji Mahmoud al Astarabadi, whose wife was
the closest friend of Nuri's wife and connected by marriage with
Nuri's friend and Minister, Dhiah Jaafar. It was a large, rambling
old house, situated in Kadhimain, the northern suburb of
Baghdad, with underground rooms, for summer use, connected
to those of other adjoining houses also belonging to the family.
There he might hide in safety. But once arrived he and they began
to think otherwise. There was the broadcast announcement of
ten thousand dinars on his head, dead or alive, and the Astarabadi
family houses might well be searched because of the known
friendship between the two families.

Madame Astarabadi and one of her women disguised Nuri
with a cloak and sent for their driver to bring their car. Then it
was remembered that the driver had been given leave that day.
Another, less experienced, man was found. He was not told about
the third passenger, who kept well veiled. They drove to the
house of Madame Astarabadi's daughter, married to Qassim
Jaafar, brother of Dhiah Jaafar, Nuri's Minister, in the Battawiin
quarter of Baghdad. It seems madness to have re-entered the city,
but Nuri by now had the fixed idea that he must reach the house
of Shaikh Muhammad al Araibi, and this they might do from the
house of Qassim Jaafar. Nuri was not very sure of the exact
position of Araibi's house himself.

Once arrived they consulted all the people in the house.
Suddenly, it is said, Nuri noticed that a turbulent young man, a
son of the house, who he felt sure had been there when they
arrived, was no longer to be seen. He suspected that he had gone
to give them away. So he hurried out, followed by Madame
Astarabadi, to find unaided the house of the Shaikh upon whom
so much depended. As he went along, pyjamas showed beneath
his cloak. 'Oh-ho, you people of Baghdad,' shouted a grocer

from his shop door—so it is said—'might that not be Nuri?
There are ten thousand dinars for us, my neighbours.'
They began to run towards him. He turned about, firing his
pistols. They, along with some men of the volunteer Police brought
up, fired in return. Madame Astarabadi, a woman of over sixty, was
killed. A moment later Nuri fell. He had been killed, whoever
may have fired the fatal shots, by action of the Army which he
himself had raised.

His body was taken by the Police to the hospital for formal
identification by doctors and then from the hospital for burial in
a cemetery beyond the North Gate. There the body remained for
a little while until, their lust unsatisfied, a party of revolutionaries
came to look for it in order to drag it through the streets. Unsure
of his grave, they hastily dug up all new graves, unearthing the
bodies of old people and children, which they left where they
were. Finding it at last, they dragged the body by a rope, after
gleefully mutilating it, along the main road to the city proper.
When a car approached they held it up and ordered the driver
to run over the body and then reverse and drive over it again.
Still not satisfied, they went on into the city and strung it up,
then lugged it down again and pulled it to bits, souvenir-hunters
having their way with it, until it was unrecognizable as the corpse
of the man who had been the best-known patriot in the Arab
world. At last the trunk was set afire. Not much petrol was
needed to consume in flame the little that remained.

In London his wife was gathering together her materials for
an Arab dinner for Nuri as soon as he arrived, the rice and con-
diments which require especial selection and careful preparation.
For a time no one dared tell her. The radio was put out of order
by Ismet, her daughter-in-law, also widowed. The newspapers
were concealed from her. After a day or two her family said that
Nuri was delayed by trouble in Iraq and so gradually began to
break the news.

Why Nuri did not in the first instance continue downriver
to Daura, a suburb where there are oil installations, Europeans
with motor-boats and other facilities of which he could make
use, is difficult to understand. From the river, like Jamil Abdul
Wahab, he might have escaped into Persia. Perhaps he felt he
was too old to face such a journey, which possibly he would have

had to make on foot, or perhaps, as once before in a crisis, he wanted to stay to find his son and be sure about the King.

The Sherif Hussain and the Princess Badiya had meanwhile, on receiving a warning in time, thanks to the devotion of the loyal officer, escaped to the house of a European neighbour, a German, with whom they sought shelter. There they were put off on the grounds that a house so large and near their own would be searched, but they borrowed a car and removed the Palace number-plate from their own car. They moved from house to house and spent the night in an empty one. In the morning, after reconnoitring the railway and road bridge north of Baghdad, and confirming that it was unguarded, they made plans to cross it to the Saudi Arabian Embassy. The Princess took off her habitual veil and gave it to the English nanny. Thus disguised, and with the party separated in two cars, they successfully ran the gauntlet of revolutionary Baghdad unharmed. The Ambassador gave them shelter and, cabling to his King the news of their arrival, received the answer that henceforth they were His Majesty's 'personal guests under his protection at his house in Baghdad' and that the Ambassador was to hold himself strictly at their service, a reply in the grand style reminiscent of that used by his father, Ibn Saud the Great.

At about nine-thirty on the morning of the revolt there had been another ghastly incident. A group of rebels arrived at the new hotel in Baghdad in search of a General and three Jordanian Ministers of the Arab Union Government. They ripped out telephones and ransacked the lower rooms. With some dozen other foreigners seized at random, the Jordanians were pushed into a truck. The first to be taken were two Britishers, who, finding themselves unguarded for a moment, slipped out of the front of the vehicle and, 'making ourselves small', managed to glide back into safety. The truck was driven to the Ministry of Defence, through streets filled by the mob. In it were the Jordanians, Ibrahim Hashim, Deputy Premier of the Union, General Sadiq Shara (who was a survivor, though injured, and later gave an account of the incident to the Press),[1] an Egyptian and some Europeans, including a German business man who had

[1] See *Time* magazine, 4th August 1958.

come to sign an important contract, together with three Californians, Robert Alcock, George S. Colley, Jr., Senior Vice-President of Bechtel Corporation, and Eugene Burns. At the gate of the Ministry the truck was stopped by a halted vehicle, and the mob attacked them. The Deputy Premier of the Union was killed almost at once by a stone flung at his head. A young Swiss or German, aged about thirty, was pulled out by the head and about eight people began slashing, stabbing and beating him with iron rods until he died, when they cut off his head. Others were being pulled out and treated in the same way. Someone got the gates of the Ministry open and the few survivors ran for it. All those who did not reach it were dismembered by the mob.

A senior officer of the Royal Air Force making his way to Habbaniya, after a visit to Baghdad in connection with Baghdad Pact duty and ignorant of the killings that had taken place at the Palace, was stopped by the mob, which had arrived there after the killing, and was stabbed several times. A big man, he struggled to free himself and reach the Iraqi Y.W.C.A. When near it, the door was opened by Miss Pilsbury, who gallantly went out to his help and drove off the attackers by her display of courage and determination, looking after him until she could get him to a doctor.[1]

The British pilot of Iraqi Airways ready to take the King to Turkey was detained at the airport for some hours, until he successfully begged to be allowed to go to his wife in their house near the Palace. He too was stopped by the mob and beaten up, until rescued by some Army personnel who sent him back to the airport.

No protecting unit of the Army was sent to the British Embassy, as it was to the American Embassy, though the arrival of the mob there cannot have been unexpected in view of the encouragement to it to rise given by the radio.

A large crowd burst through the gates into the Embassy grounds and when the Ambassador opened the door of the building a bullet whistled past his head. The situation of the Ambassador, his family and his staff was perilous and nerve-racking; and the Comptroller, Colonel Graham, was killed.

[1] Miss Pilsbury, of the British Y.W.C.A., was subsequently and very rightly awarded a decoration, the M.B.E., for her courage and devotion to duty.

Eventually, after part of the Embassy had been burnt and looted, they were extricated by the Iraq Army and were escorted, bereft of property, to the new hotel on the east bank of the Tigris. And even there safety was by no means certain, while the position of several thousand other British subjects in Iraq was unknown.

At Diwaniya, General Umr Ali, with his division, stood firm and loyal, as did other units elsewhere, until they learnt beyond doubt that there was no longer anyone to whom to be loyal. Umr Ali was persuaded to come to Baghdad the next day, where he was arrested and sent to join the other Generals in prison in Baghdad.

Twenty-four hours later the news of the death of the young King and the whole Royal family had brought revulsion of feeling against the army officers concerned, by all except the Communists and the worst of the mob. When news came of the landing first of American troops and then of British troops, at Beirut and Amman, individuals of the so-called Government prepared to leave. The opening of the prison and the arrival of the American and British troops in Iraq were expected at any moment. When none came, and the British Ambassador visited Brigadier Kassim, the rebels and the mob began to take heart again and soon arrests were continued on an even larger scale. The first arrests of over a hundred leading and key men, made at the time of the overthrow of the Royal House, were supplemented daily by arrests for nothing more than political reasons. The ordinary prison at the North Gate was emptied of the criminals there and refilled with the leading persons of the land—their names read like a guest list for a party given by one of their number. But they were twelve or so in a room and in their pyjamas.

Just under a month after the coup d'état, Sherif Hussain and the Princess Badiya with their three boys were permitted to leave by air for Cairo after negotiations through the Saudi Arabian Ambassador. They were accompanied by a one-man escort who, rather to their surprise, meekly left them in Egypt and under no duress. And equally to their surprise, and probably owing to the firmness of Ibn Saud, they were allowed to leave Egypt for

Switzerland, the only Hashimites of the Royal family living in Iraq to survive the slaughter of the 14th July 1958.

It will probably never be known for certain what preliminary details had gone to the making of the plot or the precise nature of events that led up to the moment of the murders. It was clear, however, immediately after the announcement of the names of the new Government, that they were an ill-assorted crew, unlikely to hold together long. Kassim was known to be much inclined to Communism and Abdul Salam Muhammad Arif, whom he subsequently arrested and tried, to Nasserism. Other members of the Government, though ultra-Nationalistic or chauvinists, were doubtless all for Iraq first and foremost, however misguidedly, while others were merely delinquent or born to be unhappy. Only one had much previous experience as an administrator, and two were known to be in the Red camp.

One of the first comments by an Iraqi of standing in London, on hearing an account of the events of the 14th July, was: 'You know us—that is not an Iraqi plan.' He meant that the sequence of events, the secrecy, the leaders and the whole shape of it bore every sign of having been gone over carefully by some non-Iraqi, and that it was a well-worked-out plot and not spontaneous. It was for this reason that the catch-phrase put about in some circles in London, after being used by the rebellious Military Attaché, 'It is time to come to terms with Arab Nationalism'—as if the members of the new Government were a band of young idealists—was absurd, as was shortly to be proved.

Some of the reasons listed which led an Iraqi to say that it was far from a spontaneous rising were weighty, others less so. It was no doubt spontaneous to the extent that Nasser's promises and propaganda, pumped out continuously for several years, had had their effect. A similar campaign elsewhere, if it were possible, would have a weakening effect upon even a less volatile people than the Iraqis. Imagine a powerful and easily heard station from a country that is assumed, because of the language, to be more or less of the same race (though in fact very different and mixed in blood), a country moreover accepted as having a far larger population and greater wealth, and, further, as being a country that had successfully seized an international asset and defied two great Powers—and there are already elements of a successful appeal. Ambitious Nasser, to whom the careers of Muhammad Ali and Ibrahim Pasha, great soldiers of fortune who founded the former Egyptian dynasty, no doubt acted as a stimulus, believed that by propaganda and the use of Egyptians abroad he could upset the Iraqi and other regimes in his own favour. In fact, in Iraq, he provided an opportunity for the Communists whose wiles, before the Iraqi revolution, he evidently did not fully grasp. The ill-assorted team in Iraq after the revolution reflected the temporary nature of the match between the two countries. My Iraqi friend in London felt certain that the Iraqi plot was known to and had at some stage been conned by Russians. There was seeming evidence of this in the sudden return of Khrushchev to Moscow from Berlin on 10th July; in the total destruction of the Royal family as in the Russian revolution; the release of the Communist internees on the 13th July; and the symbolically important, but otherwise senseless, burning of the British Embassy with avoidance of other provocation in the way of deliberate attempts on British lives in Baghdad or elsewhere (other than the death of Colonel Graham, the Comptroller in the Embassy, which does not seem to have been deliberate); and the absence of any threat to 'British wives and children', at Habbaniya or in the oil-fields, which could with justification have touched off British intervention.

Interesting too, as an indication of the planned nature of the attack on the Palace, was the order of the announcements from the Baghdad radio station, seized during the night of the 13th–14th. According to a Western timetable, the Baghdad announcer said at 4 a.m.: 'Noble people of Baghdad, go to the Rihab Palace and other places of slavery and humiliation.' At 5 a.m. 'a new Republic' was proclaimed and three-quarters of an hour later the new Council of State was announced, followed at 5.50 by a list of the new Cabinet and, ten minutes later, a list of the new appointments in the higher ranks of the Army.

At six o'clock in the morning the announcer said, referring to the Rihab Palace and its occupants, 'their bodies have been dragged through the streets like dogs'. Nothing of the kind had at this moment so far happened. It was about two hours later that the Royal family were killed. And every now and then the broadcasts lapsed into Egyptian Arabic.

The seizure of the Baghdad Pact headquarters and its documents, an early event, does not appear to have been announced by the radio station, again perhaps significantly. Incidentally, it is said that a European officer of the headquarters had gone to the bridge in Baghdad to check 'units going to Jordan' and ticked them off painstakingly as they went on their way, ignorantly or otherwise, to attend the slaughter of their Sovereign.

Comparatively little has been said in the foreign Press about the ending of the Baghdad Pact, though it was clearly the primary objective of the planners outside Iraq, the Russians and Egyptians, and was concerted by them with action in Jordan and the Lebanon. In Jordan the plot was partly uncovered just in time. The present Iraqi leader, Kassim, revealed his thoughts about the rebel action when he spoke at a lengthy Press conference given to Lebanese journalists, reported in the *Daily Telegraph* on the 4th August 1959.

He argued that Russia was really under a great obligation to Iraq. 'When giving us aid, Moscow is paying us only part of what she owes us for having destroyed the Baghdad Pact and with it a centre of the conspiracy against her.'

In this sentence, a year after the revolution, lies the heart of the matter.

If only Nuri and the Crown Prince, or one of them, had not returned from Turkey just at the very moment when troops were due to pass through Baghdad, the overthrow of the regime would not have taken place. It was a case for destroying all together or not at all. Some of the troops, perhaps the majority, were loyal, in particular those of General Umr Ali at Diwaniya and those at Musaiyib, but only too soon there was no one and nothing to which they could be loyal any longer.

On the 30th July 1958 I spoke the eulogy of the murdered King at a service in his memory arranged by a few of his friends in England.

The physician to the Royal family of Iraq and to the Embassy, Dr. Raymond Dixon Firth, and myself, I think, first thought of it. At the same time a friend high in the British

Government was anxious that some form of service should be held. We tried to make some arrangements with the Imam of the mosque at Regent's Park, through the helpful Jordanian Ambassador, but he thought that 'no one would attend' and was discouraging.

We then thought of holding a service at St. Margaret's, Westminster. The Vicar, who was out of London, tentatively agreed, but asked us to get in touch with his Curate, also, it turned out, a Chaplain to the Archbishop of Canterbury, in order to confirm the details. The following day the Chaplain spoke from Lambeth to say that the Palace would not agree to such a service in any church under its control. Moreover, it was understood that he said that the Archbishop in Jerusalem, whom we had asked might give the address, was totally opposed to the idea, 'which could prejudice the Anglican missionary effort in the Middle East and endanger the well-being of Christians there'.

We had at one moment thought of asking to hold the service in the Chapel of one of the Orders of Knighthood and now one of those interested in the proposal suggested the Chapel Royal Savoy, since the King, the Crown Prince and Nuri al Said were all honorary Knights Grand Cross of the Victorian Order. The Rev. Sir Cyril Cresswell, the Chaplain of the Order, agreed, having obtained Royal 'informal consent'.

A number of notices were sent out to those who might like to come and some went to the Press for publication the day before the service.

The Prime Minister said that he supported the idea and would be represented, and the Duke of Gloucester, accompanied by the Duchess, came to represent the Queen. The Duchess' brother, the Duke of Buccleuch; Mr. Selwyn Lloyd, the Foreign Secretary; Mr. Lennox Boyd, Secretary of State for the Colonies; and a number of other Ministers and Members of Parliament and Ambassadors also attended. The Jordanian Ambassador, representing the King of Jordan; Nuri's grandson Issam; and Dr. Dhiah Jaafar, the Iraq Minister of Development and a relative by marriage of the Aga Khan, who had been in hospital in England, were the chief Arab mourners. In all more than four hundred people came. Late-comers were in the end left outside. Some of the onlookers at the door clapped Sir Anthony Eden and Lady Eden as they entered. Sir Henry Channon, M.P., a brother-in-law of the Secretary for the Colonies, helped with arrangements and was the Chief Usher.

We did not forget to send a notice of the service to Miss Borland, the King's old nurse; to Miss Ramirez, his governess; or to Mr. Harwood of New Scotland Yard, attached to the Iraqi Royal family during their visits to England and since attached to Mr. Macmillan; or to Mr. Geall, a former Corporal of Horse and Mess Corporal at Knightsbridge Barracks who had been butler at the King's English residence before becoming a police officer. All of them came.

Some of the congregation were mourning the end of a dynasty that they had helped to establish. One very elderly lady, whom I helped through the crush of newcomers at the doors and up the shallow steps into the body of the church, said: 'I am Lady Richmond, sister of Gertrude Bell who put Faisal the First on the throne. May I have a seat?' Colonel Pierce Joyce, still very tall and upright, though walking only with the help of a stick, was also there. He had fought with Nuri and Faisal and Lawrence in the Arab uprising and had taken a leading part in raising the Iraqi Army. Lady Cornwallis came, though without her husband, who was, alas, too ill to attend. He had advised Faisal the First from the days of the Arab Bureau in Cairo and had been in Iraq for twenty years, finally becoming, when matters were going badly in 1941, British Ambassador. During the war, while he was in Baghdad, he had learnt that his two sons were killed. He died within a year of the end of the dynasty which he and Gertrude Bell had installed and that he himself had so long and devotedly supported.

I received a number of letters in appreciation of the Address at the Memorial Service, one of them, touchingly worded, from the Portuguese Ambassador. On the day itself many people kindly said a few words as they left the church. They were, I believe, relieved to have a means of showing sorrow not only for the loss of individuals of an allied dynasty, but for the end of a long British effort in which some of them had themselves taken part.

I gave a copy of the Order of the Service and the Address

to Neil McLean, M.P., who was leaving next day for Jordan, so that he could show it to our Ambassador and to King Hussain. I had known King Faisal the Second since he was a baby, Abdulillah since he was twelve years old and Nuri al Said since 1925.

With the dynasty in Iraq fell the great families and the best of the new middle class, including the Prime Minister, the Minister of Foreign Affairs and fifteen other Ministers or ex-Ministers, every General Officer of the Iraq Army, six Brigadiers and fifteen Colonels, nearly every Director-General in the Civil Service, most of the Senate and about half the House of Deputies. Some thousands of Iraqis were in prison in their own country and a number of them have been condemned to death or penal servitude, though only some of the death sentences have so far been confirmed. The trials continued for many months and, indeed, were still going on in 1959.

The correspondent of the *Daily Telegraph* on the 19th May 1959 wrote of the judge as 'an obscene bully'.

The mob [he continued] revel equally in the viciousness of Judge Mahdawi's depraved Punch and Judy show. Baghdad on a trial night is a terrible city, guffawing and gloating from end to end over the poor wretches in the dock.

Across the wide Tigris in the darkness the dreadful orchestration of evil can be plainly heard. The brutish laughter of the court-room, picked up on thousands of radio and television sets, is magnified by a whole city full of sadists.

From the quality of the sound, the distant listener can almost guess whether the Judge is taunting a prisoner, covering Nasser with obloquy or merely proclaiming some new bizarre aspect of liberated Arabism.

'Drag every imperialist through the streets,' his Lordship will shout, and a roar goes up from one end of the town to the other. The Western wayfarer hastening back to his hotel may be forgiven if he hastens his pace . . . one wonders if the local Communists recognize the dangerous schizophrenia and will know how to deal with it. It will certainly be a poser to their Russian mentors.

Peace, order and continuity, requisite for progress in any country and vital in a young one with a volatile urban population, have been lost. One of the first acts of the rebels was to stultify the work of the Iraqi Development Board, which was restoring economic order in a country largely ruined at the time of the Mongol invasion seven hundred years earlier.

The seed of governing profitably for the people, sown by hard-working officials, at the beginning most of them British, had begun to produce a worthy harvest, indeed a splendid one when compared with the chaos that has followed revolution. From this revolution will come no true benefit, to the Egyptians, the Russians, or to the Iraqi firebrands immediately responsible for it—least of all to the mass of the people of the countryside, left drowning in the second Great Flood to submerge their land, one of Words and Delusion.

Genealogical Table

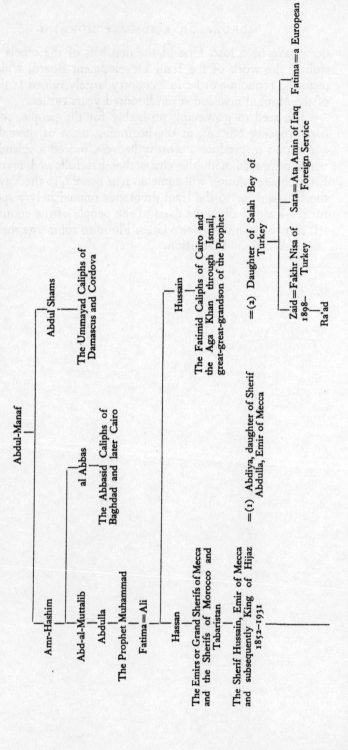

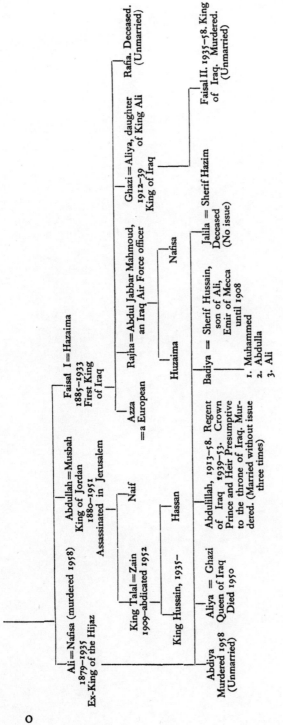

Ali＝Nafisa (murdered 1958)
1879–1935
Ex-King of the Hijaz

Abdullah＝Musbah
King of Jordan
1880–1951
Assassinated in Jerusalem

Faisal I＝Hazaima
1885–1933
First King
of Iraq

Naif

Hassan

Azza
＝a European

Rajha＝Abdul Jabbar Mahmoud,
an Iraq Air Force officer

Ghazi＝Aliya, daughter of King Ali
1912–39
King of Iraq

Rafia. Deceased.
(Unmarried)

King Talal＝Zain
1909–abdicated 1952

King Hussain, 1935–

Huzaima

Nafisa

Faisal II. 1935–58. King
of Iraq. Murdered.
(Unmarried)

Abdiya
Murdered 1958
(Unmarried)

Aliya＝Ghazi
Queen of Iraq
Died 1950

Abdulillah, 1913–58. Regent
of Iraq 1939–53. Crown
Prince and Heir Presumptive
to the throne of Iraq. Murdered. (Married without issue
three times)

Badiya ＝ Sherif Hussain,
son of Ali,
Emir of Mecca
until 1908

1. Muhammed
2. Abdulla
3. Ali

Jalila ＝ Sherif Hazim
Deceased
(No issue)

o

A Select Bibliography

ABDULLAH, King of Transjordan: *Memoirs* (Cape 1950)

ANTONIUS, G.: *The Arab Awakening* (Hamish Hamilton 1938)

ASKARI, Ja'far al-: *Five Years' Progress in Iraq* (R.C.A.S. Journal 1927)

BELL, Gertrude: *Amurath to Amurath* (Heinemann 1911)
The Letters of Gertrude Bell, selected and edited by Lady Bell. 2 vols. (Ernest Benn 1927)

BIRDWOOD, Lord, M.V.O.: *Nuri as-Said* (Cassell 1959)

BOLITHO, H. H.: *A Biographer's Notebook* (Longmans Green 1950)

BOLITHO, H. H.: *The Angry Neighbours* (Barker 1958)

BOWMAN, H. E.: *Middle East Window* (Longmans 1942)

BULLARD, Sir Reader: *Britain and the Middle East* (Hutchinson's University Library 1951)

BURGOYNE, E.: *Gertrude Bell from her Personal Papers 1889–1914* (Benn 1958)

CAROE, Sir O.: *Wells of Power* (Macmillan 1951)

CATROUX, General: *Deux Missions en Moyen Orient (1919–22)* (Plon 4. 1958)

CHURCHILL, Sir Winston, K.C., C.H., M.P.: *The World Crisis: The Aftermath* (Thomas Butterworth Ltd. 1929)

DE GAURY, Gerald: *Rulers of Mecca* (George Harrap 1951)

EDMONDS, C. J., C.M.G., C.B.E.: *Kurds, Turks and Arabs. Politics, Travel and Research in North-Eastern Iraq 1919–25* (Oxford University Press 1957)

ERSKINE, B. C.: *King Faisal of Iraq* (Hutchinson 1933)

FOSTER, H. A.: *The Making of Modern Iraq* (Williams & Norgate 1935)

GIBB, H. A. R.: *Modern Trends in Islam* (Chicago 1947)

HART, B. H. Liddell: *T. E. Lawrence, in Arabia and After* (Cape 1934)

HOOPER, C. A.: *Constitutional Law of Iraq* (Baghdad 1928)

HOURANI, A. H.: *Minorities in the Arab World* (O.U.P. for R.I.I.A. 1947)

IRELAND, P. W. (ed.): *The Near East: Problems and Prospects* (Chicago 1942)

JUNG, E.: *Les Puissances devant la Révolte Arabe—la Crise Mondiale de Demain* (Hachette 1906)

KHADDURI, M.: *Independent Iraq* (O.U.P. for R.I.I.A. 1951)

LAWRENCE, T. E.: *Seven Pillars of Wisdom* (Cape 1935)

LLOYD, Seton: *Twin Rivers* (O.U.P. 1943)

LONGRIGG, S. H.: *Four Centuries of Modern Iraq* (Clarendon Press, Oxford 1925)

LONGRIGG, S. H.: *Iraq. 1900 to 1950* (O.U.P. 1953)

LUKE, Sir H. C.: *An Eastern Chequerboard* (Lovat Dickson 1934)

LUKE, Sir H.C.: *Mosul and its Minorities* (Martin Hopkinson 1925)

LYALL, T.: *The Ins and Outs of Mesopotamia* (A. M. Philpot Ltd. 1923)

MACDONALD, A. D.: *Euphrates Exile* (G. Bell 1936)

MAIN, Ernest: *Iraq. From Mandate to Independence* (Allen & Unwin 1935)

MORTON, H. V.: *Middle East* (Methuen 1941)

MUSIL, A.: *The Middle Euphrates* (New York 1927)

NEWTON, Frances Emily: *Fifty Years in Palestine* (Coldharbour Press, Wrotham)

NICOLSON, Sir Harold: *Curzon: The Last Phase* (Constable & Co. Ltd. 1934)

NOLDE, E.: *L'Irak: Origines historiques et situation internationale* (Paris 1934)

NUTTING, Anthony: *I Saw for Myself. The Aftermath of Suez* (Hollis and Larter 1958)

PETERSON, Sir M. D.: *Both Sides of the Curtain* (Constable 1950)

PHILBY, H. St. J. B.: *Arabian Days* (Robert Hale 1948)

PHILLIPS, Sir P.: *Mesopotamia. The 'Daily Mail' Inquiry at Baghdad* (Carmelite House 1923)

PLAYFAIR, I. S. O, Maj.-General: *The Mediterranean and the Middle East.* Vols. 1 and 2 (H.M. Stationery Office 1954)

QUBAIN, Fahim I.: *The Reconstruction of Iraq 1950–1957* (Stevens & Sons Ltd., London 1959)

AL SAID, Nuri Pasha : *Arab Independence and Unity* (Baghdad Government Press 1943)

SALTER, Lord: *The Development of Iraq* (Iraq Development Board 1955 (Printed by Caxton Press, London, E.C.1))

STAFFORD, R. S. H.: *The Tragedy of the Assyrians* (Allen & Unwin 1935)

STARK, Freya :*Baghdad Sketches* (Murray 1937)

STARK, Freya: *Beyond Euphrates* (Murray 1951)

STEVENS, E. S. (Lady Drower): *By Tigris and Euphrates* (Hurst & Blackett 1923)

STORRS, Sir R.: *Orientations* (Nicholson & Watson 1937)

THOMAS, Lowell J.: *With Lawrence in Arabia* (Hutchinson 1924)

THOMPSON, Sir Geoffrey: *Front Line Diplomat* (Hutchinson 1959)

VAN ESS, J.: *Meet the Arab* (Museum Press, London 1943)

WILSON, Sir A.: *Loyalties* (O.U.P. 1930)

WILSON, Sir A.: *Mesopotamia, 1917–1920: A Clash of Loyalties* (O.U.P. 1931)

WINGATE, Sir R.: *Not in the Limelight* (Hutchinson 1959)

YOUNG, Sir Hubert, C.M.G., D.S.O.: *The Independent Arab* (John Murray 1933)

ZEINE, Zeine N.: *Anglo-Turkish Relations and the Emergence of Arab Nationalism* (Khayats, Beirut, Lebanon 1958)

A Chronology

1921   Accession of the Emir Faisal, son of King Hussain of the Hijaz, as King Faisal the First of Iraq.
An Iraq Army already in embryo, with Nuri al Said as its first Chief of Staff.

1922   10th October: First Anglo-Iraq Treaty signed at Baghdad.

1924   4th March: The Caliphate abolished by the Turks. It is assumed by King Faisal's father.
3rd October: Abdication of King Hussain of the Hijaz who is succeeded by his eldest son, Ali.
19th December: Ratifications of the Anglo-Iraq Treaty exchanged at Baghdad.

1925   August–September: King Faisal visits England—returning to Iraq via France and Egypt in November.
20th December: Exile of King Ali. The Hijaz lost by the Hashimites to Ibn Saud.
Emir Ghazi, son of Faisal the First, born in Mecca, 21st March 1912, goes to England for preparatory education with an English tutor.

1926   13th January: Second Anglo-Iraqi Treaty.
August: King Faisal visits England—returning to Iraq via Switzerland on 18th October.
January–August: Ghazi goes to Harrow.
October–December: Visit of King Faisal the First to France, Switzerland and England, 21st October to 6th December, returning via Cairo to Iraq, 15th December.
14th December: Second Treaty between U.K. and Iraq signed in London.

1930   30th June: Third Treaty of Alliance between U.K. and Iraq signed at Baghdad.

1931   26th January: Ratifications of Treaty of Alliance exchanged at Baghdad.
4th June: Death of ex-King Hussain of the Hijaz in Amman.

1932 September: End of Mandate in Iraq and achievement of Independence (League Session opened 23rd September).

1933 20th June: State visit to Britain of King Faisal the First.
11th August et seq.: Massacre of hundreds of Assyrians by Iraqi Army under General Bakr Sidqi. King Faisal returns to Iraq from Switzerland and leaves again for Switzerland.

1933 27th August: Visit of the Crown Prince, Emir Ghazi, to Mosul.
8th September: Death of King Faisal in Berne, Switzerland, and accession of his son, Ghazi.
20th September: Betrothal of King Ghazi to Emira Aliyah, his first cousin and daughter of King Ali.

1934 25th January: Marriage of Ghazi.

1935 14th January: Oil pipe-line inaugurated by King Ghazi at Kirkuk.
14th February: Death of ex-King Ali of the Hijaz in Baghdad.
27th March: Death of the Queen Mother, Faisal the First's Queen.
2nd May: A son born in Baghdad to Ghazi and named Faisal.

1936 28th October: Coup d'état by Hikmat Sulamain and General Bakr Sidqi and the Iraq Army. Murder of Jaafar al Askari, Minister of Defence, by Army officers.

1937 8th August: Murder of General Bakr Sidqi, Prime Minister, and the Commander of the Iraqi Air Force, by an Iraqi soldier at Mosul.

1938 24th December: Coup d'état by Iraq Army Generals.

1939 18th January: Murder of Rustam Haidar, Minister of Finance, in his office, by ex-police inspector of German sympathies.
1st March: Army conspiracy. Hikmat Sulaiman condemned to death; sentence mitigated through persuasion of British Ambassador.
4th April: Sudden death of King Ghazi in car accident. Succession of King Faisal the Second and beginning of Regency of Emir Abdulillah, son of King Ali of the Hijaz and uncle of the young King. British Consul at Mosul, G. Monck-Mason, killed in consequence of German propaganda. German political activity increased. (Ghazi died at 12.40 a.m. and Monck-Mason at noon on the 4th April.)
9th October: Amendment to the Constitution passed by Iraq

Parliament provided for succession to the throne in a male heir presumptive from the family of the late King Hussain, the succession having been formerly vested only in male descendants of King Faisal the First. The Emir Abdulillah in consequence became Crown Prince as well as Regent in Iraq.

1941   1st April: Revolt by Iraq Army. Rashid Ali Gailani Prime Minister. German Military Mission arrives. The Regent takes refuge in the U.S. Embassy and leaves by R.A.F. aircraft from Habbaniya. Sir Kinahan Cornwallis arrives as Ambassador. British and American Embassies invested. The boy King under 'house arrest' in Kurdistan. The Sherif Sharaf set up as puppet Ruler.
   2nd June: The Regent returns to Baghdad. The King leaves Kurdistan for Baghdad. Lines of communication through Iraq secured by British Forces during the remainder of the Second World War.

1943   November: Visit of Regent to London.

1944:   As British Forces withdraw, Iraq Army reformed. British Military Mission strengthened.

1945   June: Regent visits President of the United States, and Canada.
   July–August: Regent in London.
   September: Regent visits President of Turkey.

1946   King Faisal, the Regent and Nuri al Said attend Victory Parade, London, 8th June.

1947   Regent visits London.

1948   15th January: Treaty of Portsmouth. Leader of opposition Hikmat Sulaiman. Violent demonstrations in Iraq with many deaths.
   21st January: Treaty disavowed and ratification subsequently disapproved by Iraq Parliament.
   23rd March: Announcement that the British Military Mission to Iraq is to be terminated in May, at its own commander's suggestion.
   15th May: Iraq Army crossed into Palestine for war with Israel.
   4th October: Betrothal of Regent to Faiza el Taraboulsi, an Egyptian.

1949   King Faisal goes to Harrow School.
   P

1950 22nd December: Queen Aliya, mother of King Faisal the Second and sister of the Crown Prince, dies in Baghdad, after an operation in London in September.

1951 20th July: King Abdullah of Jordan murdered.

1952 August: Visit of Regent and King Faisal the Second to America.
September: Visit to Scotland.

1953 2nd May: Coming of age of Faisal the Second. End of the Regency.

1955 June: State visit of Faisal the Second to Turkey.

1956 June: Crown Prince marries Huyam, daughter of the Emir Rabia.
July: State visit of Faisal the Second to England.
20th September: Meeting of Faisal the Second with King Saud.

1957 British, French and Israeli advance on Suez halted. Intensification of Egyptian propaganda against Rulers of Lebanon and Iraq, and of Soviet activity.
16th September: Betrothal of Faisal the Second to Turco-Egyptian Princess Fadhila.

1958 February: Union of Jordan and Iraq kingdoms announced.
13th July: Communists released from prison in Iraq.
14th July: Murder of Royal family and Nuri al Said by Iraq Army. Imprisonment of many leaders, army commanders and staff, etc. A Republic declared. Baghdad Pact headquarters seized and looted.
31st July: British Government recognizes the new Republic.

Appendix I

Mr. Selwyn Lloyd in the House of Commons in Committee of Supply, 22nd July, 1958:

'Before I leave the subject of Iraq there is one thing that I think the Committee would wish me to do. I want to refer to the deaths of King Feisal, the Crown Prince and Nuri Said. I have not done this before, because we felt that there was not sufficient certainty about the fate which had befallen them. I do so now with great regret. Many right hon. and hon. Members have met and worked with them. His Majesty the King was educated in this country and had shown, in addition to a singular charm of manner, great capacity. I know that he was devoted to the welfare of his people; the keen interest which he took in the work of the Development Board was proof of that. I believe that he would have been a great ruler had he lived.

'The King's uncle, the Crown Prince, had an eventful life. He was always, throughout the many vicissitudes, a staunch friend of this country. I think he cared, above all, that his nephew should be a worthy King. That was his abiding interest, and his work in steering Iraq towards independence and preserving it should never be forgotten.

'Nuri Said was a great Arab patriot and nationalist. His part in the Arab Revolt in the First World War is well known. It was falsely said by those who surrounded him that he was a servant of the British. That was absolute nonsense. Anybody who had to deal with him knew of his robust independence, his toughness and his determination to get that which he thought was best for Iraq. It was due to him that, first the Mandate, and then the Treaty of 1930, were ended and he guarded and guided the independence of Iraq. He was responsible for the policy of spending the oil revenues so wisely. He laid the foundations of what we still hope will be a stable and prosperous Iraq. This country has lost three trusted friends. . . .'

Appendix II

Address by Colonel Gerald de Gaury, M.C.,
at the Memorial Service in the Queen's Chapel
of the Savoy on Wednesday, 30th July 1958:

'The men—and women and children—we are come to honour and remember were of foreign race, but we in this country throw open our gates to all the world, and the young King, nursed, taught and tutored by British, had been to an English school.

'Where he and his uncle stayed often, in their house near London, the people speak of them with affection for their kindly ways. They tell of their modesty, and praise their thought for others and their generosity.

'They were men unembittered, though their lot from childhood had been chequered with calamity. The Prince Abdulillah was obliged to leave the Hijaz as a child, with his mother, Queen Nafisa, now killed. He never returned to the land of his birth, homeland of the Hashimite family, guardians of Mecca.

'When his cousin, King Ghazi of Iraq, was killed, he became Regent for his three-year-old nephew, Faisal. He devoted himself to his Regency and to training the child for his coming role as a Sovereign —in no perfunctory way, but with all his heart.

'Experience as a Ruler brought ever-increasing wisdom, and knowledge of the West was used to the advantage of his country. His task as Regent was sharply interrupted by his enemies and ours in mid-war. The boy King was taken prisoner and so remained until order and freedom were restored.

'They were our allies in the last war, and they were the offspring of our allies in the First World War.

'In peace and war they were supported by great Arabs; one of the most outstanding of all—Nuri al Said, hero of the Arab uprising—was cut down in the same days. History will give him his place as one of the great leaders of men. Other Arab patriots fallen in Baghdad were members of the Arab Union Government.

'If there be any who doubt the devotion to their people or the verity of these Princes and leaders, let them consider whether in their place they could have done better. Consider, too, that these men knew how very little their lives were worth and that they might, had they wished, have retired from the contest, without honour though with wealth.

'The old leaders, the experienced Prince, the young King, a gentle boy, fallen after so brief a flowering—we who knew them recall their worthiness. None can uproot what is deeply planted in our minds, and so will be remembered always.

'God Rest Them All.'

Appendix III

A tentative list, indicating the comparatively modest nature, of some of the property in the Royal Palaces, Baghdad, looted in July 1958:

Pictures

Portrait of King Faisal the Second by Anthony Devas.
Portrait of the Regent by Anthony Devas.
Portrait of the Regent by Norblin.
A Scene by Monamy.
A Pair by A. H. Vicars.
A Peasant Scene, Dutch School.
A large Coastal Scene by William Shayer, senior.
A picture attributed to Claude.
A picture attributed to Gainsborough presented to King Faisal the First by a Mr. Wallack (inscription on back), of a scene with trees, cattle and magpies on a floating log.

Objects

A Chinese, beaker-shaped vessel of Ku-Shang Yin Dynasty.
A Jade Ming Vase.
A Bronze male figure by Auguste Rodin.
A Kalgan Jasper Hippopotamus.

Fabergé or similar objects in the Russian fashion. (Some of them formerly the property of the King of Greece.)

Cuff-links	Bracelet
Silver Skull Watch	Cigarette Case
Pelican	Desk Bell
Walking-stick Handle	Cane Handle
Scent Bottle	Match-box Case

The Royal Jewelry included:

A Gold Pocket Watch, inherited from his forbears, used daily by King Faisal the Second.

An Emerald Necklace of first quality, bought in the U.S.A.

A 27-carat Sapphire Ring (said to have been seen since July 1958 on the finger of the wife of a rebel leader).

A Silver and Emerald Ring and some other ancient rings and seals inherited from King Hussain of the Hijaz.

Books included a collection of illuminated Korans, some of superb quality.

Arms

A number of fine steel, ancient swords and daggers with golden sheaths, some inherited from King Hussain of the Hijaz and of great age.

Carpets

A number of fine and thin Persian rugs and carpets.

Birds and Animals

A small zoo and aviary. (Most animals and birds died from starvation.)

Thirty couple of foxhounds; the original hounds from the Brocklesbury and South Dorset Hunts in 1948, to which were added small drafts from other Hunts. (All the hounds were shot.)

Pure-bred Arab horses. (Sold by auction, many of them for a couple of pounds only.)

Index